T0215281

CONTESTING AUSTERITY AND FREE TRADE IN THE EU

The book explores the diffusion of protest against austerity and free trade agreements in the wave of contention that shook the EU following the 2008 economic crisis.

It discusses how protests against austerity and free trade agreements manifested a wider discontent with the constitutionalization of economic policy and the way economic decisions have been insulated from democratic debate. It also explores the differentiated politicization of these issues and the diffusion of protests across Western as well as Eastern Europe, which has often been neglected in studies of the post-crisis turmoil. Julia Rone emphasizes that far from being an automatic spontaneous process, protest diffusion is highly complex, and its success or failure can be impacted by the strategic agency and media practices of key political players involved such as bottom-up activists, as well as trade unions, political parties, NGOs, intellectuals, and mainstream media.

This is an important resource for media and communications students and scholars with an interest in activism, political economy, social movement studies, and protest movements.

Julia Rone is a Wiener-Anspach postdoctoral researcher at the University of Cambridge and the Université libre de Bruxelles. She has a PhD from the European University Institute in Florence with a thesis on mobilizations against free trade agreements. Julia has taught and supervised at the University of Cambridge, University of Florence, the University of Sofia, and the Heinrich Heine University in Düsseldorf. Her current research explores contestations over sovereignty in the UK, Poland, and Belgium. She has written on hacktivism, digital disobedience, and more recently, the rise of far right media in Europe.

Media and Communication Activism: The Empowerment Practices of Social Movements

Series editors: Claudia Magallanes Blanco, Alice Mattoni, and Charlotte Ryan

This Routledge series edited by Claudia Magallanes Blanco, Alice Mattoni, and Charlotte Ryan grapples with recurring issues facing practitioners, teachers, students, and scholars of communication activism; it addresses challenges to communication activism as well as emancipatory practices that build culturally resonant, richly networked, multi-faceted, movement communication systems. Core series themes include:

- The power structures of media and communication activism;
- Rights in the framework of media and communication activism;
- Outcomes, learning and sustainable futures in media and communication activism.

This is a global series published in English, and the editors welcome submissions from authors who work primarily in other languages.

Beyond Prime Time Activism
Communication Activism and Social Change
Charlotte Ryan and Karen Jeffreys

Contesting Austerity and Free Trade in the EU
Protest Diffusion in Complex Media and Political Arenas
Julia Rone

For more information about the series, please visit: www.routledge.com/Media-and-Communication-Activism/book-series/MCA

CONTESTING AUSTERITY AND FREE TRADE IN THE EU

Protest Diffusion in Complex Media and Political Arenas

Julia Rone

Routledge
Taylor & Francis Group

NEW YORK AND LONDON

First published 2021
by Routledge
52 Vanderbilt Avenue, New York, NY 10017

and by Routledge
2 Park Square, Milton Park, Abingdon, Oxon, OX14 4RN

Routledge is an imprint of the Taylor & Francis Group, an informa business

Library of Congress Cataloging-in-Publication Data
A catalog record for this book has been requested

ISBN: 978-0-367-53343-4 (hbk)
ISBN: 978-1-003-08152-4 (ebk)

Typeset in Bembo
by Apex CoVantage, LLC

To Milena, Julia, and Elena

CONTENTS

FIGURES

INTERVIEWS

19. Dorota Głowacka, Helsinki Foundation for Human Rights, Poland
20. Andrzej Tucholski, original administrator of the Nie Dla ACTA Poland Facebook page for protest against ACTA
21. Vanya Grigorova, organizer of anti-TTIP protests, founder of Solidarna Bulgaria
22. Borislav Sandov, leader of the Bulgarian Greens, active member in the anti-TTIP campaign
23. Ivaylo Popov, coordinator of the Food and Agriculture Team at "Za Zemyata", the representative of "Friends of the Earth" for Bulgaria
24. Reinhard Uhrig, campaigner at Global 2000, Friends of the Earth Austria
25. Valentin Schwarz, campaigner at Attac Austria on CETA/TTIP
26. Joachim Thaler, trade campaigner at Greenpeace Austria
27. Monika Wipplinger, project supervisor at YoUnion Austria
28. Georgi Hristov, Stop TTIP Bulgaria
29. Daniele Basso, advisor with a focus on trade policy, ETUC
30. Jesús Hernández Nicolau, accredited assistant to MEP Ernest Urtasun, Group of the Greens/European Free Alliance
31. Anne-Marie Mineur, Dutch politician, MEP for the Netherlands between 2014 and 2019, member of the Socialist Party, part of the European United Left–Nordic Green Left in the European Parliament
★ The interviews were conducted in Sofia, Brussels, Warsaw, Berlin, Oxford, Paris, and Vienna (and over Skype) in different stages in the period 2013–2020. The affiliations of the people in the list are the affiliations they had at the time of the interviews.

ACKNOWLEDGEMENTS

This book is based on my thesis, substantially revised in order to take into account everything I read, learned, and argued about since my defence in Florence in 2018. I would like to thank my supervisor Donatella della Porta for introducing me to social movement studies and to the wonderfully diverse, colourful, and intellectually rebellious community of social movement researchers in COSMOS in beautiful Florence. I especially thank her for her optimism in difficult political moments – she has always countered my pessimism with the belief that the consequences of social movements should be judged in the long run, even if in the short run they bring no radical change. I also thank Alice Mattoni, Charlotte Ryan, and Claudia Magallanes Blanco for allowing me to be part of this book series and for their advice, ideas, and encouragement while writing.

I would like to thank as well my mother Milena Popova for her unconditional love and friendship, for teaching me English and Spanish, and for introducing me to semiotics, linguistics, and Russian literature. I also thank her for reading the last version of my thesis in two days, correcting my English, and for always encouraging me to write a novel (I hope I will one day!). Most importantly, I thank her for asking always the right questions about the purpose of what I do and for being the strongest, smartest, and most wonderful person I know.

I am also deeply grateful to my aunt Julia, whom I am named after and who after her night shifts used to read children's books to me and introduced me to the most anarchist female character in literature – Pippi Longstocking. My aunt's love for life, her strength and charming stubbornness, and crucially her talent and tasty recipes have always been inspiring.

I would also like to thank three women who are no longer among us. We lost my beautiful cousin Elena while I was writing this book. She was the first person to teach me how to use a computer and was the coolest, funniest, and sweetest hacker of my youth. We lost you too early! I would also like to thank my grandmother Elena, whom I've never known. She was a resistance fighter and loved to recite revolutionary poetry. I somehow hope that she would like a book on protests (even though it would certainly not be revolutionary enough for her). Finally, I thank Britta Baumgarten, whom I have never actually met but whose work on the Portuguese protests inspired a lot of what I wrote.

After thanking so many women, I would like to say a huge thank you to Manès Weisskircher, who was the protagonist of my Florence PhD years and with whom we drank white wine in Oblate and Café Atlantic, conquered Aurelio Saffi and Matteo Palmieri, and climbed the Great Wall of China (and Vitosha mountain!). Thank you for the soap bubble maker, for always being an intellectual inspiration, and for allowing me to steal your interesting books even before you read them – both *Globalists* and *Global Inequality* influenced much of the writing of this book, so your generosity was not in vain! Thanks also to Elfriede, Elisabeth, Veronika, Günter, and Luise, in whose houses I wrote parts of the thesis that formed the basis of this book. You have been exceptionally kind to me and I remember this. I hope Fenno as a fellow Bulgarian behaves well!

Thanks also to Kimon, Fabio, Sergiu, Johannes, Rutger, Liam, Ola, Anna, Lyuba, Vesco, Marita, Elitsa, and Tom for sharing the beauty of Florence! I would like to thank as well my first supervisor in Sofia, Ivaylo Ditchev, for introducing me to the world of academia, and to my other mentors and good friends in Sofia: Mila Mineva, Todor Hristov, Valya Gueorgieva, Orlin Spassov, Desislava Lilova, Nikoleta Daskalova, Kristina Dimitrova, Teodor Grigorov, Lea Vajsova, and the other heroes of my BA years. Thanks also to Georgi Hristov, whom I met while interviewing him for this book and with whom we have since discussed political economy, TV series, and political strategy (in this order) in times of quarantine, at cold-floored social centres and at "Bolyarka", the last non-hipster кръчма in Sofia.

Crucially, I thank my current supervisors – Amandine Crespy, Chris Bickerton, Nathalie Brack, and Ramona Coman for allowing me to become part of their Wiener-Anspach project on conflicts of sovereignty and for helping me find clarity in key concepts such as democracy and sovereignty while analyzing the messy realities of Brexit and free trade. A big thank you also to Niels Gheyle, who appeared out of Twitter and read the final draft of this book, providing extremely relevant and life-saving comments on how to improve the text. I want to mention also all the great people I befriended in Cambridge: Rob, Felix, Sophia, Olga, Paul, Richard, and Michaela, who were there for me in a very tough year of my life.

Finally, I would like to thank Jelle Lever, whom I met the very week I submitted the official proposal for this book and with whom I spent the key months finishing the book itself. Thank you for letting me into your life and house during the pandemic and for teaching me the names of birds and plants I had never known, showing me how to plant pumpkins and tomatoes, and making me so happy despite the worst global crisis. Amidst the non-deterministic chaos surrounding us, you have been an anchor and a light, lieve Dr. Lever. This book is also for you.

INTRODUCTION

Most books on social movements start with a powerful description of an important protest. They make you picture the crowds, the police, the excitement of being surrounded by thousands of people who share the same strong indignation. Eventful protests capture the imagination, stir emotions, change people's biographies and occasionally also the world. Indeed, if asked about the protest cycle in the aftermath of the 2008 economic crisis, I would immediately mention the Spanish Indignados protesters occupying the "Puerta del Sol" square in Madrid with demands for "Real Democracy now!", the thousands of people marching in Berlin to oppose the Transatlantic Trade and Investment Partnership (TTIP) with the US, or the Greek Syntagma Square, where thousands of citizens across the political spectrum opposed austerity measures again and again, to no avail. I had seen Syntagma Square so many times on the news that when I finally saw it live for the first time in 2015, I felt I knew it well already. Still, focusing on big protests with a lot of media exposure gives a very partial view of what happened after the 2008 economic crisis.

If one wants to really understand opposition to free trade agreements and austerity policies in the European Union, one should focus also on smaller protests and on "failed" non-events (della Porta and Mattoni, 2014; Roberts, 2008). In fact, my very first experience of anti-austerity protests was a complete failure. The Bulgarian Occupy protest took place on November 11, 2011, in the small park between the National Assembly and Sofia University. It was a cold, dark evening, and even though students from the university were passing by all the time, only a few people joined. I know this because I was there. This is hard to prove, however, because the activist-produced video of the event on YouTube is quite amateurish and completely dark, and nothing can be seen on it.

There were similarly few people at the Sofia event in solidarity with the French "Nuit Debout" on May 15, 2016. This time even fewer people showed up – no more than 30. I knew most of them: the activists from a local left-wing social centre, friends who had been on Erasmus in Southern European countries, an editor from a magazine I occasionally contribute for, and a favourite professor of mine who was just finishing her own book on protests in Bulgaria. And there was I again, a social movements PhD, among fellow-minded people in what could admittedly be considered a not particularly successful event.

There are also all the cases in between. While Italy did not have Indignados-style occupations, it did have several well-attended trade union strikes and protests that sent a powerful message to ruling politicians and made it into international media. Similarly, resistance to the Anti-Counterfeiting Trade Agreement (ACTA) in the EU took place along a broad spectrum of participation – from thousands of protesters in Bulgaria, Germany, and Poland to small events in London, Brussels, and Stockholm, and virtually no one on the streets in Italy and Spain. Why was there such a big difference in the ways protests against austerity and free trade diffused in the EU?

An important caveat is needed before addressing this question. Protests in the EU have been simply an episode in a truly global protest cycle that started with protests in Iceland and the Arab Spring in Middle Eastern and North African countries before continuing to the EU, but also occurred in the US, Brazil, and South Africa, among others. The reason why I focus on the EU in this book is two-fold. First, purely practically, the book is based on extensive research and interviews conducted in different EU countries. I am European, even though writing this is problematic for me because I am from Eastern Europe, and for people from my region such a statement is never simply stating a matter of fact but always a strange mixture of a normative statement, wishful thinking, and an act of self-assertion. In any case, despite globalization, I have been outside of the EU only three times and outside of the European continent only once, so I do not feel expert enough to comment on protests in other regions, as important as they might be. This is not to say that protests elsewhere do not matter or that one should not study the differentiated politicization of the 2008 economic crisis across the globe. It is just to say that this needs to be done by other researchers with more knowledge about protest in these regions. Second and more theoretically speaking, taking the EU as a case for studying differentiated politicization is particularly fruitful since the EU has exclusive competence over trade policy and thus negotiated as a unitary actor. Furthermore, countries within the Eurozone in particular have a common monetary policy but a lot less integration on fiscal matters, where national states have been reluctant to give up their authority. Still, after the Maastricht Treaty, member states wishing to adopt the euro as their currency have had to abide by certain common fiscal rules, such as not having a budget deficit larger than

3% of GDP and no public debt larger than 60% of the GDP, etc. Asking how the crisis was politicized on the protest arena in different EU member states gives us the perfect opportunity to explore divergence among states that are part of the same union and share a common institutional framework, at least in some aspects.

Most broadly defined, politicization is "the act of transporting an issue or an institution into the sphere of politics – making previously unpolitical matters political" (Zürn, 2019, 977). Politicization is usually operationalized using three main indicators – "issue salience (visibility), actor expansion (range), and actor polarization (intensity and direction)" (Hutter and Kriesi, 2019, 999). Following this definition, both free trade and austerity, to some extent assumed as given in the high period of neoliberalism, were dramatically politicized in the aftermath of the 2008 crisis. They were politicized across various levels of governance – national, European, and international (Zürn, 2019) – and across different institutional and non-institutional arenas: parliaments, mass media and digital media, electoral politics, and the protest arena, among others (Kriesi, 2014). Starting from the premise that both free trade and austerity became objects of a "comprehensive politicization" across multiple levels and arenas (Gheyle, 2019, 231–232) in a number of countries, this book focuses on one particular manifestation of politicization – street protests and the ways they diffused across the EU.

In some countries, the politicization of austerity and free trade through protest was strongly connected to politicization in parliamentary settings, mass media, and party politics and even caused profound systemic changes in these settings: the birth of Podemos as a political party from the Indignados protests in Spain is a case in point. In the case of resistance to austerity in Spain, different manifestations of politicization had mutually dependent and reinforcing logics, creating virtuous circles of salience, actor expansion, and polarization. In other cases, such as protests against TTIP and the Comprehensive Economic Trade Agreement (CETA) with Canada in Eastern European countries, protests attempted to politicize free trade also in other arenas but ultimately failed to do so. While the resonance of protests and their effects on other forms of politicization are key issues to explore, in this book I focus above all on the success of protest diffusion itself, that is, on protest diffusion as the phenomenon to be explained, and not so much on how protest diffusion affects politicization in other arenas.

Explaining why and how different types of protests managed or failed to diffuse across the EU is the main contribution of this book. It is an important question because the key social movements literature on the post-crisis protest cycle primarily explores successful protests (della Porta, 2015; della Porta et al., 2017; Gerbaudo, 2012, 2017; Kriesi, 2015) and thus might create the impression that opposition to austerity and free trade in the EU is natural and logical. What is more, a growing number of political economists have paid attention to the anger provoked by the non-democratic EU economic policy and the corresponding "revolt" from bellow (Blyth and Lonergan, 2020; Nachtwey, 2018; Streeck, 2016). Yet, they have similarly focused on successful protests and have treated mobilization of anger as an almost automatic response to economic policies. Complementing these two perspectives, there has been a powerful narrative in both academic research and mass media according to which digital media helped protests spread like wildfire across the world – in Europe, North Africa, Brazil, Turkey, and the US (Castañeda, 2012; Kwon and Hemsley, 2017; Mercea, 2013, 2016; Vasi and Suh, 2013). What all these accounts cannot account for, however, is that the politicization of economic policy in the EU has been neither inevitable nor uniform. Focusing on protest in particular, anti-austerity protests simply failed to diffuse in Eastern Europe, while anti-ACTA protests failed to diffuse in Southern Europe, for instance.

If the economic crisis was some kind of a major external shock, the political response to it in the EU was surprisingly consistent – after an initial flirtation with Keynesian policies in some member states, the political recipe for the next decade became a mixture of austerity measures, low interest rates, and encouragement of free trade. On the contrary, the response of citizens to these policies was much less uniform.

This is not to say that all EU member states were in the same economic situation when the crisis hit or that all of them imposed the same measures. Far from it. There are persisting deep structural differences and divides between the Western and Eastern EU countries, between the North and the South, not to mention that not all EU countries are part of the Eurozone. Still, unlike issues such as the construction of a bridge or the appointment of a controversial politician, opposition to austerity and free trade by default had a larger potential to diffuse transnationally in the EU. Austerity policies affected large parts of the South and the East of Europe, and increasingly core European countries such as Belgium, France, or Finland (Rathgeb and Tassinari, 2020). Free trade agreements, being a competence of the European Union, also had the potential to be politicized in all EU countries. Yet, despite this, protests against austerity and against free trade diffused far from everywhere and followed very different patterns. Why?

The book addresses this puzzle by breaking it into two sub-questions. First, I ask: *why did different types of protests diffuse in very different ways?* Here, I want to compare the diffusion of protests against austerity with the diffusion of protests against different trade agreements. Second, I ask: *why did anti-austerity and anti-free trade protests diffuse in some cases but completely fail to diffuse in others?* Ultimately, both questions address the differentiated politicization (Crespy, 2016) of economic policy, especially when it comes to protests. The answer to both research questions, the book suggests, lies in the strategic agency of various political players and the ways in which they have navigated different media arenas in order to inform, mobilize, and organize. It is precisely these different political players and their diverse media practices that are the focus of the book.

To begin with, media activism has always been a crucial and challenging part of social movements' efforts to raise particular issues, organize, and reassert particular frames of key debates (Gamson and Wolfsfeld, 1993; Ryan, 1991). In recent years, social movement scholars have been preoccupied predominantly with how activists use digital media. But important new research has shown that instead of exploring single media use (such as Twitter or Facebook) or even all digital media in isolation, we need to focus on the ways activists navigate between all kinds of different media arenas (both online and offline) in their day-to-day media practices (Mattoni, 2009, 2017; Treré, 2019). This book applies this insight to the field of protest diffusion and explores the multiple media practices involved in the process of protest diffusion.

Furthermore, the book expands and enriches the media-centred focus, emphasizing that there are not only multiple media but also multiple types of political actors involved in protest diffusion. Protest is diffused not only by activists, but also by intellectuals, NGOs, media, trade unions, and political parties and only by paying attention to the characteristics of each type of player can one understand the type of media they prefer and the paths of diffusion that follow from this. If one wants to understand the complexity of media practices in protest diffusion, one needs to acknowledge also the complexity of players involved, going beyond bottom-up social movement activists.

An analysis of how different political players in each concrete case engage in protest diffusion and navigate complex arenas is extremely important, as it can help predict what pathways of diffusion are more likely to be observed and whether diffusion, in general, will be successful. The book engages in theory building and uses as "test cases" the protests against austerity and free trade in the EU.

The Introduction proceeds as follows. In the second section, I discuss why austerity and free trade agreements provoked a democratic backlash. Then, I compare the patterns of diffusion of protests against austerity and free trade agreements and emphasize the importance of studying failure. In the fourth section, I present the main theoretical contribution of the book – the claim that protest diffusion can be explained with the strategic agency of a variety of political players – including intellectuals, NGOs, media, trade unions, and parties – who navigate multiple media, including mainstream newspapers, books, digital media platforms, email lists, TV studios, and many more – to make their message heard. Politicization is not a black box. Protest diffusion is not a black box. They are the result of concrete actions taken by actual political players who organize political action and convince other people to join them. The final, fifth section of the Introduction provides a brief overview of the main chapters of the book and their main topics and approaches.

Democracy in Danger: What's Wrong With Austerity and Free Trade Agreements?

A well-known image from the European campaign against the Transatlantic Trade and Investment Partnership with the US shows a young activist setting up a model of the German Reichstag in the open space in front of the building (Figure 0.1). Behind the fake model, far in the background, one can see the real Reichstag with the famous glass dome designed by Norman Foster to allow people to walk above the debating chamber. The symbolism of the dome is clear: the people are "above" their representatives.

But on the small-scale model of the Reichstag, instead of the transparent cupola, one can see a big dome-like ticking bomb with the abbreviation TTIP written on it. A larger than life cartoon figure of Angela Merkel applies a flame to the bomb wire, risking to blow up the whole Reichstag. As if the metaphor wasn't clear enough, the authors of the model have written with big letters "democracy" on the model Reichstag building. Democracy, in short, is about to explode.

One can hardly find a better visual summary of the battles between technocratic decision-making, on the one hand, and popular sovereignty and democracy, on the other. A number of authors have paid attention to the increasing constitutionalization of economic policy at the EU level (Bickerton, 2016; Quaglia, 2003; Slobodian, 2018), i.e. the process by which crucial economic decisions

FIGURE 0.1 Protest against the Transatlantic Trade and Investment Partnership in Berlin, October 9, 2015

Source: © Michael Kappeler/dpa/Alamy Live News

are as if "lifted" above the sphere of political contestation and established through legal norms. This insulation of markets from democratic control has been recently traced to the intellectual and political project of a group of thinkers from the collapsed Habsburg Empire, including Friedrich Hayek. The so-called globalists contemplated how to establish a global free market (or, in a compromise solution for some of them, an EU free market) that could coexist with at least nominally standing nation states and democratic practices (Slobodian, 2018).

The globalists' project was further supported by intellectual currents such as public choice theory that helpfully portrayed politicians as self-serving agents who care only about their egoistical goals or, at best, their constituencies, to the detriment of the general public (Hay, 2007). The alternative to the "egoistical" and "partial" behaviour of politicians was to delegate decision-making to impartial technocrats who think of the general interest (Bickerton and Accetti, 2017). This meant, of course, no democratic discussion of policies. Why did people need to deliberate, to argue or agree with each other, if the technocrats already knew what was best?

In the aftermath of the economic crisis, this technocratic approach reached unprecedented heights. The European Commission, the European Central Bank, and the International Monetary Fund formed a non-elected decision-making group, popularly known as the Troika. The Troika imposed tough austerity measures on countries such as Greece and Portugal who could not repay their sovereign debt. With default not even considered as an option (Roos, 2019), these countries were coerced into taking loans with strict conditions, including retrenchment of the welfare state, the freezing of wages, and increasing flexibilization of the labour market. The same fix was applied to other countries such as Italy, Spain, and Ireland. Eastern European countries such as Latvia, Romania, and Hungary also entered in negotiations with the International Monetary Fund (IMF), and Bulgaria imposed tough austerity measures on its own initiative.

In countries such as Greece, austerity measures were imposed explicitly against the democratic will of the people. In early July 2015, the government of Alexis Tsipras organized a democratic referendum on whether to accept the agreement plan submitted by the Troika to the Eurogroup, which comprised another set of austerity reforms in exchange for lending money to the Greek government. The Greek people overwhelmingly voted against these conditionalities, knowing that a "No" answer (the famous OXI) might mean an exit from the Eurozone. After a combative and dramatic Euro Summit that lasted 16 hours and went well into the night of the 13th of July, Greek Prime Minister Tsipras saw himself forced to ignore the referendum result and accept a further swathe of austerity measures and economic reforms. According to EU officials, Tsipras was "crucified" during the meeting and looked like a "beaten dog" (Beattie, 2015).

But austerity measures lacked not only legitimacy. They lacked also effectiveness and led to highly problematic results. An increasing body of research has shown that "the pro-cyclical turn in fiscal policy started in 2010 intensified recessions, increased job losses, reduced the path of output growth, and contributed to rising poverty and income inequality" (Perez and Matsaganis, 2019, 259–260). Even in Ireland, which became the poster boy of reforms, economic recovery could be explained better with other reasons, including foreign direct investment by Silicon Valley companies encouraged to settle their European offices in Ireland by a mix of low taxes and cultural and linguistic proximity (Regan and Brazys, 2018).

So why did the Troika insist on such measures? Both economic ideas and class interest undoubtedly played a crucial role. But authors such as Fritz Scharpf have insisted that austerity is not the result simply of class interest or irrational stubbornness in face of contradicting facts. On the contrary, austerity policies have been the product of a rational concentrated effort to achieve structural convergence across the EU and transform Southern European economies into export-oriented ones (2016). Structural convergence was to be pursued even at the price of suppressing domestic consumption and triggering social crises in these societies. Scharpf emphasizes that had it been subjected to a public debate, this dramatic structural transformation would have provoked serious controversy. This is why it was done by European elites surreptitiously, in a highly undemocratic fashion and avoiding public scrutiny at any cost.

Transforming economies to encourage export made perfect sense in a worldview according to which more trade liberalization means more prosperity. In fact, this was the key to Germany's economic success after severe structural reforms in the early 2000s. Consequently, it is no surprise that the EU not only attempted to increase export competitiveness but also embarked on a series of ambitious new trade agreements. The European Commission tried to solve the problem of stagnating economic growth with more trade liberalization and even deeper market integration with Canada, the US, and later on Japan and a number of other economic powers (Siles-Brugge, 2013). In the aftermath of the crisis, EU's internal economic agenda played "a crucial role in the legitimation of an external free trade agenda, and vice versa" (de Ville and Orbie, 2014, 152). After the Greek crisis, the European Commission opted for a discourse according to which further liberalization was the necessary solution for future growth in a context where fiscal policy was no longer on the table (ibid., 159). Free trade agreements such as ACTA, but especially TTIP and CETA, were portrayed as absolutely key for stimulating exports and the economy in general. The geopolitical factor of fostering transatlantic cooperation and setting higher standards in the face of an increasingly expanding Chinese economy was also often given as an argument in favour of CETA and TTIP in particular (de Ville and Siles-Brugge, 2016). Still, the effects of EU trade agreements on third countries are less than certain (Siles-Brugge and de Ville, 2015). What is certain is that they bring even further liberalization of EU's economies and more power in the hands of private actors. Furthermore, it is far from clear how trade-induced growth is distributed among different strata of society, and there are strong reasons to believe it might actually increase inequality. Finally, similarly to austerity measures, most EU agreements have been negotiated outside of democratic purview in order to avoid the risks of politicization.

The fact that one can observe similar threats to democracy in both the field of austerity policy and free trade is far from a coincidence. Both types of policies are symptomatic of the same attempt to insulate economic decision-making from democratic oversight that Quinn Slobodian explored in *Globalists*. Yet, the remarkable assault on national sovereignty and democracy went too far. The Indignados protesters in Spain famously proclaimed, "We are not goods in the hands of politicians and bankers who do not represent us". Austerity measures and free trade stopped being a matter of "quiet politics" (Culpepper, 2011) and became a matter of public contestation. Slobodian's book on the globalist project ends with the protests against the World Trade Organization (WTO) in Seattle in 1999. In a sense, the current book starts from where *Globalists* ends – the politicization of economic policy on the streets – and explores how protests against austerity and free trade spread in the EU. The ruling elites' misguided responses to the economic crisis, the bailout of banks deemed too big to fail, and the outright class assault of the poorest members of society and the middle class disrupted the everyday lives of millions of people and provoked massive resistance and contestation (della Porta, 2015; Kriesi, 2015).

European activists clearly perceived the commonalities between what was going on in different EU countries and did everything they could to spread protest. According to a famous anecdote, there was a poster during the Spanish Indignados protest with the words "Quiet, we might wake up the Greeks". The presence of such a poster has remained unproven, but once the Greeks started protesting, they put up posters declaring "Quiet, you might wake up the Italians" and "Silence! The French are Sleeping. They dream of '68", thus urging protesters in other countries to the streets. Activists consciously tried to connect their struggles and to diffuse protest across time and space.

This book studies the diffusion of protest from the perspective of political and social sciences and aims to explain why and how activists succeeded or failed in their attempts to diffuse protest. Protests against free trade and austerity diffused in very distinct ways and with various rates of success. It is precisely these differences in the diffusion of protest that I try to explain by focusing on the agency of different political players in complex media environments.

Comparing the Diffusion of Protest Against Austerity and Against Free Trade Agreements

A number of authors have noticed that unlike previous protests such as the massive alter-globalization protest wave in the late 1990s, the anti-austerity protests have been much more national in their frames, demands, and repertoires (Crespy, 2016; della Porta, 2015; Gerbaudo, 2017). Important attempts have been made to bridge national anti-austerity protests and to create transnational alliances (Pianta and Gerbaudo, 2015), but they have remained rather scattered – most protest events driven by bottom-up activists remained confined to Southern Europe, while attempts for more transnational coordination were initiated by the European Trade Union Confederation but also ended up confined in Southern Europe, and even there with dubious success. There has certainly been a cross-national diffusion of protest and protest frames and repertoires (Baumgarten and Díez García, 2017; Díez García, 2017; Romanos, 2016), but its success and scope have strongly varied, with the types of actors involved being very different even in neighbouring countries such as Spain and Portugal (Carvalho, 2019).

On the contrary, protests against free trade agreements have been substantially more transnational in terms of organization structures, frames, and protest repertoires, and in this aspect similar to previous protests from the alter-globalization movement (Siles-Brugge and Strange, 2020). To begin with, back in 2012, both Eastern European and Western European countries protested against the Anti-Counterfeiting Trade Agreement, signed by the EU and 22 of its member states in January 2012 in order to enhance the enforcement of intellectual property rights. While the spontaneous bottom-up protests against ACTA came as a surprise to Brussels-based NGOs in the campaign (Parks, 2013, 2015), NGOs quickly reacted and used popular protest in order to legitimize their lobbying efforts. NGOs did everything possible to diffuse a set of common depoliticized frames that could be used to oppose the agreement throughout the EU. The protests against ACTA led to the first ever rejection of a trade deal by the European Parliament and served as an important case to inform future campaigns. The mobilizations against TTIP and CETA that followed were more centralized and coordinated from the very beginning, with German and Brussels-based NGOs producing and disseminating a common set of frames and repertoires across a number of EU countries. Again, these more centralized and transnationally coordinated attempts at diffusion of protests against TTIP and CETA succeeded only in some countries, while largely failing in Eastern Europe.

This difference in the process of diffusion is especially interesting considering the important commonalities between protests against austerity and free trade. Not only did they form part of the same protest cycle, but they were also both protests against the lack of democratic oversight over key economic decisions. The most convincing explanation proposed so far about the different ways in which these protests diffused points to the political opportunity structure (Kriesi, 1991) activists faced in these two very diverse types of protests (della Porta and Parks, 2018). Trade policy in general has been transferred to the EU level as a competence of the European Commission. The Lisbon Treaty has given power also to the European Parliament that can now veto trade agreements. This institutional arrangement allowed protesters to have a clear target at the transnational level and encouraged transnational cooperation, often led by transnational NGOs that had both the resources and experience to organize a campaign. On the contrary, the informal nature of the Troika made it difficult for anti-austerity protesters to formulate a clear target at the EU level, so they chose to pressure their national representatives instead (who were also ultimately the ones to introduce austerity measures) (ibid.).

Yet, the political structure opportunity explanation cannot account for the ways in which protests against two different types of trade agreements – ACTA and TTIP – diffused. Indeed, both types of protests were preceded by the organized efforts of transnational NGOs lobbying members of the European Parliament. But the pattern of diffusion of anti-ACTA protests was very different from that of anti-TTIP protests. Anti-ACTA mobilization was driven by a variety of players interested in Internet freedom and digital rights, whereas the mobilization against TTIP was the result of a broader coalition of players generally supportive of the alter-globalization movement and, surprisingly, far right players as well (Rone, 2018). These different types of players had a diverse presence in various EU countries and distinct media strategies.

Mobilizations against austerity were organized and diffused predominantly by bottom-up activists or, as already mentioned, trade unions. In contrast, mobilizations against free trade agreements were often led by the concerted efforts of NGOs, and in the case of TTIP and CETA especially, also by political parties and trade unions, with bottom-up protesters playing a more marginal role. These diverse actors engaged in very different types of media practices and had varying levels of control over the diffusion process. Anti-austerity protesters initially had much less access to mainstream media and focused on distributing information through alternative channels, apart from engaging in pre-figurative action and innovative media projects. Trade unions used their own channels for mobilization and counted on good old press releases to attract the attention of mainstream media. On the contrary, NGOs leading anti-free trade protests not only created purpose-built platforms but also had good access to mainstream media, which allowed them to keep their control over the narrative.

Thus, complementing the explanation based on the political opportunity structure, the current book focuses more on strategic agency and explains the differences between the types of diffusion observed in anti-austerity protests and various anti-free trade protests with the different constellations of players involved and the diverse ways in which these players navigated complex media arenas. This approach enriches existing studies on protest diffusion by bringing insights from the literature on players and arenas (Duyvendak and Jasper, 2015) and on media practices (Mattoni, 2012, 2017).

Complex Media and Political Arenas

Diffusion studies as a field has a long history dating back to the post-war years in the United States. A modernist belief in progress combined with scientific advances created a fertile ground for sociologists to study the conditions under which communities were ready to embrace innovations. Some of the earliest studies in the process of diffusion in fact explored the diffusion of hybrid seeds, antibiotics, and hard tomatoes (Rogers, 2003). With time, scholars moved beyond studying the diffusion of objects or practices (such as the practice of boiling water) and started exploring also how ideas, news, and – most relevant to this book – protests diffuse (della Porta and Mattoni, 2014; Givan et al., 2010; Soule, 2007; Tarrow, 2010; Tarrow and McAdam, 2005).

Classical diffusion studies focused a lot on who diffuses an innovation and to whom – the transmitters and adopters. This made sense since the diffusion processes they explored often included a transmitter recruiting members of a community and convincing them of using the new invention, be it a seed, a drug, or a complex new machine. For example, diffusion studies revealed that members of the community with greater social capital are more successful at convincing others and spreading innovations. What is more, it emerged that the diffusion of most innovations followed an S curve with only few adopters in the beginning, followed by a peak of adopters, and then another fall (Rogers, 2003).

As social movement scholars started paying attention to the problem of diffusion, the focus on who diffuses protest was displaced by a focus on *what* diffuses (ideas, forms of contention such as sit-ins, for example) and *how* it diffuses. Scholars distinguished between relational direct diffusion, non-relational diffusion (most often through the media), and brokered diffusion (done by intermediators such as NGOs). An increasing number of studies also started paying attention to *why* protests diffuse (Flesher Fominaya, 2015; Gerbaudo, 2013; O'Connor, 2017; Zamponi, 2012). Various researchers emphasized the role of pre-existing protest traditions, timing, and political opportunity structure. But unlike classical diffusion studies, few social movement studies focused on *who* exactly diffuses protest. It was simply presupposed that bottom-up activists and social movements drove diffusion. This book aims to fill in this gap and show that all other questions of diffusion – *what* diffuses, *how* and *why* – can be, at least to some extent, explained by identifying *who* drives diffusion.

In order to do this I count on the literature on players and arenas (Duyvendak and Jasper, 2015) that focuses on the strategic agency of a multiplicity of players. I complement their approach with the latest literature on complex media ecologies (Mattoni, 2017; Treré, 2019) to explore how different players engage in multiple media practices in order to spread protest.

The first main claim of the book is that protest is diffused not only by protesters but also by a variety of other players, including intellectuals, NGOs, media, trade unions, and political parties. Even though the social movement literature focuses mostly on activists, protest is diffused also by intellectuals who make incendiary statements on public TV, parties that provide funding, NGOs that create slogans and distribute leaflets, and trade unions that have the capacity to mobilize workers across countries. To ignore all these activists is to ignore the very complexity of social protests and reduce it to some idealized spontaneous bottom-up action, which rarely happens in practice.

The second claim that the book makes is that these diverse political players choose different types of media to diffuse protests based on their ideology and the resources they possess. In this respect, the book resonates very much with resource mobilization theory (McCarthy and Zald, 1977). Political parties have a privileged access to television studios that activists simply would not have. On the contrary, as it became clear in anti-austerity protests, activists would often experiment with all kinds of alternative platforms in order to engage in movement building (Magallanes-Blanco and Rodriguez Medina, 2016; Ryan, 2005; Valencia and Magallanes, 2016) to organize, mobilize, and reach the public. What is more, intellectuals and critical communities (Rochon, 1998) use not only mainstream and digital media but also more old-style media such as books to diffuse their ideas. Let's not forget that the very name of the Spanish protesters who called themselves Indignados (The Outraged) came from Stéphane Hessel's French book *Indignez-Vouz!*, translated in Spanish as *¡Indignaos!* (Time for Outrage). Finally, while media are treated most often as an arena, they can also behave as a player. This was particularly clear in the case of several Polish media that participated in the blackout against ACTA or in the campaign the Austrian *Die Kronen Zeitung* launched against TTIP.

The third claim that the book makes, following logically from the first two, is that what type of diffusion would be observed and whether it would be successful at all depends on the particular constellations of players and the media they use. The book uses as test cases the European mobilizations against austerity and the trade agreements ACTA, TTIP, and CETA.

Throughout the book, I have identified the main political actors and their media practices based on qualitative content analysis of activists' documents, websites, and media appearances, of social network analysis on directions of information diffusion (in the case of ACTA), and based on interviews with key figures in the mobilizations. I started the analysis with six types of players, identified deductively based on existing theory, but other (often unexpected) players emerged from the analysis – among whom were hacktivists, city and regional councils, and torrent trackers – and I added them to the description. The analysis of the types of actors involved and their media practices is meant to facilitate theoretical predictions about future processes of diffusion. This book does not start with hypotheses about what types of diffusion to expect from different constellations of actors and in which cases diffusion is successful, since the main goal is theory building. The book aims, however, to offer some key generalizable findings that can be tested in further research on other empirical cases.

Chapter Description

Chapter 1 outlines the theoretical framework of the book and introduces the rationale for moving beyond the comparative approach and for studying instead diffusion in complex systems. The chapter presents the notion of "protest cycles" to explain the clustering of protests in time and space and explores how diffusion dynamics interact with exogenous shocks and endogenous factors (such as the strength of local actors) in order to make the appearance of common frames and protest repertoires across a number of countries possible. After discussing briefly the history of diffusion studies, I provide an introduction to the "players and arenas" framework as presented by Duyvendak and Jasper (2015) and present the key players in the process of protest diffusion.

Chapter 2 begins with a critical reading of the post-crisis economic governance regime in the EU, drawing on a wide-range of contemporary writings in political economy. It provides a comprehensive account of austerity measures across the EU, showing that they took place not only in the Eurozone, most often explored in academic texts, but also in Eastern European countries. The chapter then proceeds to outline the diffusion of protests against austerity in Southern Europe, where it was led by bottom-up activists experimenting with innovative digital practices to actively diffuse protest frames and repertoires. I draw attention also to the role of trade unions, political parties, and intellectuals as key for spreading protest. Next, the chapter moves on to Eastern Europe and shows that even though countries such as Bulgaria and Romania experienced substantial austerity cuts, protests there focused primarily on corruption and demands for democratic deepening (Rone, 2017). There was a conspicuous absence of critique to austerity from a left-wing perspective. Countries such as Latvia and Lithuania, on the other hand, did not have any protest at all. These cases of failed diffusion of anti-austerity protest can be largely explained with the dearth of political players who could mobilize on the issue and popularize it. Yet, such players started slowly appearing as a result of diffusion following the eventful wave of protests. The chapter ends with several practical takeaways for activists, including the importance of reaching out to players they do not already have connections with. There is a lot of unexplored potential for building connections between activists in Southern Europe and Eastern Europe and between activists from different Eastern European countries as well.

Chapter 3 explores the transnational bottom-up protests against ACTA. First, I explain briefly what ACTA was and why it provoked so much controversy. Then, I explore the politicization of intellectual property and the way it was connected to international trade, provoking a wave of contestation. Analyzing the diffusion of mobilization against ACTA, I focus on Poland, Germany, and Bulgaria as three of the countries with the biggest protests. The comparison between these three cases is particularly interesting since in each of them the leading players were different – NGOs and activists in Poland, Pirate Parties and activists in Germany, and mainly bottom-up activists in Bulgaria. Nevertheless, the key actors for the success of the protest were Brussels-based NGOs that produced expertise and lobbied European policy makers. These transnationally oriented NGOs managed to impose a set of depoliticized frames that were shared across the EU, used in interviews with mainstream media and in lobbying governments.

The chapter then addresses the failed diffusion of protest against ACTA in Spain. I show that Spanish activists were already very much invested in the anti-austerity protests that had started in 2011 and thus unable to invest time or attention to a single-issue protest. The chapter ends with few important takeaways for activists on how to achieve more sustainable mobilization across borders and not lose control of the diffusion process.

Chapter 4 explores the transnational diffusion of protest against TTIP and CETA. As in the previous chapters, I first provide some background on what TTIP and CETA entailed and why they provoked massive resistance across the EU. I then move to explore the diffusion of protest led by German and Brussels-based NGOs, outlining the leading players involved in diffusion and their media practices. An important development in the mobilization has been the engagement of city and regional councils, a practice known from earlier resistance to neoliberal globalization (Siles-Brugge and Strange, 2020) but reinvigorated by a rising municipalist movement that came out of the 2011 anti-austerity protests. The chapter then traces the diffusion of opposition to TTIP and CETA from the Green left to the far right and analyzes the strategic agency of far right players in the process. I show that there was a deliberate attempt by far right parties to appropriate frames and repertoires coined by left and Green progressive actors, emphasizing once more that protest diffusion is a highly political and contested process in which players often have very different agendas. Finally, I explore the failed diffusion of protests against TTIP and CETA in Eastern Europe and find that, similar to the case of anti-austerity protests, in Central and Eastern Europe there were few players with experience from the alter-globalization movement and, what is more, they had almost no access to mainstream media. In the conclusions of the chapter, I provide some ideas for activists on how to avoid their cause being appropriated by the far right.

Overall, the book shows that any study of protest diffusion should take into account the wide variety of political players involved and their media strategies. Intellectuals, bottom-up activists, NGOs, parties, trade unions, and media professionals themselves strive to diffuse their own particular "version" of the frames, ideas, and events taking place and to incite into action. Far from being an automatic process of "contagion", diffusion is an agentic political process in which different players cooperate, help each other, or enter into conflict.

Such an approach tries to be movement-relevant (Bevington and Dixon, 2005; Croteau, 2005; Flacks, 2005; Ryan et al., 2010) and allows activists to predict when and where their protest can diffuse. Identifying players that can be receptive to protesters' messages in another country and engaging in adequate types of media strategies can be crucial for the success of protest diffusion. What is more, based on the analysis of the concrete cases, the book encourages activists to establish connections to players in new countries they have not contacted before, engage actively and strategically with trade unions, NGOs, and political parties, and fight attempts by far right players to co-opt their causes.

Protests against austerity and free trade agreements have shown that there is deep discontent with the constitutionalization of economic policy and the way economic decisions have been insulated from democratic debate. If activists want to have their voice heard and organize successful transnational actions in defence of democracy, they need a better knowledge of how and why protests diffuse across countries and a viable strategy for the most difficult cases. In times of a crisis of the world-system and a proliferation of anti-systemic movements (Arrighi et al., 1989), systemic knowledge of protest diffusion is needed more now than ever.

References

Arrighi, Giovanni, Terence Hopkins and Immanuel Wallerstein (1989): *Antisystemic Movements*. London: Verso Books.

Baumgarten, Britta and Rubén Díez García (2017): More Than a Copy Paste: The Spread of Spanish Frames and Events to Portugal. *Journal of Civil Society*, 13:3, 247–266.

Beattie, Jason (2015): Greek Prime Minister Alexis Tsipras 'Beaten Like a Dog and Crucified' by EU Sanctions. *The Mirror*. Retrieved from www.mirror.co.uk/news/world-news/greek-prime-minister-alexis-tsipras-6059935.

Bevington, Douglas and Chris Dixon (2005): Movement-Relevant Theory: Rethinking Social Movement Scholarship and Activism. *Social Movement Studies*, 4:3, 185–208.

Bickerton, Christopher (2016): *The European Union: A Citizen's Guide*. New York: Penguin, Random House.

Bickerton, Christopher and Carlo Invernizzi Accetti (2017): Populism and Technocracy: Opposites or Complements? *Critical Review of International Social and Political Philosophy*, 20:2, 186–206.

Blyth, Mark and Eric Lonergan (2020): *The Political Economy of Anger*. New York: Columbia University Press.

Carvalho, Tiago (2019): *Contesting Austerity: A Comparative Approach to the Cycles of Protest in Portugal and Spain Under the Great Recession (2008–2015)*. PhD Thesis, Department of Sociology, University of Cambridge, Cambridge.

Castañeda, Eduardo (2012): The Indignados of Spain: A Precedent to Occupy Wall Street. *Social Movement Studies*, 11:3–4, 309–319.

Crespy, Amandine (2016): *Welfare Markets in Europe: The Democratic Challenge of European Integration*. London: Palgrave Macmillan.

Croteau, David (2005): Which Side Are You on? The Tension Between Movement Scholarship and Activism. In: *Rhyming Hope and History: Activists, Academics and Social Movement Scholarship*. Minneapolis: University of Minnesota Press, 20–40.

Culpepper, Pepper (2011): *Quiet Politics and Business Power*. Cambridge: Cambridge University Press.

della Porta, Donatella (2015): *Social Movements in Times of Austerity*. Cambridge: Polity Press.

della Porta, Donatella, Massimiliano Andretta, Tiago Fernandez, Francis O' Connor, Eduardo Romanos and Markos Vogiatzoglu (2017): *Late Neoliberalism and Its Discontents in the Economic Crisis*. London: Palgrave Macmillan.

della Porta, Donatella and Alice Mattoni (2014): *Spreading Protest: Social Movements in Times of Crisis*. Essex: ECPR Press.

della Porta, Donatella and Louisa Parks (2018): Social Movements, the European Crisis and EU Political Opportunities. *Comparative European Politics*, 16, 85–102.

de Ville, Ferdi and Jan Orbie (2014): The European Commission's Neoliberal Trade Discourse Since the Crisis: Legitimizing Continuity Through Subtle Discursive Change. *The British Journal of Politics and International Relations*, 16, 149–167.

de Ville, Ferdi and Gabriel Siles-Brugge (2016): *TTIP: The Truth About the Transatlantic Trade and Investment Partnership*. London: Polity Press.

Díez García, Rubén (2017): The 'Indignados' in Space and Time: Transnational Networks and Historical Roots. *Global Society*, 31:1, 43–64.

Duyvendak, Jan Willem and James Jasper (eds.) (2015): *Players and Arenas: The Interactive Dynamics of Protest*. Amsterdam: Amsterdam University Press.

Flacks, Richard (2005): The Question of Relevance in Social Movement Studies. In: *Rhyming Hope and History: Activists, Academics and Social Movement Scholarship*. Minneapolis: University of Minnesota Press, 3–19.

Flesher Fominaya, Cristina (2015): Debunking Spontaneity: Spain's 15-M/Indignados as Autonomous Movement. *Social Movement Studies*, 14:2, 142–163.

Gamson, William A. and Gadi Wolfsfeld (1993): Movements and Media as Interacting Systems. *The Annals of the American Academy of Political and Social Science: Citizens, Protest, and Democracy*, 528, 114–125.

Gerbaudo, Paolo (2012): *Tweets and the Streets: Social Media and Contemporary Activism*. London: Pluto Press.

Gerbaudo, Paolo (2013): Protest Diffusion and Cultural Resonance in the 2011 Protest Wave. *The International Spectator: Italian Journal of International Affairs*, 48:4, 86–101.

Gerbaudo, Paolo (2017): *The Mask and the Flag: Populism, Citizenism and Global Protest*. London: Hurst and Company.

Gheyle, Niels (2019): Conceptualizing the Parliamentarization and Politicization of European Policies. *Politics and Governance*, 7:3, 227–236.

Givan, Rebecca, Sarah Soule and Kenneth Roberts (eds.) (2010): *The Diffusion of Social Movements*. Cambridge: Cambridge University Press.

Hay, Colin (2007): *Why We Hate Politics*. London: Polity Press.

Hessel, Stéphane (2010): *Indignez-vouz!* Montpellier: Indigène Éditions.

Hutter, Swen and Hanspeter Kriesi (2019): Politicizing Europe in Times of Crisis. *Journal of European Public Policy*, 26:7, 996–1017.

Kriesi, Hanspeter (1991): *The Political Opportunity Structure of New Social Movements: Its Impact on Their Mobilization*. FS III 91–103 Discussion Paper. Berlin: Wissenschaftszentrum Berlin für Sozialforschung.

Kriesi, Hanspeter (2014): The Political Consequences of the Economic Crises in Europe: Electoral Punishment and Popular Protest. In: Nancy Bermeo and Larry M. Bartels (eds.), *Mass Politics in Tough Times: Opinions, Votes and Protest in the Great Recession*. Oxford: Oxford University Press, 297–333.

Kriesi, Hanspeter (2015): Political Mobilization in Times of Crises: The Relationship Between Economic and Political Crises. In: Marco Giugni and Maria T. Grasso (eds.), *Austerity and Protest: Popular Contention in Times of Economic Crisis*. Burlington: Ashgate, 19–33. References to the pages on this file. Retrieved 14 June 2016, from www.eui. eu/Projects/POLCON/Documents/Kriesicrises2014.pdf.

Kwon, Hazel and Jeff Hemsley (2017): Cross-National Proximity in Online Social Network and Protest Diffusion: An Event History Analysis of Arab Spring. *Proceedings of the 50th Hawaii International Conference on System Sciences*. Retrieved from http://hdl. handle.net/10125/41414.

Magallanes-Blanco, Claudia and Leandro Rodriguez-Medina (2016): Give Me a Mobile and I Will Raise a Community. In: *Communication and Information Technologies Annual (Studies in Media and Communications, Vol. 12)*. Bingley: Emerald Publishing, 315–343.

Mattoni, Alice (2009): *Multiple Media Practices in Italian Mobilizations Against Precarity of Work*. PhD Thesis, European University Institute, Florence.

Mattoni, Alice (2012): *Media Practices and Protest Politics: How Precarious Workers Mobilize*. London: Routledge.

Mattoni, Alice (2017): A Situated Understanding of Digital Technologies in Social Movements: Media Ecology and Media Practice Approaches. *Social Movement Studies*, 16:4, 494–505.

McCarthy, Matthew and Mayer Zald (1977): Resource Mobilization and Social Movements: A Partial Theory. *The American Journal of Sociology*, 82, 1212–1241.

Mercea, Dan (2013): Probing the Implications of Facebook Use for the Organizational Form of Social Movement Organizations. *Information, Communication and Society*, 16:8, 1306–1327.

Mercea, Dan (2016): The Social Media Overture of the Pan-European Stop-ACTA Protest: An Empirical Examination of Participatory Coordination in Connective Action. *Convergence*, 22:3, 287–312.

Nachtwey, Oliver (2018): *Germany's Hidden Crisis: Social Decline in the Heart of Europe*. London: Verso.

O'Connor, Francis (2017): The Presence and Absence of Protest in Austerity Ireland. In: *Late Neoliberalism and Its Discontents in the Economic Crisis*. London: Palgrave Macmillan, 65–98.

Parks, Louisa (2013): *Political Process, Popular Protest and the EU: The Case of ACTA*. Paper Presented at the ESA Conference – Crisis, Critique and Change, Turin, 28–31 August.

Parks, Louisa (2015): *Social Movement Campaigns on EU Policy: In the Corridors and in the Streets*. London: Palgrave Macmillan.

Perez, Sofia and Manos Matsaganis (2019): Export or Perish: Can Internal Devaluation Create Enough Good Jobs in Southern Europe? *South European Society and Politics*, 24:2, 259–285.

Pianta, Mario and Paolo Gerbaudo (2015): In Search of European Alternatives: Anti-Austerity Protests in Europe. *Subterranean Politics in Europe*, 31–59.

Quaglia, Lucia (2003): European Monetary Integration and the 'Constitutionalization' of Macroeconomic Policy Making. *Constitutional Political Economy*, 14, 235.

Rathgeb, Philip and Arianna Tassinari (2020): How the Eurozone Disempowers Trade Unions: The Political Economy of Competitive Internal Devaluation. *Socio-Economic Review*, mwaa021.

Regan, Aidan and Samuel Brazys (2018): Celtic Phoenix or Leprechaun Economics? The Politics of an FDI-Led Growth Model in Europe. *New Political Economy*, 23:2, 223–238.

Roberts, Kenneth (2008): The Mobilization of Opposition to Economic Liberalization. *Annual Review of Political Science*, 11:327–349.

Rochon, Thomas (1998): *Culture Moves: Ideas, Activism and Changing Values*. Princeton: Princeton University Press.

Rogers, Everett (2003): *Diffusion of Innovations*, 5th edition. New York: Free Press.

Romanos, Eduardo (2016): From Tahrir to Puerta del Sol to Wall Street: The Transnational Diffusion of Social Movements in Comparative Perspective. *Revista Española de Investigaciones Sociológicas*, 154, 103–118.

Rone, Julia (2017): Left in Translation: The Curious Absence of an Austerity Narrative in the Bulgarian 2013 Protests. In: Donatella della Porta (ed.), *The Global Diffusion of*

Protest: Riding the Protest Wave in the Neoliberal Crisis. Amsterdam: Amsterdam University Press.

Rone, Julia (2018): Contested International Agreements, Contested National Politics: How the Radical Left and the Radical Right Opposed TTIP in Four European Countries. *London Review of International Law,* 6:2, 233–253.

Roos, Jerome (2019): *Why Not Default? The Political Economy of Sovereign Debt.* Princeton: Princeton University Press.

Ryan, Charlotte (1991): *Prime Time Activism.* Boston: South End Press.

Ryan, Charlotte (2005): Successful Collaboration: Movement Building in the Media Arena. In: *Rhyming Hope and History: Activists, Academics, and Social Movement Scholarship.* Minneapolis: University of Minnesota Press, 115–136.

Ryan, Charlotte et al. (2010): Making Research Matter . . . Matter to Whom? *International Journal of Communication,* 4, 845–855.

Scharpf, Fritz (2016): *Forced Structural Convergence in the Eurozone – Or a Differentiated European Monetary Community.* MPIfG Discussion Paper 16/15. Köln: Max-Planck-Institut für Gesellschaftsforschung.

Siles-Brugge, Gabriel (2013): The Power of Economic Ideas: A Constructivist Political Economy of EU Trade Policy. *Journal of Contemporary European Research,* 9:4, 597–617.

Siles-Brugge, Gabriel and Ferdi de Ville (2015): The Transatlantic Trade and Investment Partnership and the Role of Computable General Equilibrium Modelling: An Exercise in Managing Fictional Expectations. *New Political Economy,* 20:5, 653–678.

Siles-Brugge, Gabriel and Michael Strange (2020): National Autonomy or Transnational Solidarity? Using Multiple Geographic Frames to Politicize EU Trade Policy. *Politics and Governance,* 8:1, 277–289.

Slobodian, Quinn (2018): *Globalists: The End of Empire and the Birth of Neoliberalism.* Cambridge: Harvard University Press.

Soule, Sarah (2007): Diffusion Processes Within and Across Movements. In: Hanspeter Kriesi, David Snow and Sarah Soule (eds.), *The Blackwell Companion to Social Movements* Oxford: Blackwell.

Streeck, Wolfgang (2016): *How Will Capitalism End?* London: Verso Books.

Tarrow, Sidney (2010): Dynamics of Diffusion: Mechanisms, Institutions, and Scale Shift. In: Rebecca Givan, Sarah Soule and Kenneth Roberts (eds.), *The Diffusion of Social Movements.* Cambridge: Cambridge University Press.

Tarrow, Sidney and Doug McAdam (2005): Scale Shift in Transnational Contention. In: Donatella della Porta and Sidney Tarrow (eds.), *Transnational Protest and Global Activism.* New York: Rowman & Littlefield.

Treré, Emiliano (2019): *Hybrid Media Activism: Ecologies, Imaginaries, Algorithms.* London: Routledge.

Valencia, Juan Carlos and Claudia Magallanes (2016): Prácticas Comunicativas y Cambio Social: Potentia, Acción y Reacción. *University of Humanistic Studies,* 81, 15–31.

Vasi, Ion and Chan S. Suh (2013): *Protest in the Internet Age: Public Attention, Social Media, and the Spread of "Occupy" Protests in the United States.* Draft. Retrieved from https://www.politicsandprotest.ws.gc.cuny.edu/files/2012/07/PPW-2-Vasi.pdf.

Zamponi, Lorenzo (2012): 'Why Don't Italians Occupy?' Hypotheses on a Failed Mobilisation. *Social Movement Studies,* 11:3–4, 1–11.

Zürn, Michael (2019): Politicization Compared: At National, European, and Global Levels. *Journal of European Public Policy,* 26:7, 977–995.

1

STUDYING PROTEST DIFFUSION

1.1. Hard to Be a God: Diffusion in Protest Cycles

In the 1967 Russian sci-fi novel *Hard to Be a God* (Strugatsky and Strugatsky, 2014), Anton, an undercover operative from the future planet Earth, is sent on a mission to a distant planet inhabited by human beings who still have not advanced beyond the Middle Ages. Anton can only observe but is not allowed to interfere, because this might change the course of history. This, however, proves to be increasingly difficult for him as difficult moral dilemmas arise. The fictional plot of *Hard to Be a God* points to some of the crucial dilemmas of social science. Is it possible to observe a foreign society and assume it is completely independent from ours, as if it were on a different planet? How long can "separate" cases remain isolated from each other before diffusion of ideas or practices takes place?

For a long time, social and political sciences have championed a comparative approach that treats different country cases as separate and comparable, setting aside the many ways in which they could influence each other. Contrary to this classical type of sociology that treats the world as an empty experimental space, this book understands the world as a complex system, which is constantly transforming itself. What matters in complex systems are not their different components analyzed separately from each other, but the very process of interaction and communication between components forming a part of a single whole. As the philosopher of information Paul Cilliers insists, "complex systems display behaviour that results from the interaction between components and not from characteristics inherent to the components themselves. This is sometimes called emergence" (Cilliers, 2005, 257). Cases cannot be neatly distinguished from each other as they form part of the same system – one case would not be the same without the other.

What follows from this epistemological principle in terms of approaching the topic of the book is that protests against austerity and free trade in different countries cannot simply be compared to each other as if there were no diffusion processes between them. Similarly, protests against austerity and protests against free trade agreements have influenced each other across time, being part of the same protest cycle. This is the reason why instead of studying them as separate cases, I am interested in the diffusion processes between them, perceived in both their spatial and temporal dimensions. It is impossible to understand protest cycles and their inner logic without paying attention to diffusion processes.

Before turning to the history and theory of diffusion studies, however, a brief discussion of protest cycles is due. This term is so widespread by now that it is treated almost as self-evident in most books on protests. Yet it is anything but self-evident.

One amazing thing about large protests is that they are not evenly distributed across time and space but tend to cluster. While there are of course single-event protests, some of the most prominent and significant historical examples of protest formed part of larger cycles: the 1848 Spring of the People, the 1968 student movements wave, the 1989 pro-democracy protests in Eastern Europe, the late 1990s/early 2000s alter-globalization protests, and of course, the post-economic-crisis protests against austerity and free trade that I am interested in.

According to the classical definition, a protest cycle or a "cycle of contention" is

> a phase of heightened conflict across the social system, with rapid diffusion of collective action from more mobilized to less mobilized sectors, a rapid pace of innovation in the forms of contention employed, the creation of new or transformed collective action frames, a combination of organized and unorganized participation, and sequences of intensified information flow and interaction between challengers and authorities.
>
> *(Tarrow, 1998, 199)*

The most characteristic feature of cycles of contention is their innovative nature and the role they play for the creation of transformed symbols, frames of meaning, and ideologies to justify collective action that later enter the culture in more diffuse and less militant form (Tarrow, 1998, 204). Snow and Benford, the pioneers of framing theory, emphasize that social movements do not simply carry extant ideas and meanings that emerge as if automatically out of structural arrangements, unanticipated events, or existing ideologies. On the contrary, movement actors actively produce and maintain meaning for their constituents, antagonists, and bystanders (Snow and Benford, 2000, 613). During protest cycles new ideas, frames, and practices diffuse both in space and in time, from one protest to the next.

The notion of a protest cycle presupposes that different protests clustered in time in space are not happening in isolation but influence each other in terms of ideas, frames, protest repertoires, or sometime even in terms of actors involved. This does not mean that all protests in the same cycle are "the same" or share many common features. It rather means that they share some features, and that makes it even more interesting to explore which beliefs, general ideas, frames, and protest repertoires diffuse within the same protest cycle and which do not. For example, demands for more "real democracy now" and beliefs in the power of digital media did diffuse from Indignados-style protests in Southern Europe to protests in Eastern Europe. But left-wing anti-austerity frames did not. Thus, while protests in Bulgaria and Romania in 2013 formed part of the same post-cycle crisis of contention, they cannot be conceptualized as "anti-austerity" protests. Why was there such a gap in diffusion? This is one of the questions this book tries to address.

There is also another, broader understanding of cycles of contention that I do not engage with but has been fundamental for conceptualizing cycles of contention in the 1980s and 1990s. According to this understanding, clusters of protests reoccur cyclically, and this is how one gets to the concept of protest cycles. Scholars in this tradition posed several fundamental questions, most of which led to a dead end, but this doesn't make them less interesting. One such fundamental question was, what causes the reoccurrence of protest cycles, starting with the 1848 Spring of the People all the way to the 1989 pro-democracy protests? Different authors have tried to find a connection between protest cycles and so-called Kondratieff waves – hypothesized cycle phenomena in the modern world economy, consisting of periods of high economic growth alternating with periods of low economic growth. Nevertheless, economists do not agree on whether Kondratieff waves exist or are just an attempt to see a pattern where there is none (Frank and Fuentes, 1994). Even if one accepts the existence of Kondratieff waves, it seems that the connection with protest cycles is rather tenuous – evidence shows that protests tend to happen both during the downward turn of the cycles and during periods of dynamic expansion and economic growth (Frank and Fuentes, 1994). This means that one can expect protest cycles to take place both in times of economic crises, such as the protest cycle we explore in this book, and in times of relative affluence and economic boom, as experienced in 1968. Other authors have searched for connections between protest cycles and demographic changes, claiming that state breakdowns and social movements, at least in the early modern period, could be explained with population growth that leads to changes in prices, shifts of resources, and increasing social demands (Goldstone, 1991, quoted in Frank and Fuentes, 1994). Yet, these connections are difficult to prove for the 20th and 21st centuries. All things considered, there is still no definite academic opinion on whether there is indeed such a thing as protest cycles reoccurring in time, following a pattern. What is even more remarkable is that this question that seemed to be essential in the 1990s seems to have been completely forgotten in the literature since then. Rather than answering this question, this book has the much more modest ambition to explore the diffusion of protest events, and the corresponding frames, protest repertoires, and ideas, within the same protest cycle following the 2008 economic crisis.

Of course, one might argue that there was no diffusion present in the cycle and the fact that many EU member states experienced protest more or less at the same time is largely due to the exogenous shock of the 2008 economic crisis that created grievances in many places at the same time. Yet, such an exogenous shock-based explanation cannot explain why not all EU countries had protests. Refining this hypothesis, one might say protests were not triggered by the crisis per se, but by governments' adoption of austerity measures, i.e. protest often emerged as a reaction to particular types of policies, not as a reaction to economic grievances (Kriesi, 2015). Nevertheless, after the 2008 economic crisis, there were many countries in which the government adopted tough austerity measures – Ireland, the Baltic countries, Bulgaria, and Romania, among others, but no serious anti-austerity protests took place. Thus, an exogenous shock alone cannot explain the incidence of protest.

What about endogenous reasons? The classical explanation why protests succeed in some cases but fail in others points to diverging political opportunity structures. Political opportunities have been defined as a combination of increasing access for movements, shifting political alignments, divided elites, influential allies, limited repression, and low state strength, among others (Tarrow, 1998, 78–85), even though this list has been regularly refined and updated since its first appearance. Yet, most of the EU countries that adopted austerity measures did not have political opportunity structures so radically different that they could explain why protests occurred or failed to occur. What was different seemed to be rather whether their players were ready to seize political opportunities. In the Baltic countries, as in other Eastern European countries, there were simply no players ready to mobilize on the left. Incidentally, this was also the case for Ireland for quite some time (O'Connor, 2017). Recently, authors have also begun drawing attention to the presence and strength of local organizations and players as a key endogenous factor as well (Kriesi, 2012). Social movements with resources and strong protest traditions have a key role in offering a diagnosis of the political situation and a prognosis of what could be done to improve it (Flesher Fominaya, 2017). They can also use the experience from previous mobilizations, resources, and contacts to mobilize. This is exactly what happened in Southern Europe's mobilizations against austerity, where social movements stepped in to mobilize action, often in alliance or competition with trade unions, NGOs, and political parties.

Thus, if one wants to understand the protest cycle in the EU after 2008, one should take into account both the economic crisis as an exogenous factor and the national presence and strength of players capable of organizing protest as an endogenous factor. Both explanations are crucial and necessary for understanding the dynamics of the protest cycle. But they are not sufficient. One important question cannot be answered by either of these explanations, namely, why did protests in different countries often share the same slogans and protest repertoires, such as occupying squares and organizing assemblies? What explains the striking similarities between protests in different countries? And why were protests often clustered in particular regions: protests against austerity in Southern Europe; anti-ACTA protests mainly in Eastern Europe, Austria, and Germany; and protests against TTIP and CETA in Austria and Germany, with strong instances also in Belgium and Spain? What explains the predominance of certain types of protest within certain regions where countries have close cultural ties?

Beyond both exogenous and endogenous explanations of the dynamics of the protest cycle, I argue that what was at play in all these cases was clearly a dynamic of diffusion of information and resources between countries, often facilitated by sharing the same language or having similar cultures. Different countries influenced each other and could not be treated as fully separate and independent. What is more, while at the beginning of the protest cycle many Eastern European countries had almost no left-wing players, by the end of the cycle, such players had appeared and were gaining strength. The main way in which these players emerged was in fact through diffusion of ideas and discourses from the West to the East. This book thus focuses on the multiple processes of diffusion taking place within the same protest cycle. I argue that cross-national diffusion introduces a dynamic element to the interaction between exogenous shocks and endogenous players, allowing also new types of players to emerge, even where they did not exist before. Diffusion does not happen "spontaneously" but most often is the result of the conscious efforts of diffusers, that is transmitters, to spread their message and of adopters to transform it for the local circumstances. Before discussing the key players driving diffusion, I first present in more depth the rationale behind studying diffusion processes and their key elements.

1.2. Diffusion Studies: From Hard Tomatoes to Sit-Ins and Occupations

Diffusion studies have a long history that predates their application to the study of social movements. The field's origins can be traced to post-war US agricultural science when agricultural universities were interested in how to diffuse innovative knowledge, practices, or objects, such as genetically modified seeds or new machinery, among farmers (Rogers, 2003). Starting from topics such as the diffusion of hybrid corn, antibiotics, and hard tomatoes – easier to pick mechanically but much less tasty – diffusion studies gradually consolidated as a field and generalized across cases in order to outline typical rates of adoption and the common characteristics of successful innovations and of early adopters and laggards, among others.

In the early 1990s, social movement studies as a field started paying increasing attention to research in diffusion, with several seminal collections published since then (Givan and Roberts, 2010; della Porta and Mattoni, 2014). Studies of diffusion in social movements analyzed not only contemporary events but also went back in history to explore the diffusion patterns of strikes in 19th-century US and Paris (Biggs, 2003, 2005) or diffusion processes in the American civil rights movement (Andrews and Biggs, 2006, 2010; Mansour, 2014). The analysis of diffusion of sit-ins in the 1960s, for example, showed that what mattered for successful diffusion was above all news media, plus a dedicated cadre of activists, rather than mass membership in organizations. Studies of the global protests after the economic crisis, in turn, revealed that despite the prevailing opinion that digital media have drastically sped up the process of diffusion, the 1848 protest cycle had in fact diffused much more quickly (Gerbaudo, 2013). In the aftermath of 2008, protest travelled "slowly and tortuously" from Middle East and North African countries, where the so-called Arab Spring erupted, to the Mediterranean and then to the US's Occupy Wall Street, because as it turned out local protest cultures and cultural context still matter greatly, "even in an era of instantaneous communication technologies" (ibid., 86).

Despite the slow speed of diffusion, protest, protest frames, and repertoires did spread also in the post-2008 protest wave (Baumgarten and Díez García, 2017; Flesher Fominaya, 2017). What is more, some of the key messages of the post-2008 protest cycle could be traced back to the American new left protests in the 1960s (Díez García, 2017), showing that protest diffusion takes place not only within the same protest cycle but also in time between different cycles. Tracing diffusion even further back in time, Chabot and Duyvendak explored the connections between the 1960 American freedom movement and the Gandhian repertoire in India and tried to explain how diffusion between such different contexts was made possible (Chabot and Duyvendak, 2002). As we already discussed, scholars so far have been unable to answer the question of what causes protest cycles and whether there is some common "master variable" that explains all protest cycles. What research has shown for sure, however, is that there are diffusion processes at play not only within the same cycle but also between different protest cycles, which involve the transmission of resources and information such as descriptions of protest practices, pledges, declarations of solidarity, etc.

While explanations of social processes often focus on exogenous structural factors, approaches that focus on diffusion emphasize the importance of communication, imitation, and learning processes for the occurrence of any social event. If there was a series of protests across the EU in the aftermath of the crisis, this was certainly because citizens in many countries were angry at how their governments reacted to the economic shock. But it is also due to the fact that citizens observed what citizens in other countries, both across the globe and in Europe, did, communicated with them, and actively exchanged resources and information. It is diffusion that could explain how the occupation of squares as the signature tactic of the latest cycle of protests spread from Tahrir Square in Egypt to Puerta del Sol in Spain and Zuccotti Park in New York (Gerbaudo, 2017). And it is also diffusion that could explain why many of the slogans and explanations used by the protesters were similar to the ones from previous cycles of protest, including both the late 1990s and early 2000s alter-globalization movement (Gerbaudo, 2017; Flesher Fominaya, 2017) and even the American civil rights movement (Díez García, 2017).

Within social movement studies, diffusion has been famously defined as

> the acceptance of some specific item, over time, by adopting units – individuals, groups, communities – that are linked both to external channels of communication and to each other by means of both a structure of social relations and a system of values, or culture.
>
> *(Katz, quoted in McAdam and Rucht, 1993, 59)*

According to this definition, there are four main elements of diffusion:

> (1) a person, group, or organization that serves as the emitter or transmitter; (2) a person, group, or organization that is the adopter; (3) the item that is diffused, such as material goods, information, skills, and the like; and (4) a channel of diffusion that may consist of persons or media that link the transmitter and the adopter.
>
> *(McAdam and Rucht, 1993, 59)*

Most research on diffusion in social movements so far has focused on the latter two elements of diffusion: what is diffused and how. Some authors have added another dimension focusing on why diffusion takes place (della Porta and Mattoni, 2014; Soule and Rogeband, 2018). What I claim is that much more attention in social movement studies needs to be paid on the diffusers and adopters of protest, that is, the strategic players driving the process and their media practices. Basically, what I propose is to place in the centre of analysis the players who diffuse protest. Only by analyzing who does the diffusion can we understand better what is being diffused, how, and why. The framework that allows us to do this is Duyvendak and Jasper's work *Players and Arenas*.

1.3. Players and Arenas in Protest Diffusion

Scholars of social movements have consistently emphasized that protest diffusion should not be treated as some sort of biological "automatic" contagion but as an agentic political process (Tarrow and McAdam, 2005). At the same time, there have been few attempts to study systematically all the players involved in diffusion. In the literature so far, protest diffusion has been considered primarily a concern of protesters and studied mainly from the perspective of bottom-up activists. But this view has unnecessarily narrowed the question and has precluded us from a simple yet important insight: protest is diffused not only by bottom-up activists or even only by activists and NGOs acting together, but also by a variety of other actors, including intellectuals, media, NGOs, political parties, and trade unions. Each of these players can be highly important for the diffusion of protest.

The emphasis on players is important also because it helps us understand better why some pathways of diffusion are more prominent in particular cases. Different types of players engage in diverse types of media practices, have distinct types of networks, and are connected transnationally to a different extent. They also have mixed levels of expertise, institutional authority (if any), and levels of access to mass media or digital media. Thus, identifying the types of actors and their background and resources can help us significantly in predicting which diffusion they will opt for.

The focus on players in this book is inspired by the innovative research of Duyvendak and Jasper on players and arenas and the interactive dynamics of protest (2015). The authors distinguish between simple players – individuals, and compound players – ranging from "loose, informal groups to formal organizations all the way up to nations tentatively or seemingly united behind some purpose" (Duyvendak and Jasper, 2015, 10). Compound players are never completely unified and, following Gamson's analysis, are treated as "necessary fictions" (ibid.). Interestingly, Jasper and Duyvendak insist that players can also be treated as arenas:

> a compound player almost always devotes more time to internal interactions – making decisions, performing rituals of solidarity, eating or occupying together – than to external engagements. . . . A player that looks unified from the outside is still going to be an arena for contestation within.
>
> *(ibid., 12)*

Within this framework, an arena is identified as "a bundle of rules and resources that allow or encourage certain kinds of interactions to proceed, with something at stake" (ibid., 14). Somewhat like light that can be treated as both a particle and a wave depending on the instruments of the observer, compound players involved in contention can be treated as both players and arenas, depending on the observer. Ultimately, Duyvendak and Jasper claim that if we want to understand

> how protest arises, unfolds, and affects (or does not affect) the world around it, research needs to begin with catalogues of the players involved on all sides. These lists often need to be quite extensive, and include the multiple goals and many capabilities a player has at its disposal. The goals and the means, furthermore, change over time, as do the players themselves.
>
> *(ibid., 13)*

Applying these insights to the diffusion of protest against free trade and austerity, what I propose is to analyze how different types of political players navigated complex media arenas in order to diffuse protest. In the next section, I focus in more detail on a selection of different types of players that are key for protest diffusion, specifically bottom-up activists, intellectuals, NGOs, media, political parties, and trade unions. Accepting that protest diffusion is driven not only by activists opens up a series of important questions and has important consequences for our understanding of what diffuses in a protest and how.

First, if one accepts that protest diffuses not only between individuals but also between organizations such as trade unions and political parties, or that it can be driven also by media organizations, the question of institutions looms large. This question is essential and shows the deficiencies of many studies that treat diffusion of protest as a form of contagion (Bonnasse-Gahot et al., 2018; Saideman, 2012). While contagion theories of protest diffusion have been around for quite some time, they became particularly popular in the age of big data when troves of information from Twitter and Google became available for researchers to test hypotheses on diffusion. The problem is that models that compare protest diffusion to contagion often focus exclusively on individuals and their networks or on populations as a whole. This might work for spontaneous events such as riots (Bonnasse-Gahot et al., 2018) but is much more problematic when it comes to the diffusion of protests that often require extensive preparation and organization. Only rarely do mathematical models of diffusion as contagion pay attention to the role of groups or collectives of actors in diffusion (Newton and Sercombe, 2020), and they almost never account for the role of institutions in protest diffusion. When I urge my 800 friends on Facebook to follow me tomorrow to a protest, this statement has a very different effect from a situation in which a trade union leader urges the 800 members of the union to go to the streets to protest. What matters is not only how many connections a node has but also the nature of these connections. Authority, power, and path-dependence all come into play in important ways when an institution decides whether to support a particular protest and try to diffuse it. Analyses that treat diffusion as "contagion" that happens between individuals completely overlook the importance of institutional actors.

The role of institutional players is crucial also in understanding what diffuses. With viruses and bacteria, there is an easily traceable biological substratum. But what spreads when protest spreads? Apart from protest itself (della Porta and Mattoni, 2014), the content of diffusion can occur in two primary dimensions: behavioural and ideational (Givan et al., 2010: 5), i.e. what is diffused are movement tactics, collective action repertoires, and frames. The importance of paying attention to the players involved in diffusion and their strategic actions becomes even clearer when exploring how diffusion takes place. Indeed, this has been a key topic in the literature so far: in a further development of the original 1993 theory of McAdam and Rucht's on mechanisms of diffusion, Givan and colleagues outlined three general mechanisms of diffusion: relational (based on direct network ties between individuals and organizations), non-relational (based mainly on mass media that allow geographically distant actors to get acquainted with the latest developments from distant contexts), and mediated diffusion, known also as brokerage (based on actors' connection to a third actor, "who is able to facilitate the diffusion of information and actions") (Givan et al., 2010, 212). With the rise in the use of Web 2.0 applications, research on mechanisms of diffusion drew attention to the role of the Internet, and social media in particular, as a specific channel that blurs the distinctions between relational and non-relational diffusion: users can often connect directly to each other and spread information (Bailón et al., 2013; Kwon and Hemsley, 2017; Mercea, 2016). Furthermore, it has been famously suggested that social media change the nature of protest mobilization and diffusion and lead to a new type of "connective action" instead of the collective action of the past, which was driven mainly by collective actors such as classes or nations (Bennett and Segerberg, 2012).

In this book I put digital media "in their place" and explore them as only one among many other channels for diffusion, including relational diffusion through personal contact, as seen in the marches of Spanish activists to Brussels, and non-relational diffusion through mainstream media reports or through more classic "media" such as books, for example. I explore how different political players engage in a wide variety of media practices (Mattoni, 2012), including but not reducible to digital media. Clearly, different types of players have very diverse personal networks and varied levels of access to both mainstream media and digital media networks. Studying diffusion independently of the type of players that drive it overlooks these important differences and the reasons for the dominance of particular types of diffusion.

Crucially, there is no such thing as simple "diffusion", as actors often transform information while diffusing it through time and space. What is more, "transnational diffusion processes are circuitous, complex and reciprocal rather than linear as the transmitter-adopter model would suggest" (Flesher Fominaya, 2017, 11). Flesher Fominaya gives the example of protest diffusion between Spain and Portugal: the Portuguese Geração à Rasca movement took place in March 2011 and inspired Spanish protesters who occupied Puerta del Sol in Madrid in May the same year. The Spanish occupation in turn inspired similar occupations in Lisbon. The line between transmitter and adopter is not always clear, and the same players can engage in creative translation on both sides (Anderl, 2016).

Overall, even though existing research on diffusion in social movements has made remarkable progress in the last 20 years, there is still no overarching explanation of why diffusion succeeds or fails or why it takes the shape it does. Instead, there are a number of separate, often disconnected hypotheses. Beyond describing pathways of diffusion, can researchers convincingly predict whether protest diffusion will be successful? The foundational scholars of the field declared explicitly this is not what they aimed to answer (Tarrow and McAdam, 2005, 145). Yet, this is precisely what activists want to know: how can we make diffusion work?

One of the reasons for the lack of such a unifying model, according to this book, is that the field of social movement studies has consistently underplayed the question of "transmitters" and "adopters" that has dominated classic diffusion studies, i.e. who are the main players involved in the diffusion process, what are their properties, and how do they interact with each other? But only by analyzing who does the diffusion can we understand what is being diffused and how, and as a consequence how successful diffusion will be in terms both of reach and of convincing people to protest.

1.4. Key Players

Following Duyvendak and Jasper's approach in *Players and Arenas*, in the next section I describe in more detail the key players for protest diffusion that I focus on in this book. I have identified these players deductively based on an extensive review of the existing literature on protests and social movements. The following list is by no means exhaustive but outlines the most essential players that researchers need to consider when analyzing diffusion. Other types of players can and will be added in the process of analysis, but I argue that these are the most basic players that each analysis of protest diffusion needs to take into account as a starting point:

Bottom-Up Protesters

Quite expectedly, bottom-up protesters and activists have been the most explored player when it comes to protest diffusion. Almost all existing literature on protest diffusion focuses on bottom-up protesters and social movements (della Porta and Mattoni, 2014; Givan et al., 2010). There have been a number of important studies on activists' media practices (Gerbaudo, 2012; Mattoni, 2009, 2012; Treré, 2018) and on the role of Internet use for protest diffusion (Castells, 2012; Kwon and Hemsley, 2017; Mercea, 2013; Vasi and Suh, 2013). To be sure, a number of authors emphasized that protest diffusion cannot be explained with the spontaneous spread of messages thanks to digital media but rather with activists' histories, pre-existing networks, and protest traditions (Flesher Fominaya, 2013, 2015; Gerbaudo, 2013; Zamponi, 2012; Zamponi and Daphi, 2014; Zamponi and Fernández González, 2017). Interestingly, most research so far has focused on progressive social movements, and only recently have researchers started paying attention to the diffusion of far right protests (Berntzen and Weisskircher, 2016; Gattinara and Pirro, 2019).

In any case, an exclusive focus on protest activists does not grasp diffusion in its full complexity and dynamics. Activists are a crucial player in protest diffusion but not the only player involved. The frames that can be found in protesters' slogans, interviews, and online manifestos often predate the concrete protest and are the result of knowledge production by movements (Cox, 2014; Díez García, 2017) but also by researchers, scientists, epistemic communities, or what can be broadly called intellectuals (Rochon, 1998). Protest frames and forms of contention travel via embodied social movement practices and via digital media, but also via books, university lectures, newspaper articles, opinion pieces, TV shows, internal trade union communications, party newspapers, and so on. The complexity of these media arenas reflects the complexity of political players involved. This is why bottom-up protesters are the first but definitely not the only players that I look for when analyzing diffusion processes.

Intellectuals

The role of intellectuals for articulating particular ideologies and visions of society has already been convincingly demonstrated by socialist thinker Antonio Gramsci in the beginning of the 20th century (O'Neill et al., 2017; Ramos, 1982). What is more, intellectuals as key players in triggering change together with social movements (with all potential problems their relationship might entail) have received renewed attention in the last decades (Baud and Rutten, 2010; Borg and Mayo, 2007; Kurczewsky, 1997; Rochon, 1998).

That said, it must be noted that while the importance of neoliberal thought collectives and the intellectual origins of neoliberalism as a project have been extensively explored (Mirowski, 2009; Slobodian, 2018), a comprehensive intellectual history of resistance to neoliberalism is still missing. The renewed interest in capitalist social movements and the role of think tanks in promoting conservative ideas and expertise (Sklair, 2016; Stahl, 2016) has not yet been matched by a similar wave of publications tracing the connections between different progressive social movements and intellectuals trying to influence policy. At the same time, intellectuals have greatly influenced progressive social movements.

For example, authors such as Ernesto Laclau and Chantal Mouffe have been pivotal for the political strategies of the new left in countries such as Spain and Greece. What is more, authors such as Manuel Castells have influenced strongly with their techno-enthusiasm activists and researchers across the world, but especially in Spain. The techno-political experiments of the Spanish Indignados movement have also produced important organizational experience and expertise that activists diffused in other countries and that became the object of extensive academic research.

The borders between research and activism are sometimes extremely porous. And while a lot of attention has focused on the role of digital media, one of the most powerful media for the diffusion of protest is still books. The very name of the Spanish protesters who called themselves Indignados (The Outraged) came from Stéphane Hessel's book *Indignez-Vouz!*, translated in Spanish as ¡*Indignaos!* (Time for Outrage). It is not a coincidence that the period of contention following the Indignados protests in Spain has also been a period of active translation of foreign thinkers into Spanish in an attempt to conceptualize and steer the deep political transformation of Spanish society (Fernández, 2020).

Political Parties

Political parties might seem to be an unlikely player in diffusing protest. Didn't the post-2008 protest movements gain support precisely because citizens are more and more disappointed with political parties? As the title of a research paper on the Spanish Indignados succinctly states, "Young People Took to the Streets and All of a Sudden All of the Political Parties Got Old" (Hughes, 2011). Indeed, anti-austerity protesters in countries like Spain and Italy were very suspicious of political parties and defined their protests as explicitly independent from them. This suspicion towards political parties has been a common feature of many of the protests of the latest wave of contention. Yet, attitudes have varied from country to country. While Spanish anti-austerity protests were dominated by bottom-up protesters, anti-austerity protests in Portugal and Greece were to a large extent co-organized by both trade unions and left-wing political parties (Carvalho, 2019; Kanellopoulos et al., 2017). What is more, even in Spain, the peak of protests coincided with a massive boom in the establishment of new political parties – only in the period between 2011 and 2012, 492 political parties were created (Tormey and Feenstra, 2015). The role of political parties was even more pronounced in anti-free trade protests, where radical left and Green parties from across the EU actively collaborated with NGOs and trade unions to oppose agreements such as TTIP and CETA (Bauer, 2016).

Scholars both of the far left and of the far right explored the rise of so-called movement parties in the last decade and have emphasized the fuzzy empirical boundaries between parties and movements (della Porta et al., 2017). A recent large-N comparative analysis of movement–party interactions across Europe revealed that party-sponsored protests have been a crucial feature of protest in contemporary Europe (Borbáth and Hutter, 2019). In highly differentiated contexts, where protests sponsored by parties are rare, the typical protestor party very much mirrors the image of movement parties – it does not belong to mainstream party families and has no governing experience (ibid.). In less differentiated contexts, where parties often support protests, parties are driven to the streets by more strategic considerations, for example when they are in opposition (ibid.; Andretta, 2018).

It was mainly left-wing and Green political parties that took part in the protests against free trade and austerity that I explore. Yet, opposition to TTIP and CETA was increasingly appropriated by the far right parties such as AfD in Germany and Lega Nord in Italy (Rone, 2018). In the protests against ACTA, Pirate Parties were instrumental, especially in Germany, where they had already gained popularity and media influence and had a good position to frame the public debate. When exploring political parties as players in the process of diffusion, I explore not only their ideology and media practices but also the ways they cooperate with other actors and advance different media strategies.

Trade Unions

Theories of new social movements have treated labour unions as firmly embedded within capitalist industrial relations and increasingly defined by the "iron law of oligarchy", very similar to political parties. In this context, it is not surprising that in the last few decades, social movement scholars rarely perceived trade unions as agents of progressive social change. Instead, they expected that new social movements (fighting on issues such as women's rights or the environment) would assume this progressive role. Nevertheless, already in the mid-1990s, some authors challenged this perspective and insisted that trade unions were actually receptive to broader social problems and ready to forge alliances (Carroll and Ratner, 1995). What is more, a powerful new vision of "social movement unionism" emerged, envisaging unions fighting for social justice beyond the narrow economic confines of old trade unions that dealt primarily with workplace issues, payment, and terms and conditions (Engeman, 2015; Fairbrother, 2008; Moody, 1997).

Indeed, far from being "remnants from the past" co-opted by the state, trade unions have increasingly cooperated with social movements in a variety of contexts. A number of authors have shown that trade unions played a crucial role in anti-austerity mobilizations across Southern Europe (Andretta, 2018; Baumgarten, 2013; Carvalho, 2019; Kanellopoulos et al., 2017; Zajak, 2018). Unions were also important in the mobilization against TTIP (Gortanuti, 2016). But not only did trade unions take part in protest diffusion, they also shaped it in distinctive ways depending on their relative prominence. A key question for labour politics in recent years has been whether trade unions can forge robust transnational cooperation in order to mobilize against the increasingly non-democratic features of EU's new economic governance regime (Erne, 2018). The Stability and Growth Pact and other EU instruments of economic governance set targets for states to aim for (in an almost managerial way), thus nationalizing social conflict and compelling states to compete with each other (Erne, 2017). Following up on Erne's research and drawing on the unsuccessful attempts of Spanish trade unions to transnationalize the fight against austerity, this book makes a strong appeal for more collaboration between Eastern and Western trade unions.

NGOs

Unlike trade unions and political parties that have often been considered as compromised by their connections to established power, for a long time NGOs have been perceived by social movements and researchers alike as an important and independent ally for progressive causes. That said, the relations between NGOs and social movements have been quite complex. Social movement scholars have often paid attention to the dangers of moderation and co-optation related to the NGO-ization of movements. What is more, in recent years a number of authors have noticed an increasing disconnect between these two types of players (Esteves et al., 2009) and even between the literatures studying them (della Porta, 2014). In many parts of Eastern Europe, social movements have explicitly targeted NGOs as inauthentic and serving foreign interests (Rone, 2016), contributing to significant rifts in relations between these two players. The history of the establishment of NGOs can be a particularly important factor to explain their ideology and also appetite (or lack thereof) for confrontation. For example, many NGOs in Eastern Europe were established in the 1990s to promote democracy and the free market, perceived as inseparable. Thus, it is no surprise that they have rarely sided with left-wing social movements.

At the same time, NGOs often have more resources than social movements have, which makes them valuable allies. NGOs such as Association pour la Taxation des Transactions financières et pour l'Action Citoyenne (ATTAC), Seattle to Brussels, and Campact played a crucial role in the mobilizations against CETA and TTIP, for example, thanks to their funding, organizational expertise, and media strategy that successfully targeted mainstream media and used digital media in a centralized and efficient fashion. NGOs in the cases I analyze in this book had superior access to legal expertise that gave their claims an additional authority and impact in public debates and in lobbying. In fact, this book claims that one of the main reasons for the different paths of diffusion observed in anti-free-trade campaigns as compared to anti-austerity campaigns was the varying level of involvement of NGOs. While in the protests against free trade agreements transnational NGOs were early comers that defined the problems, in the case of anti-austerity protests, mostly national NGOs followed suit after popular mobilizations and had less influence over mobilization and diffusion processes.

Media

Media are an important player with high levels of agency and impact in diffusing protest. There has been substantial research on the dilemmas activists face when trying to attract journalists' attention and the unequal power relations between social movements and mass media (Gamson and Wolfsfeld, 1993). Furthermore, activists and mass media often clash over the framing of events. For instance, scholars have shown the highly tendentious way in which mainstream media such as *Der Spiegel* reported on Greek protests against austerity (Mylonas, 2015). While most of the time media have the upper hand, activists sometimes manage to push forward alternative framings as seen, for example, in the battle over framing the US war in Nicaragua (Ryan, 1991).

The functions of gate-keeping, priming, and agenda setting might seem radically transformed by new digital media (Bro and Wallberg, 2014), where everyone can publish what they decide (as long as it doesn't violate the terms of service, one must add). Digital platforms such as Facebook deliberately reinforced this image by insisting that they are not publishers but simply platforms that do not engage in moderation. Nevertheless, numerous authors have shown that platforms do moderate and govern, even if their human moderators are largely an appendix to algorithms (Gillespie, 2018). What is more, digital media and politics scholars have increasingly drawn attention to the role of algorithms as the material underpinning many digital platforms and have shown that they follow a logic very different from the logic of activism and collective change (Couldry, 2014; Klinger and Svensson, 2018). Media are not just channels but important players in the process of protest diffusion.

I am particularly interested in the interplay between traditional and digital media in protest diffusion. Purportedly neutral "channels" of communication such as Google, Tumblr, Twitter, and Wikipedia participated in a massive "blackout" in protest of the US Stop Online Piracy Act (SOPA) and the Protect IP Act (PIPA), thus declaring a clear political position. Following their example, a number of Polish websites, including Wykop.pl, JoeMonster, and Helion.pl, participated in a blackout to protest against ACTA and thus further attracted the attention of mainstream media that was eager to explain what was going on. But mainstream media are not always in the position of laggards who try to understand what is going on. A particularly poignant example of mainstream media as key players for mobilization and protest diffusion is the way the widely circulated Austrian print newspaper *Die Kronen Zeitung* embraced the anti-TTIP and anti-CETA cause and massively swayed public opinion in the country. What is more, in many of the protest diffusion cases I discuss, there was a significant feedback loop in which protests starting online drew attention to mainstream media whose videos and information were then shared to make the protests even bigger online.

1.5. Conclusions

Each of the types of players outlined earlier is important for protest diffusion. But the crucial question for explaining diffusion is how these different players interact – what particular constellations of players can be observed and what their media practices are. The hypothesis forwarded in this book is that diverse patterns of protest diffusion can be explained by the different constellations of actors acting as original transmitters and adopters, and their media practices. Bottom-up protesters count more on their personal networks and diffuse ideas through direct contact – both live and on user-friendly online platforms such as Facebook, Twitter, or alternative open source platforms. On the contrary, intellectuals and members of political parties, NGOs, and trade unions count not only on personal contacts but often have privileged access to mainstream media's networks of distribution. They might also have the financial resources to build purpose-oriented digital platforms and media solutions. In addition, each of these players might have a very different idea of what is to be diffused and what the best way is of doing it. This focus on players and their strategic interactions does justice to the idea that protest diffusion is not an act of "contagion" but a political process with different strategic considerations involved.

The book focuses on the empirical cases of diffusion of protest against austerity and free trade in the EU. But beyond exploring these protests in depth, the book aims also to build a theory that can be useful more generally for understanding why protest diffusion fails or succeeds and how it happens.

The idea is that once I analyze and compare the anti-austerity and anti-free trade protests, I would be able to tell what types of transmitters and adopters account for successful or failed diffusion of protest. I will not pretend that my analysis is definitive and exhaustive and includes all relevant players – a "full description" of all players involved can be an endless task. It would also be a pointless task – a bit like creating a map of the territory that coincides completely with the territory in Borges's famous short story "On the Exactitude in Science".

Instead, drawing on rich qualitative data, I identify the constellations of players that can be involved in the diffusion of protests and explore their media practices. In terms of methodology, throughout the book, I have triangulated social network analysis with qualitative content analysis of media reports and activists' documents, and most crucially, with interviews with key figures in the mobilizations. The book has also relied extensively on secondary literature on protests within Europe after the economic crisis and attempts to provide a summary and systematization of a number of studies that have focused on particular country cases but not so much on the connections between them. While the analysis is centred on the six types of players I identified in this chapter and the relations between them, other (often-unexpected) players emerged inductively in the process of research – among whom are small- and medium-sized businesses, hacktivists, city councils, and torrent trackers. I also added these players in my analysis.

Overall, this chapter has traced the history and theory of protest diffusion and has outlined the theoretical and methodological foundations of the book. I have tried to show why studying diffusion processes is crucial if one wants to understand the dynamics of the protest cycle after the 2008 crisis. In the next chapter, I explore in more depth the anti-austerity protests across the EU after 2008 and try to account for the particular pattern of diffusion of these protests based on the players involved and their specific media practices.

References

Anderl, Felix (2016): The Myth of the Local. *The Review of International Organizations*, 11, 197–218.

Andretta, Massimiliano (2018): Protest in Italy in Times of Crisis: A Cross-Government Comparison. *South European Society and Politics*, 23:1, 97–114.

Andrews, Kenneth and Michael Biggs (2006): The Dynamics of Protest Diffusion: Movement Organizations, Social Networks, and News Media in the 1960 Sit-Ins. *American Sociological Review*, 71:5, 752–777.

Andrews, Kenneth and Michael Biggs (2010): From Protest to Organization: The Impact of the 1960 Sit-Ins on Movement Organizations in the American South. In: Rebecca Kolins Givan, Sarah A. Soule, and Kenneth M. Roberts (eds.), *The Diffusion of Social Movements: Actors, Frames, and Political Effects*. Cambridge: Cambridge University Press, 187–203.

Bailón, Sandra González, Javier Borge-Holthoefer and Yamir Moreno (2013): Broadcasters and Hidden Influentials in Online Protest Diffusion. *American Behavioral Scientist*, 57:7, 943–965.

Baud, Michiel and Rosanne Rutten (eds.) (2010): *Popular Intellectuals and Social Movements: Framing Protest in Asia, Africa, and Latin America*. Cambridge: Cambridge University Press.

Bauer, Matthias (2016): *Manufacturing Discontent: The Rise to Power of Anti-TTIP Groups*. Retrieved from http://ecipe.org/app/uploads/2016/11/Manufacturing-Discontent.pdf.

Baumgarten, Britta (2013): Geração à Rasca and Beyond: Mobilizations in Portugal After 12 March 2011. *Current Sociology*, 61:4, 457–473.

Baumgarten, Britta and Rubén Díez García (2017): More Than a Copy Paste: The Spread of Spanish Frames and Events to Portugal. *Journal of Civil Society*, 13:3, 247–266.

Bennett, Lance and Alexandra Segerberg (2012): The Logic of Connective Action: Digital Media and the Personalization of Contentious Politics. *Information, Communication & Society*, 15:5, 739–768.

Berntzen, Lars Erik and Manès Weisskircher (2016): Anti-Islamic PEGIDA Beyond Germany: Explaining Differences in Mobilisation. *Journal of Intercultural Studies*, 37:6, 556–573.

Biggs, Michael (2003): Positive Feedback in Collective Mobilization: The American Strike Wave of 1886. *Theory and Society*, 32:2, 217–254.

Biggs, Michael (2005): Strikes as Forest Fires: Chicago and Paris in the Late 19th Century. *American Journal of Sociology*, 110:6, 1684–1714.

Bonnasse-Gahot, L., H. Berestycki and M. Depuiset (2018): Epidemiological Modelling of the 2005 French Riots: A Spreading Wave and the Role of Contagion. *Scientific Reports*, 8, 107.

Borbáth, Endre and Swen Hutter (2019). A Comparative Analysis of Parties Protest Involvement Across Europe. *Party Politics*. Doi:10.1177/1354068820908023.

Borg, Carmel and Peter Mayo (2007): *Public Intellectuals, Radical Democracy and Social Movements, a Book of Interviews*. New York: Peter Lang.

Bro, Peter and Filip Wallberg (2014): Digital Gatekeeping. *Digital Journalism*, 2:3, 446–454.

Carroll, William K. and R.S. Ratner (1995): Old Unions and New Social Movements. *Labour/Le Travail*, 35, 195–221, January. Retrieved from www.lltjournal.ca/index.php/llt/article/view/4965.

Carvalho, Tiago (2019): *Contesting Austerity: A Comparative Approach to the Cycles of Protest in Portugal and Spain Under the Great Recession (2008–2015)*. PhD Thesis, Department of Sociology, University of Cambridge, Cambridge.

Castells, Manuel (2012): *Networks of Outrage and Hope: Social Movements in the Internet Age*. Cambridge: Polity Press.

Chabot, Sean and Jan Willem Duyvendak (2002): Globalization and Transnational Diffusion Between Social Movements: Reconceptualizing the Dissemination of the Gandhian Repertoire and the 'Coming Out' Routine. *Theory and Society*, 627–640.

Christiansen, Jonathan (2009): *Four Stages of Social Movements*. EBSCO Publishing Inc. Retrieved from www.ebscohost.com/uploads/imported/thisTopic-dbTopic-1248.pdf.

Cilliers, Paul (2005): Complexity, Deconstruction and Relativism. *Theory, Culture, Society*, 22, 255–266.

Couldry, Nick (2014): The Myth of 'Us': Digital Networks, Political Change and the Production of Collectivity. *Information, Communication and Society*, 18:6, 608–626.

Cox, Laurence (2014): Movements Making Knowledge: A New Wave of Inspiration for Sociology? *Sociology*, 48, 954–971.

della Porta, Donatella (2014): Democratization from Below: Civil Society Versus Social Movements? In: T. Beichelt, I. Hahn-Fuhr, F. Schimmelfennig and S. Worschech (eds.), *Civil Society and Democracy Promotion: Challenges to Democracy in the 21st Century Series*. London: Palgrave Macmillan.

della Porta, Donatella and Alice Mattoni (2014): *Spreading Protest: Social Movements in Times of Crisis*. Essex: ECPR Press.

della Porta, Donatella et al. (2017): *Movement Parties Against Austerity*. London: Polity Press.

Díez García, Rubén (2017): The 'Indignados' in Space and Time: Transnational Networks and Historical Roots. *Global Society*, 31:1, 43–64.

Engeman, Cassandra (2015): Social Movement Unionism in Practice: Organizational Dimensions of Union Mobilization in the Los Angeles Immigrant Rights Marches. *Work, Employment and Society*, 29:3, 444–461.

Erne, Roland (2017): How to Analyse a Supranational Regime That Nationalises Social Conflict? The European Crisis, Labour Politics and Methodological Nationalism. In: E. Nanopoulos and F. Vergis (eds.), *The Crisis Behind the Euro-Crisis: The Euro-Crisis as Systemic Multi-Dimensional Crisis of the EU*. Cambridge: Cambridge University Press.

Erne, Roland (2018): Labour Politics and the EU's New Economic Governance Regime (European Unions): A New European Research Council Project. *Transfer: European Review of Labour and Research*, 24:2, 237–247.

Esteves, Ana Margarida, Sara Motta and Laurence Cox (2009): 'Civil Society' vs Social Movements, Editorial. *Interface: A Journal for and About Social Movements*, 1:2, 1–21.

Fairbrother, P. (2008): Social Movement Unionism or Trade Unions as Social Movements. *Employee Responsibilities and Rights Journal*, 20, 213.

Fernández, Fruela (2020): Tool-Box, Tradition, and Capital: Political Uses of Translation in Contemporary Spanish Politics. *Translation Studies*. Doi:10.1080/14781700.2020.1731589.

Flesher Fominaya, Cristina (2013): Movement Culture Continuity: The British Anti-Roads Movement as Precursor to the Global Justice Movement. In: Laurence Cox and Cristina Flesher Fominaya (eds.), *Understanding European Movements New Social Movements, Global Justice Struggles, Anti-Austerity Protest*, London: Routledge, Advances in Sociology, 109–124.

Flesher Fominaya, Cristina (2015): Debunking Spontaneity: Spain's 15-M/Indignados as Autonomous Movement. *Social Movement Studies*, 14:2, 142–163.

Flesher Fominaya, Cristina (2017): European Anti-Austerity and Pro-Democracy Protests in the Wake of the Global Financial Crisis. *Social Movement Studies*, 16:1, 1–20.

Frank, Andre Gunder and Maria Fuentes (1994): On Studying Cycles in Social Movements: Research in Social Movements. *Conflicts and Change*, 17, 173–196.

Gamson, William A. and Gadi Wolfsfeld (1993): Movements and Media as Interacting Systems. *The Annals of the American Academy of Political and Social Science: Citizens, Protest, and Democracy*, 528, 114–125.

Gattinara, Pietro Castelli and Andrea L.P. Pirro (2019): The Far Right as Social Movement. *European Societies*, 21:4, 447–462.

Gerbaudo, Paolo (2012): *Tweets and the Streets: Social Media and Contemporary Activism.* London: Pluto Press.

Gerbaudo, Paolo (2013): Protest Diffusion and Cultural Resonance in the 2011 Protest Wave. *The International Spectator: Italian Journal of International Affairs*, 48:4, 86–101.

Gerbaudo, Paolo (2017): *The Mask and the Flag: Populism, Citizenism and Global Protest.* London: Hurst and Company.

Gillespie, Tarleton (2018): *Custodians of the Internet: Platforms, Content Moderation, and the Hidden Decisions That Shape Social Media.* New Haven, CT: Yale University Press.

Givan, Rebecca, Sarah Soule and Kenneth Roberts (eds.) (2010): *The Diffusion of Social Movements.* Cambridge: Cambridge University Press.

Goldstone, Jack (1991): *Revolution and Rebellion in the Early Modern World: Population Change and State Breakdown in England, France, Turkey and China, 1600–1850*, 25th anniversary edition. Berkeley: University of California Press.

Gortanuti, Giulia (2016): *The Influence of Trade Unions and Social Movements on EU Trade Policy.* Retrieved 20 March 2017, from goo.gl/qufCxK.

Hughes, Neil (2011): 'Young People Took to the Streets and All of a Sudden All of the Political Parties Got Old': The 15M Movement in Spain. *Social Movement Studies*, 10:4.

Kanellopoulos, Kostas, Konstantinos Kostopoulos, Dimitris Papanikolopoulos and Vasileios Rongas (2017): Competing Modes of Coordination in the Greek Anti-Austerity Campaign, 2010–2012. *Social Movement Studies*, 16:1, 101–118.

Klinger, Ulrike and Jacob Svensson (2018): The End of Media Logics: On Algorithms and Agency. *New Media and Society*, 1–18.

Kousis, Maria and Christina Karakioulafi (2013): *Labour Unions confronting Unprecedented Austerity in Greece, 2010–2013.* Paper for Panel P301, Southern European Labour Contention: New and Old Repertoires, Social Alliances, and Party Relations, ECPR General Conference, Bordeaux, 4–8 September.

Kriesi, Hans-Peter (2012): The Political Consequence of the Financial and Economic Crisis in Europe: Electoral Punishment and Popular Protest. *Swiss Political Science Review*, 18:4, 518–522.

Kriesi, Hans-Peter (2015): Political Mobilization in Times of Crises: The Relationship Between Economic and Political Crises. In: Marco Giugni and Maria T. Grasso (eds.), *Austerity and Protest: Popular Contention in Times of Economic Crisis.* Burlington: Ashgate, 19–33.

Kurczewsky, Jacek (1997): Intellectuals and Social Movements in Process of Transformation. *Polish Sociological Review*, 119, 211–226.

Kwon, Hazel and Jeff Hemsley (2017): Cross-National Proximity in Online Social Network and Protest Diffusion: An Event History Analysis of Arab Spring. *Proceedings of the 50th Hawaii International Conference on System Sciences.* Retrieved from http://hdl.handle.net/10125/41414.

Mansour, Claire (2014): The Cross-National Diffusion of the American Civil Rights Movement: The Example of the Bristol Bus Boycott of 1963. *Miranda*, October. Online Since 23 February 2015, Connection on 19 April 2019. Retrieved from http://journals.openedition.org/miranda/6360. Doi:10.4000/miranda.

Mattoni, Alice (2009): *Multiple Media Practices in Italian Mobilizations Against Precarity of Work*. PhD Thesis, European University Institute, Florence.

Mattoni, Alice (2012): *Media Practices and Protest Politics: How Precarious Workers Mobilize*. London: Routledge.

Mattoni, Alice (2017): A Situated Understanding of Digital Technologies in Social Movements: Media Ecology and Media Practice Approaches. *Social Movement Studies*, 16:4, 494–505.

McAdam, Doug and Dieter Rucht (1993): The Cross-National Diffusion of Movement Ideas. *The Annals of the American Academy of Political and Social Science*, 528:1, 56–74.

Mercea, Dan (2013): Probing the Implications of Facebook Use for the Organizational Form of Social Movement Organizations. *Information, Communication and Society*, 16:8, 1306–1327.

Mercea, Dan (2016): The Social Media Overture of the Pan-European Stop-ACTA Protest: An Empirical Examination of Participatory Coordination in Connective Action. *Convergence*, 22:3, 287–312.

Mirowski, Philip (2009): *The Road from Mont Pelerin: The Making of the Neoliberal Thought Collective*. Cambridge: Harvard University Press.

Moody, Kim (1997): Towards an International Social Movement Unionism. *New Left Review*. Retrieved from https://newleftreview.org/issues/I225/articles/kim-moody-towards-an-international-social-movement-unionism.pdf.

Mylonas, Yannis (2015): Austerity Discourses in 'Der Spiegel' Magazine 2009–2014. *Triple C: Communication, Capitalism and Critique*, 13:2, 248–269.

Newton, Jonathan and Damian Sercombe (2020): Agency, Potential and Contagion. *Games and Economic Behavior*, 119, 79–97.

O'Connor, Francis (2017): The Presence and Absence of Protest in Austerity Ireland. In: *Late Neoliberalism and its Discontents in the Economic Crisis*. London: Palgrave Macmillan, 65–98.

O'Neill, Deirdre and Mike Wayne (2017): *On Intellectuals, in Considering Class: Theory, Culture and the Media in the 21st Century*. Boston: Brill.

Portos García, Martín and Tiago Carvalho (2019): Alliance Building and Eventful Protests: Comparing Spanish and Portuguese Trajectories Under the Great Recession. *Social Movement Studies*. Doi:10.1080/14742837.2019.1681957.

Ramos, Valeriano (1982): The Concepts of Ideology, Hegemony, and Organic Intellectuals in Gramsci's Marxism. *Theoretical Review*, 27, March–April.

Rochon, Thomas (1998): *Culture Moves: Ideas, Activism and Changing Values*. Princeton: Princeton University Press.

Rogers, Everett (2003): *Diffusion of Innovations*, 5th edition. New York: Simon and Schuster.

Rone, Julia (2016): The People Formerly Known as the Oligarchy: The Cooptation of Citizen Journalism, Citizen Media and Public Spaces. In: Mona Baker and Bolette Blaagaard (eds.), *Critical Perspectives on Citizen Media*. London: Routledge.

Rone, Julia (2018): Contested International Agreements, Contested National Politics: How the Radical Left and the Radical Right Opposed TTIP in Four European Countries. *London Review of International Law*, 6:2.

Ryan, Charlotte (1991): *Prime Time Activism*. Boston: South End Press.

Saideman, Stephen M. (2012): When Conflict Spreads: Arab Spring and the Limits of Diffusion. *International Interactions*, 38:5, 713–722.

Sklair, Leslie (2016): The Transnational Capitalist Class, Social Movements, and Alternatives to Capitalist Globalization. *International Critical Thought*, 6:3, 329–341.

Slobodian, Quinn (2018): *Globalists: The End of Empire and the Birth of Neoliberalism*. Cambridge: Harvard University Press.

Snow, David and Robert Benford (2000): Framing Processes and Social Movements: An Overview and Assessment. *Annual Review of Sociology*, 26, 611–639.

Soule, Sarah and C. Rogeband (2018): Diffusion Processes Within and Across Movements. In: Hanspeter Kriesi, David Snow and Sarah Soule (eds.), *The Blackwell Companion to Social Movements*. Oxford: Blackwell.

Stahl, Jason (2016): *Right Moves: The Conservative Think Tank in American Political Culture Since 1945*. Chapel Hill: The University of North Carolina Press.

Strugatsky, Arkady and Boris Strugatsky (2014): *Hard to Be a God*, translated by Olena Bormashenko. Chicago: Chicago Review Press.

Tarrow, Sidney (1998): *Power in Movement: Social Movements and Contentious Politics*, 3rd edition. Cambridge: Cambridge University Press.

Tarrow, Sidney and Doug McAdam (2005): Scale Shift in Transnational Contention. In: Donatella della Porta and Sidney Tarrow (eds.), *Transnational Protest and Global Activism*. New York: Rowman & Littlefield.

Tormey, Simon and Ramón A. Feenstra (2015): Reinventing the Political Party in Spain: The Case of 15M and the Spanish Mobilisations. *Policy Studies*, 36:6, 590–606.

Treré, Emiliano (2018): *Hybrid Media Activism: Ecologies, Imaginaries, Algorithms*. London: Routledge.

Vasi, Ion and Chan S. Suh (2013): *Protest in the Internet Age: Public Attention, Social Media, and the Spread of 'Occupy' Protests in the United States*. Draft. Retrieved from https://www.politicsandprotest.ws.gc.cuny.edu/files/2012/07/PPW-2-Vasi.pdf.

Zajak, S. (2018): Social Movements and Trade Unions in Cross-Movement Counter Mobilization. In: J. Grote and C. Wagemann (eds.), *Social Movements and Organized Labour: Passion and Interests*. London: Routledge, 82–108.

Zamponi, Lorenzo (2012): 'Why Don't Italians Occupy?' Hypotheses on a Failed Mobilisation. *Social Movement Studies*, 11:3–4, 1–11.

Zamponi, Lorenzo and Joseba Fernández González (2017): Dissenting Youth: How Student and Youth Struggles Helped Shape Anti-Austerity Mobilisations in Southern Europe. *Social Movement Studies*, 16:1, 64–81.

Zamponi, Lorenzo and Daphi Priska (2014): Breaks and Continuities in and Between Cycles of Protest: Memories and Legacies of the Global Justice movement in the Context of Anti-Austerity Mobilisations. In: Donatella della Porta and Alice Mattoni (hgs.), *Spreading Protest: Social Movements in Times of Crisis*. Essex: ECPR-Press, 193–226.

2

QUIET, YOU MIGHT WAKE
UP THE GREEKS

The Diffusion of Protests Against Austerity

2.1. Lo Spread

In the 2012 film *Every Blessed Day* by Italian director Paolo Virzì, a young couple in crisis-hit Italy tries to have a child. The man, a brilliant translator from Latin, works as a hotel receptionist, while the woman, a talented singer-songwriter, works at a car rental company. They have not been on vacation for ages and they barely see each other despite living in the same flat: she goes to work the moment he comes back from his night shift. During an important visit to the gynaecologist, as the girl spreads her legs for examination, one can hear on the radio news about "Lo Spread" – the difference between borrowing costs for Italy and for Germany. In 2012, the Italian debt to GDP ratio reached 120% and the country paid around 5% of its GDP to service its interest rates (Statistical Data Warehouse, 2020). Such was the fascination of the Italian public with the topic of "Lo Spread" that even in the gynaecologist's office one could not escape from reports on it.

What the "spread" scene in Virzì's film does is to show in a playful way the intricate connection between often vague and abstract macro-economic indicators and the very concrete real-life experiences of the "lost generation" of the 2008 economic crisis. This generation has had to deal with unprecedented unemployment levels, precarious jobs, and the postponing of key life decisions such as moving out of their parents' home or having a child due to complete existential insecurity. But the crisis hit not only the young generation. In Eastern Europe, in countries like Bulgaria, Latvia, and Romania, the crisis affected strongly also retired people and state employees of every age, showing that no one was safe. As Spanish citizens took to the streets en masse to protest austerity, Bulgaria saw a series of more than 20 fatal self-immolations, as people from the age of 21 to 82 set themselves on fire for personal, political or economic reasons. Many of them were either pensioners or unemployed. The first self-immolation that attracted widespread media attention and to some extent inspired subsequent ones was that of 36-year-old photographer and mountain climber Plamen Goranov, who protested against the capture of Varna municipality by a local oligarchic circle. While anti-austerity protests in Spain were public and angry but also cheerful and involving a collective attempt to prefigure a different future, the series of self-immolations in Bulgaria were often a private affair of desperation and lonely suffering. After instances of this most dramatic type of protest multiplied, even the media stopped reporting on them for fear that paying too much attention might stimulate further attempts. Between these two poles – the mass street protests and the lonely suicides by fire – the period after the 2008 economic crisis was marked by the everyday struggles of people such as the characters of Paolo Virzì's film, who just tried to live their life the best as they could while the radio aired news on spreads, possible sovereign debt default, and protesters clashing with the police.

In this chapter, I explore how macro-level economic policies in a variety of EU countries provoked very different responses from their citizens – from innovative forms of protest (such as occupations and protest marches from all corners of Spain towards Brussels) to emigration, self-immolations, or simply acquiescence. I explore this differentiated politicization of the 2008 economic crisis by paying special attention to processes of diffusion and exchange between key players in different EU countries. I start the chapter with a brief description of the unfolding of the 2008 economic crisis and the imposition of austerity policies across the EU, often against the democratic will of the people.

2.2. A Brief History of the Economic Crisis and Austerity Measures in the EU

Democracy in Danger: Two Scenes From Cannes and Brussels

In August 2011, at the height of the Eurozone crisis, with worries about Italy's ability to service its national debt dramatically increasing, the outgoing and incoming presidents of the European Central Bank, Jean-Claude Trichet and Mario Draghi, sent a letter to Italian Prime Minister Silvio Berlusconi urging him to engage in a series of structural reforms, including pension reforms, the privatization of local public services, and labour flexibilization, among others, in order to restore the confidence of international markets (Verney and Bosco, 2013, 403). Needless to say, these were politically toxic reforms that enjoyed little public support. But what was at stake was not only the confidence of markets. When asked at the end of the European Council Summit in October whether they had confidence in Berlusconi, Germany's Chancellor Angela Merkel and France's President Nicolas Sarkozy famously smirked (Bickerton, 2016). During the G20 summit in Cannes that followed, Berlusconi had to accept an IMF supervision of the country's reform commitments, which was unprecedented considering that Italy had not taken a loan from the IMF. Greek Prime Minister George Papandreou was summoned to the same G20 summit, despite not being a leader of a G20 country, and was reprimanded for his decision to call a referendum on the second bailout for Greece (the first bailout had taken place already in 2010). During the meeting, the French and German leaders made it clear that if Greece failed to implement the measures required from it, an exit from the Eurozone was on the table (Verney and Bosco, 2013).

Soon after the eventful Cannes meeting, Papandreou withdrew the referendum and transformed an already announced vote of confidence in the government into a vote of confidence that would allow him to form a new government in which he wouldn't take part. While these highly unusual events were taking place in Greece, members of Berlusconi's own party called for his resignation, and Italy's longest serving prime minister since World War II resigned on November 12, 2011. The president of the country, Giorgio Napolitano, appointed as his successor the technocrat Mario Monti, who was now leading an expert government supported by a broad parliamentary majority formed by Berlusconi's Party of Freedom, the Democratic Party, and the Centrist Union. Monti was appointed to get through Parliament the tough austerity package for the country, including measures to freeze public sector salaries until 2014, raise the retirement age for women, increase value-added tax (VAT), and fight tax evasion.

The BBC article on the Italian events stated, "Mr Monti, a well respected economist, is exactly the sort of man that the money markets would like to see take charge at this time of crisis" (BBC, 2011). This sentence, in one of the world's most authoritative news media, is impressive because of the way it treats money markets as an entity that has its own desires and would even "like to see" particular developments. The metaphor, because this is nothing but a metaphor, seemed so obvious to the authors of the text that they felt no need to explain it. The fact that a democratically elected prime minister such as Berlusconi, even if he was considered to be a "buffoon" by the crowds (BBC, 2011), could be replaced to satisfy "the markets" remained unproblematized and received no further commentary in the short news piece. Unlike most news reports, however, political scientists did not fail to notice that the way Berlusconi was removed posed a serious challenge to democracy (Bickerton, 2016; Culpepper, 2014). If a country's leader can be swiftly replaced in order to satisfy other countries' leaders or the abstract entity of the "markets", why bother organizing elections to begin with?

As further developments in Greece revealed, this question could be expanded also to "why bother organizing referenda?" After several tumultuous protest years that brought to power in Greece the far left Syriza, in early July 2015 Greek Prime Minister Alexis Tsipras followed up on what Papandreou had attempted and announced a democratic referendum on whether to accept the agreement plan for the, by that point, third bailout of Greece. The bailout agreement submitted by the European Commission, the European Central Bank, and the International Monetary Fund (collectively known as the Troika) to the Eurogroup comprised a further set of austerity reforms in exchange for lending money to the Greek government. Considering that both previous bailouts had utterly failed, Greek people overwhelmingly voted against these conditionalities, in full knowledge that a "No" answer (the famous OXI) might mean an exit from the Eurozone.

After a combative and dramatic Euro Summit in Brussels that lasted 16 hours and went well into the night of the 13th of July, Prime Minister Tsipras saw himself forced to ignore the result of the referendum and accept a further swathe of austerity measures and economic reforms in a blatant contradiction to popular will. According to EU officials, Tsipras was "crucified" during the meeting and looked like a "beaten dog" (Beattie, 2015). The international Twitter Hashtag #thisisacoup started trending in sign of protest to the treatment of Greece but to no avail (Hänska and Bauchowitz, 2018). Greek opposition was broken and an "agreekment", in the playful words of Donald Tusk, was reached. On July 15, 2015, the governing radical left (at least back then) party Syriza voted together with the opposition to accept the conditionalities of the Troika.

These highly publicized episodes of intervention into the national politics of Italy and Greece show clearly that austerity measures in these countries were imposed in a far from democratic way (Bickerton, 2016). What is more, as recurring problems with debt and state deficit in Greece continued, even the IMF admitted that the Greek programmes were unsuccessful. But what made the imposition of such harsh measures necessary? And how did countries such as Italy and Greece end up in a situation of such spectacular loss of sovereignty? As happens in TV series, we need a flashback in time, from the 2011 removal of Berlusconi and Papandreou and the 2015 Greek referendum back to 2008 when the US Lehman Brothers financial services company collapsed, marking the beginning of an economic crisis the scale of which the world had not seen since the 1930s. This crisis had dramatic effects across the EU. And while academic attention has focused mainly on the Eurozone – countries that have the euro as their currency, Eastern European countries such as Romania, Hungary, and Latvia that were not in the Eurozone in this period also experienced serious difficulties and had to ask the IMF for help, while countries such as Bulgaria imposed austerity even without external pressure.

Flashback: The Crisis Hits

During the 2000s as belief in algorithms and the use of increasingly complex financial instruments soared, the US witnessed an increase in both housing speculation and subprime mortgage lending, that is, lending for high-risk mortgages that were later bundled together in mortgage-based securities (MBS) and resold. As the US housing bubble burst and the prices of housing started going down, more and more mortgage owners defaulted on their payments, thus decreasing the value of mortgage-based securities. Hedge funds and investment companies that had borrowed from global investors to buy such securities saw themselves forced to offer collaterals or pay back immediately, causing a crisis across the system and numerous bankruptcies. The 158-year-old US financial company Lehman Brothers had to close its mortgage lending unit BNC and, after a year of turmoil, declared bankruptcy in September 2008, setting the record for the largest bankruptcy in the history of the United States (Singh, 2018). In October the same year, the US voted for an emergency bailout of its banking system amounting to 700 billion dollars of tax payers' money in order to prevent full collapse.

Many European banks were strongly exposed to US subprime mortgages, and governments across the EU had to step in and provide bailouts to their banks as well in order to prevent the collapse of their whole financial system. The bailouts were done with public money leading to substantial budget deficits. In normal situations, countries could borrow money on the financial markets, but as countries such as Greece, Ireland, and later Italy started losing the confidence of markets and investors, it became prohibitively expensive for them to borrow. With interest rates so high, such countries had to pay a large per cent of their GDP just to service the interests. It was this situation that forced them into the role of debtors accepting tough conditions in exchange for loans. From 2010 to 2012 Greece, Ireland, Portugal, and Spain entered into negotiations with the Troika with the former three countries receiving a full-fledged bailout package and Spain a bailout for its banking sector. While Italy did not receive a bailout, it agreed, as already mentioned, to allow the IMF to scrutinize its finances to restore confidence among investors and to try to stop the increasing spread between its borrowing costs and those of Germany (the famous "Lo Spread").

In all these cases, the Troika insisted on "structural reforms" – a term that has been generally clouded in ambiguity and has included different requirements for each country. Still, "despite floating meaning, the notion of structural reforms exhibits a persisting core consisting of typically neoliberal policy recipes such as the liberalization of products and services markets, the deregulation of labour markets, and public administration reform" (Crespy and Vanheuverzwijn, 2019). The Troika openly advocated a policy of austerity. Its function was to allow governments to service their debt, but it was also justified as promoting growth through supply-side reforms that were meant to encourage businesses to invest and export. This type of austerity has been justified as expansionary austerity (Meloni, 2017), and by targeting predominantly state employees and the sectors of the social state, it offered more of the same logic that had contributed to rising levels of state and private indebtedness in the European peripheries to begin with.

Across the EU, the welfare state had been retrenched in vital spheres such as housing and healthcare already before the crisis, and thus the financial burden was increasingly passed on to citizens themselves as part of "the privatization of the welfare state" (Crouch, 2009; Nachtwey, 2018). As middle-class wages stagnated in many Western countries, due to the effects of both globalization (Milanovic, 2016) and a class-interest-driven rise in inequality (Harvey, 2005), the only way for citizens to keep up with a middle-class lifestyle was to borrow money. The system of private credit amounted thus to yet another attempt at "buying time" for an increasingly unequal global capitalism (Streeck, 2014). This dynamic became especially pronounced in the EU's southern periphery during the economic boom of the 2000s, when the banks of core EU states provided easy credit to consumers in the South to fund private consumption, but also investment. This was easier than ever since in the Eurozone area all countries shared a common currency and a single interest rate (Scharpf, 2016; Regan, 2017). The influx of cheap credits led to asset price bubbles in Southern Europe and made its countries "extremely vulnerable to financial markets and a sudden stop in capital inflows" (Regan, 2017, 11). And this is precisely what happened once the financial crisis hit the US. But not only private citizens were in debt. States were also increasingly indebted for a variety of reasons, including weak economic growth, rising unemployment, increasing inequality, growing tax resistance, and declining political participation, thus giving rise to what political economist Wolfgang Streeck has called "the debt state" (2013, 2014). The increased tax avoidance of the rich and the offshoring of money led to an additional decrease in tax revenues, further emptying the coffers of the state (Zuckerman, 2015). In a sense, it was precisely the "shrinking of the state" that increased public and private indebtedness that in turn was "cured" after the economic crisis by even more shrinking of the state forced on states by the Troika.

Beyond bailouts for individual countries, in 2012 all governments of the EU, with the exception of the Czech Republic and the UK, signed the Treaty on Stability, Coordination and Governance in the Economic and Monetary Union (TSCG). The "Fiscal Compact", as the treaty is better known as, envisaged among other things that all countries should adopt a balanced budget rule in their binding legislations (Morlino and Sottilotta, 2019). EU instruments strengthening budgetary discipline turned out to be much stricter in terms of surveillance and enforcement than any initiative aiming to improve social investment in the EU (de la Porte and Heins, 2015). The consequences of this were clear: with strict limits on budget deficits, crisis-hit governments could not afford investing in healthcare, education, or research and development, not to mention in government-financed projects to boost demand. In this way, austerity trapped countries that were already in trouble in a vicious circle.

But there was also a second element of austerity policies that is crucial for understanding the Eurozone crisis in particular. In the context of the Eurozone, the Troika promoted austerity also with the stated goal of increasing the "export competitiveness" of Southern countries caught in a dynamic of persistent trade imbalances with the North. This has led several authors to talk about "competitive austerity" (Meloni, 2017) as connected to and expanding on the (supposedly) expansionary austerity discussed earlier. The policy of competitive austerity was premised on the assumption that the imbalances in the Eurozone were due to Southern countries' low external competitiveness. Considering that all these countries were members of the euro, they could not devalue their currency, and the only way to increase their competitiveness, the Troika narrative went, was to slash wages and social contributions and make the price of labour cheaper in order to stimulate exports. Instead of following Keynesian economic ideas of boosting domestic demand, the Troika insisted on the necessity of internal devaluation (that is, making the cost of labour cheaper) to boost competitiveness and external exports. The embattled governments of Greece, Italy, Ireland, Portugal, and Spain did not have much room to manoeuvre. While countries like Spain had experimented with Keynesian politics in the beginning of the crisis (Portos, 2019, 49), subsequently they all agreed to some extent to impose austerity measures, even if this meant a full-blown social crisis, increased unemployment (especially among the youth), and high levels of out-migration.

Greece has been the most well-known example of the disastrous consequences of austerity: the controversial bailouts of the country amounted to transferring German taxpayers' money as a loan to Greece, which then had to "give them back" to French and German banks (Varoufakis, 2017). This amounted ultimately to transferring money from ordinary citizens to financial elites. Meanwhile, the country saw its GDP plummet and experienced a full-blown social catastrophe with a notable deterioration of healthcare and retirement schemes and a massive outflow of young people. Ireland, the poster child of austerity, did recover and regain the confidence of financial markets, but that was due not so much to austerity reforms as to the considerable investments of US tech companies that were attracted by a mix of low corporate taxes, cultural proximity, and, more generally, the path-dependent effect of its liberal market economy model (Regan, 2014).

Why Austerity?

Why did the Troika insist so much on austerity policies even if they turned out to have disastrous consequences? The rhetorical justification of austerity policies often included the invocation of the proverbial example of the Swabian housewife who never spends too much and always has a balanced account. While the fallacy of this approach when extended from the household level to the country level has been convincingly demonstrated (Blyth, 2013), moralistic tales of hard-working Germans as opposed to Greeks who waste money on "booze and women" were often put forward by politicians from the North to justify their strictness (DW, 2017). Needless to say, northern self-righteousness and moralistic tales of southern laziness did not resonate too well in the South. What is more, recent experimental research has shown that the household metaphor as a way to explain complex economic issues also doesn't affect citizens' preferences over government budgets, but is mainly invoked ex-post by politicians to justify their actions (Barnes and Hicks, 2020).

So did the Troika insist on the "dangerous idea" of austerity (Blyth, 2013) just out of ideological stubbornness? Or was it a clear class-interest-driven project to redistribute wealth from the poor to the rich? One explanation that tries to find a rationale for austerity, beyond stubbornness and outright class war, claims that the aim of such policies was to achieve structural convergence in the Eurozone between the Southern economies, whose growth model is based on domestic demand, and Northern European economies that are much more export-driven (Scharpf, 2016). Austerity policies thus could be seen as having the double aim of reducing the imbalances within the Eurozone and improving the export performance of the Eurozone as a whole. Improving export competitiveness fit well with the external trade offensive by the European Commission that engaged in negotiations for a number of bilateral free trade agreements in the 2010s with the aim of opening new markets to EU exporters. This trade-oriented agenda in the EU made strategic sense in a world where China rose as a key actor and the US had pivoted towards the East and initiated talks for a Trans-Pacific Partnership (TPP). In this changing international environment, the EU aimed to overcome the economic crisis and reassert itself as a key trade actor on the global scene. In hindsight, the failure of EU's strategy to promote export competitiveness in Southern Europe was to be matched by the shock to the world trading system caused by the 2016 election of Donald Trump as president of the US and the 2020 coronavirus crisis.

And while the election of Trump and the rise of protectionism would have been difficult to predict, the problem with EU's austerity policies as a way to increase export competitiveness in the South lay in a diagnosis that was faulty from the very beginning: "focusing on external competitiveness and unit labour costs misdiagnoses the problem and the cure" (Regan, 2017, 5). One could not make all countries within the Eurozone export champions considering that the monetary union functions as a semi-closed trading economy, in which a gain for competitiveness for one country can only come at the expense of a loss of another country (Regan, 2017, 6–7). The export success of Germany was closely connected to the increase in imports by Southern European countries. What is more, the very weakness of Southern economies prevented the euro from becoming more expensive and thus stimulated even further German exports to third countries. The attempt to transform the domestic-consumption-driven economies of Italy or Greece into export-driven ones through supressing wages – what the Troika demanded – hit Southern economies exactly where their strength was without delivering a substantial increase in export competitiveness, i.e. improving their weak side. The human cost of this experiment was dramatic, with serious cutbacks in welfare, education, and quality of life and numerous families being separated due to emigration. But even if one decides to ignore the human losses and suffering and cold-heartedly accept competitiveness as the ultimate goal, austerity policies fail to deliver.

The even bigger problem with EU's austerity policies was that in many cases they were negotiated in non-democratic ways, and they constrained democratic choice in the future as well. Whatever one might say about the disastrous consequences of austerity policies in Latvia and Lithuania, it would be a stretch of imagination to insist that the governments or populations of these countries strongly opposed them through voting or street protests (even if they might have disapproved of them). Nevertheless, in countries such as Italy, Spain, and Greece austerity policies did provoke mass protests and resistance. Yet, citizens were made to accept them for their own good in the longer run. "No pain, no gain" was the motto of the decade. And yet, as the decade drew to a close, it seemed that what had happened was a lot of economic and personal biographic pain, and still no gain. To paraphrase the famous Shakespeare play "Love Labour's Lost", the 2010s were EU's labour lost.

All Quiet on the Eastern Front?

Even though most analyses focus on austerity policies in the EU and especially on the Eurozone crisis, similar developments could be observed in EU's eastern periphery, as well as in countries that had not adopted the euro. Eastern European countries such as Latvia and Hungary entered into negotiations with the IMF already back in 2008, followed by Romania in 2009. Even in the absence of such negotiations, Bulgaria, mentioned in the introduction of the book, implemented harsh austerity policies justified with the colourful rhetoric of the financial minister Simeon Dyankov (former chief economist of the finance and private sector vice-presidency of the World Bank), who compared the country's budget to a shrinking pizza. In the years of the crisis, Dyankov even proposed to constitutionalize measures that would not allow the budget deficit to go over a 3% threshold (Rone, 2017). Despite the almost complete focus in both the political economy and social movement literature on the Eurozone, the economic crisis in fact spread also to other EU countries, where national elites often readily accepted austerity measures. Even countries which could devaluate their currency, such as Romania or Hungary (Bulgaria and Latvia could not devaluate since their currencies at the time were pegged to the euro for different reasons), opted for tough austerity reforms that led to even further retrenchment of the welfare state in the region.

In the early days of the economic crisis, the European Commission had pledged to help struggling economies in the East, but as it failed to find broad support for such type of action, it ultimately let the IMF lead the politically controversial programmes that aimed at cutting state spending in states with serious problems of growth (New York Times, 2009). Hungary was the first Eastern European state to find itself in dire straits after the collapse of Lehman Brothers – as the financial crisis deepened, investors started carefully assessing the risk profiles of countries, and Hungary with its high budget deficit and government indebtedness didn't score very high in terms of credibility (Horvath, 2009). In addition, by 2008, Hungarian household debt had reached 40% of the GDP

(Trading Economics, 2020) as numerous Hungarian citizens had taken mortgage loans in foreign currencies because of their lower interest rates. As markets reassessed perceived risk, "the forint started to weaken, financial institutions faced insufficient liquidity and numerous citizens saw their debts in foreign currencies increase" (Horvath, 2009). Unable to avert bankruptcy not only for private borrowers but also for the country, Hungary saw itself forced to search for a bailout and concluded the agreement with the IMF for a bailout programme in October 2008 (Kickert and Ongaro, 2019, 1353). The loan came with demands for austerity measures such as cuts in social benefits that hit mostly pensioners and civil servants (Connolly and Trayner, 2008). The programme was highly disputed and was ultimately left unfinished. It was precisely the scandal around the bailout deal that facilitated the coming to power of Victor Orban's Fidesz in 2010. One of Orban's most popular economic policies was the conversion of all foreign-denominated debt into forints.

Even though Latvia's bailout deal encountered political problems in the beginning, including the resignation of the prime minister, the deal was successfully approved in December 2008 and finished as initially negotiated in 2011 (Kickert and Ongaro, 2019, 1353). The bailout came again with requirements for structural reforms and fiscal tightening leading to similarly harsh outcomes for key state sectors and a rise in emigration. Still, Latvia saw much less unrest both in party and protest politics in comparison to Hungary or Southern European states.

Finally, Romania also had to ask for a bailout from the IMF in the early years of the crisis. Among the key measures imposed by the agreement were

> Decreasing wages in the public sector by 25% and the elimination of many extra-benefits; Public pensions cuts by 5% – this measure was declared unconstitutional by the Constitutional Court and was compensated by a VAT increase from 19% to 24% and the imposition of a tax for the health insurances; Decreasing the total number of positions for employees paid by the state by 200,000 during the 2009–2011 period; 15% cut in unemployment and child benefits; Structural reforms of 141 government agencies; Tax increases for owners of more than one house or car; – Institutional reform to decrease tax evasion; Privatization of various state companies like Oltchim, Cupru-Min, Transelectrica, Transgaz, TAROM, and Posta Română.
>
> *(Todor, 2014, 35)*

In addition, in 2011 the Parliament approved a new Labour Code that was marked by "increased flexibility of employing and dismissing employees, the implementation of fixed-term work contracts, and decreasing the immunity of trade union leaders" (ibid., 35). As if these measures were not enough, strict austerity measures were also employed in the healthcare system with 67 hospitals closed and an ambitious plan to privatize the emergency system, transfer health insurance to private companies, and privatize hospitals or transform them into foundations (ibid., 36).

One of the most shocking aspects of the Romanian austerity programme, but also of austerity measures recommended across the EU, has been their clearly regressive character. State finances were consolidated by consistently cutting expenditure with insufficient focus on the necessity of taxation. Wherever revenue was to be raised through taxes, indirect taxes such as VAT were recommended. Such an approach entrenched inequality and had catastrophic social consequences. Romania was one of the countries with the most regressive austerity measures, and this was due not to any economic reason but primarily to ideological convictions (Todor, 2014, 39).

Indeed, Eastern Europe is such an important case for studying austerity measures since in many Eastern European countries national elites fully embraced these measures. Policy makers in countries such as Romania had internalized neoliberal ideas to such an extent that they went even further than what the IMF proposed and the IMF had to restrain them, warning of the dangerous effects of austerity policies on their own populations (Ban, 2016). Countries such as Latvia and Lithuania had adopted tough neoliberal reforms already in the beginning of the 1990s, opting for the promotion of nationalism as a way to foster solidarity in the face of crumbling systems of welfare and social support (Bohle and Greskovits, 2012).

But while governments in many Eastern countries openly embraced austerity measures, this did not necessarily mean that the population of these countries was so enthusiastic. A growing feeling of lack of representation and resentment towards the political system was prevalent among citizens in the East. In countries like Bulgaria and Romania, the famous apathy towards street politics gave way to an "end of patience" (Beissinger and Sasse, 2014) and a series of mass street protests, even if they were rarely formulated as anti-austerity ones. In the following sections, we will compare the eruptions of protests in reaction to austerity measures across the EU, exploring who the main players were that diffused these protests and their media practices.

2.3. The Diffusion of Anti-Austerity Protests in Southern Europe: The Main Players and Their Media Practices

Bottom-Up Protesters: The Beginning

In January 2011, the neo-fado Portuguese group Deolinda performed at a concert hall their song "*Parva que Sou*", which translates into English as "What a fool I am". The magnetic vocalist of the group sang the sometimes ironic, sometimes sad and slightly angry lyrics describing the life of a young person from a generation that lives without pay in mom and dad's house and has to study only in order to be enslaved afterwards.

The song is written in the tradition of the Portuguese *música de intervenção*, intervention music, that was a powerful part of resistance to dictatorship in the years leading to the Carnation Revolution of 1974. In the same way the song repeated a musical form from the past and playfully reinvented it, the protests it inspired followed in the footsteps of past traditions and yet brought forward new forms of resistance and powerful new coalitions. During the first performances of the song, the audience spontaneously burst into applause after every chorus. Soon, recordings from the concert became viral online and, weeks before an official version of the song was released by the group, people were already sharing it on YouTube and various social networks.

In February 2011, a group of friends on Facebook issued a call for a protest on March 12 with the name "Geração à Rasca" (GaR) – a word play referring to a 1990s journalist's description of student protesters as "Geração Rasca"- "lousy generation", which however acquired, with the addition of "à", the meaning of a "generation that has difficulties to make ends meet" (Carvalho, 2019, 97). The activists posted their message on Facebook and on a dedicated blog and achieved an impressive success in attracting popularity online and subsequently mainstream media attention that increased their reach even further. One of the descriptions on the blog read:

> We, unemployed, five hundred-euristas, and other underpaid workers, disguised slaves, sub- and term-hired, fake independent workers, intermittent workers, trainees, scholarship holders, working students, mothers, fathers and offspring of Portugal . . . We protest so that those responsible for our current situation – politicians, employers and ourselves – act together towards a rapid change in this reality that has become unsustainable.
>
> (Protesto de *Geração Rasca, text translated by and quoted in Acornero, 2018, 196)*

The protest was organized by a group of activists that split in two – four of them were doing the media interviews and communications with mainstream media, while another group of activists was working behind the scenes, taking care of the organizational aspects of protest (Carvalho, 2019, 93). The protest organizers were remarkably capable of using social media to influence the mainstream media framing of protest: the movement wanted to emphasize the precariousness that its members have to deal with and the spontaneity of organization, and both of these self-descriptions were picked up by mainstream media (Acornero, 2018). Thus, contrary to the protest paradigm (Chan and Lee, 1984), according to which mainstream media marginalize protesters as irrational, Portuguese media were surprisingly sympathetic to the movement. Portuguese activists certainly benefited from the strong enthusiasm about the Internet and democratization in the aftermath of the Arab Spring, which was crucial in influencing coverage. Thus, the use of digital media had not only a practical organizational character but also a performative one, designating the belonging of Portuguese activists to the wave of global protest. While in March 2011, GaR activists in Portugal did not occupy squares like Egyptian protesters had done, they continued their actions by creating the Facebook page Forum de Geraçãoes that allowed for online debates of ideas and political proposals and also the platform M12M, which was further involved in organizing the Global Day of Demonstrations on October 15, 2011 (Acornero, 2018).

A network analysis of the M12M platform reveals that the platform had connections with important civil society organizations that embraced it – the Associação 25 de Abril (Association 25 of April), the Movement of the Armed Forces, that had played an important role in toppling the 1974 dictatorship; the Provedor de Justiça (Ombudsman) site set up to hear citizen claims; and the NGO Aprofundamento da Democracia (Deepening of Democracy) movement (Rosas, 2014, 319). The fact that the movement was also embraced by communist writer and Nobel laureate José Saramago added an additional level of legitimacy and public acceptance (ibid.). Nevertheless, while they were well connected at home and received relatively favourable media coverage, Portuguese protesters had fewer international links.

Thus, the Spanish anti-austerity movement, albeit close in a geographical sense and well informed of Portuguese developments, followed its own rhythms and logic. In February 2011, the Organization Juventud Sin Futuro was formed by several Madrid University collectives that had been involved in mobilizations against student reforms associated with the Bologna Process in 2008–2009. The collectives decided to form an organization prompted by the 2010 reforms of labour law and the pension system (15MPedia, 2020a). Juventud sin Futuro took active part in the minority trade union protests against the pension reform in January 2011 and on March 31 announced a protest march on April 7, which was attended by around 10,000 people (ibid.).

Indeed, the months from January to May 2011 saw increased social activity and mobilization among activist circles in Spain. On February 14, 2011, Ley Sinde – a law curbing Internet freedom for the sake of protecting copyright – was approved. This law, discussed in more detail in the next chapter, provoked strong resistance by free and open source activists and the Spanish blogosphere, which launched a campaign known as No les Votes (Don't vote for them). (15MPedia, 2020b). Still in February 2011, a new discussion group was built – Plataforma de coordinación de grupos pro-movilización ciudadana (Coordination platform for citizen pro-mobilization groups). The invitation to participate was distributed online – on blogs, webpages, all kinds of different web fora and collectives, and by March 10, 2011, more than 40 Spanish collectives had joined. It was this discussion group that later was renamed Democracia Real Ya (Real Democracy Now) and coined the key slogan: "*Democracia Real Ya! No somos mercancía en manos de políticos y banqueros*" (Real Democracy Now! We are not goods in the hands of politicians and bankers) (15Mpedia, 2020c). It was all these groups, as well as the

Barcelona-based Plataforma de Afectados Por La Hipoteca – PAH (Platform for Those Affected by Mortgages) formed in 2009, that took part in organizing the massive protests on May 15, 2011, that came to be known as the Indignados or 15M protests.

On May 15, 2011, thousands of people in Madrid, Barcelona, Granada, and other Spanish cities marched on the streets with the slogan "We are not goods in the hands of politicians and bankers". The evening of the same day, after clashes with the police, a group of activists headed to Puerta del Sol and started an occupation that at first was to last until the local elections of May 22, but ultimately it continued for several more weeks. After an attempt by the police to clear the camp on May 17, activists who organized themselves using social media took not only to Puerta del Sol but also to the main squares of over 30 other Spanish cities. In the following months, another form of contention was added: protest marches. From June 20 to June 29, groups of indignant citizens started marching from their cities to Madrid (Iniesta, 2011), and having reached the capital, a group of 50 activists continued towards Brussels. Spanish protesters opposed the striking lack of democratic representation observed in the imposition of austerity measures, the measures themselves, and government and elite corruption seen as an all-pervasive system-defining phenomenon. At the same time, they put forward visions for democratic deepening that were influenced by a strong faith in digital technologies. Rather than subsiding or radicalizing after the first few months, the Spanish protest cycle lasted long and involved innovative actions such as discussion and debates returning to neighbourhood assemblies, the creation of the so-called *Mareas* (Tides) that functioned as working groups on topics such as healthcare or education, and the springing up of numerous innovative digital initiatives (Mattoni, 2017; Portos, 2019).

What is particularly important for the analysis in this book, however, is that at the early stages of protest there was almost no alliance building between activists from Spain and Portugal. Activists from one country surely knew what their counterparts in the other country were doing. A search in the Factiva database, for example, shows that between March and the end of April 2011, Spanish mainstream press, including *El País* and *La Vanguardia*, published 19 articles discussing the Portuguese Geração à Rasca movement. José David, one of the representatives of "Democracia Real Ya", was recorded telling protesters at the occupied Puerta del Sol,

> The demonstrations that took place a few months ago in Portugal were a reference for us . . . Much was said here about what was happening in Portugal and it made us ashamed that we had done nothing here. In Portugal, they showed that one should not be afraid, that one should go out into the street.
>
> *(Jornal de Notícias, 2011)*

Indeed, it seemed that the "generation 'why should I complain'" described in Deolinda's song had grown to political maturity and was ready not only to start complaining but also to take to the streets. And while Spanish Indignados quoted the Portuguese GaR as an inspiration (Jornal de Notícias, 2011), there were in fact few direct connections between activists at this point (Baumgarten and Díez García, 2017, 255).

Reverse connections were, however, present. In May 2011, soon after the occupation of Puerta del Sol, similar actions were taken in Portugal, where Rossio Square in Lisbon was occupied. In fact, as an activist commented, there were more Spanish people at the square originally than Portuguese. Yet, as time progressed more and more Portuguese versions of Spanish organizations appeared, showing clear diffusion of the Spanish model that came later in time but in a sense was considered as a good example of "successful mobilization" (Baumgarten and Díez García, 2017, 254). A Factiva search reveals that the Portuguese mainstream press had a striking number of 502 publications on the Indignados in the month following the protests – more than 25 times the quantity of 19 publications in Spain on the Portuguese GaR protests. Portuguese mainstream newspapers clearly chose to focus on the protests in their neighbouring country, giving them considerable exposure and popularizing their messages, tactics, and leading collectives. Thus, beyond Spanish activists living in Lisbon, the Portuguese mainstream press played a key role in the diffusion of frames and repertoires related to the protest. At the same time, it mattered greatly who the local adopters of protest messages were. In the Portuguese context, trade unions were in fact stronger and more present than bottom-up activists in anti-austerity mobilizations, and they strongly modified the messages of the Spanish Indignados to focus primarily on issues of precarity, inequality, and labour rights – issues that unions traditionally care about (Carvalho, 2019).

Yet, the importance of activists' direct connections and efforts to spread protests should not be underestimated. According to an urban legend, protesters in Spain held a poster with the words, "Quiet, we might wake up the Greeks", thus ironically urging their Greek counterparts suffering from austerity to go to the streets. While the existence of the original poster is yet to be confirmed, once Greek protesters took to the streets, they replied by raising a banner with the words "¡Estamos Despiertos! ¿Qué hora es? ¡Ya es hora que se vayan!" (We have woken up! What's the time? It's time for them to go!) (della Porta and Mattoni, 2014). The protests in Athens were organized on the Facebook page "Aganaktismenoi Sto Syntagma" (Angry ones at Syntagma), and more than 30,000 people attended the first demonstration on May 25, followed by weeks of square occupation and protests (Figure 2.1). In these early days, Greek protesters established a live link on Skype with their Spanish counterparts and also tried to urge activists in other austerity-stricken countries to mobilize. The Greek Indignados – the Aganaktismenoi – held banners with the words "Zitti

FIGURE 2.1   Greek protesters at Syntagma Square, Athens

Source: © Ggia/Wikimedia Commons/CC-BY-SA-3.0

che svegliamo gli italiani" (Be quiet or you will wake up the Italians) and *"Silence! Les Français dorment! Ils rêvent de '68"* (Silence! The French are sleeping! They dream of '68) (Himanen, 2012, 156).

Interestingly enough, the first attempt at occupying Syntagma Square had taken place already on February 23, 2011, yet due to the small number of participants and the decisive actions by the police, it was soon dismantled (Simiti, 2014, 5, quoted in Ferra, 2020). Thus, it was only after the successful mobilization in Spain that Greek protesters moved on to successfully occupy Syntagma. This is a clear example of how and why protest diffusion matters. Clearly, Greece had been anything but quiet by the time Spanish activists occupied Puerta del Sol: by May 2011, Greece had already had five general strikes and at least two large demonstrations against austerity (Kousis and Karakioulafi, 2013). The country had strong and experienced political players in the face of trade unions, far left parties, and bottom-up activists, all of which had engaged in anti-austerity actions in different configurations (Kanellopoulos et al., 2017). Yet, the emergence of the Greek Aganaktismenoi as such was directly inspired by the Spanish occupation as a successful example. It was the protest in the other country that pushed the Greeks to action in this specific form.

Protesters from Spain and Greece clearly cooperated. By September 2011, the Puerta del Sol Economics Working Group and occupants from Syntagma published a joint statement expressing their indignation and inviting "all the squares around the world to join". The groups analyzed the economic measures imposed on Spain and the memorandum of understanding which Greece had to sign and declared:

- The policies of cut-backs that they are applying will not lift us out of the crisis – on the contrary, they push us even further in. They are stretching us to the limit, applying present and future bail-outs which in reality go to the creditor banks and result in serious attacks on our rights, family finances and our national assets.
- We must stand up and protest against these violations. We are the15M movement in Sol and the Popular Assembly of Syntagma.
- Stop adjustment plans and bailouts.
- No to the payment of illegitimate debt. This is not our debt. We owe nothing, we sell nothing, we pay nothing.
- For real and direct democracy NOW.
- For the defence of public interests. Not one sale of public property or services.
- Let all indignados in all the squares join together.

(Joint Statement, 2011)

The statement was republished by radical media such as *ROAR Magazine* and grassroots organizations such as the Committee for the Abolition of Illegitimate Debt. Meanwhile, despite calls of activists for their counterparts in Italy to take to the streets, May and June 2011 passed in Italy without any significant street mobilization or occupation. The Spanish protests were widely commented on in the Italian mainstream press, which, according to Factiva, published over 220 articles containing the word "Indignados". Yet, no "awakening" of street activists in Italy took place.

Italy did have players that could start an occupation similar to those in Spain, Greece, and Portugal. In fact, Italian activists had been early mobilizers against austerity with massive student protests already in 2008 (Zamponi, 2012). Yet, precisely because mobilization had started earlier in Italy, by the time the Indignados protests unfolded, Italian activists had already moved to a next stage of mobilization, involving both more exhaustion and specialization, far removed from the spontaneous indignation that could take people to the streets (ibid.) In July 2011, the youth section of the Trade Union CGIL had a four-day meeting with the indicative name "*Ora, tocca a noi*" (Now, it's our turn), where they had invited activists from Tunisia and Spain to share their stories of mobilization on the squares (Gazzari, 2011). Yet, the Italian turn to protest didn't come all the way until the Global Day of Action on October 15, 2011, when "Indignados" from many nations went to the streets in their respective countries on the same day.

Take the Square: 15M Goes Global

The October 15 Global Day of action was organized by activists from different countries connecting online with the help of Facebook, Twitter, the open source alternative to Facebook N1, a variety of mailing lists, and the platform Mumble for conversations. The initial impetus for the mobilization came from the Spanish Indignados movement that created the webpage "Take the Square" with the explicit goal to spread the movement around the world. The page had sections with political analyses, activist history, news, and tutorials on how to use different types of media such as the N1 network, for example, but also collaborative maps where activists from around the world could add their planned protest events (Take the Square, 2011). One could read on the website posts with catchy titles such as "How to Cook a Non-Violent Revolution" that gave detailed explanations not only of the movement's ideology but also of how labour was divided within the Indignados and how they planned to reach wider audiences, including through the use of Twitter (@acampadasol) and Facebook (Spanish revolution) and through the creation of three complementary websites: takethesquare.net was to be the international one; tomalaplaza.net – the national one, and finally tomalosbarrios.net – the one for operation at the neighbourhood level (Carolina, 2011). Meanwhile, on September 17, 2011, the Occupy Wall Street movement was born in New York. The Spanish Indignados movement had been often interpreted as a precedent and a precursor for Occupy (Castañeda, 2012; Gerbaudo, 2013; Oikonomakis and Roos, 2016). Indeed it was Spanish activists who did the important work of "cultural translation" between the Arab Spring protests and Western democracies, taking up the square occupation as a repertoire and adapting anti-dictatorship frames into frames that focused on austerity, inequality, and demands for direct democracy, relating to a master frame in Western social movements that can be traced back all the way to the American civil rights movement (Díez García, 2017). Indeed, when the Canadian anti-consumerist magazine *Adbusters* launched a call to #OccupyWallStreet in July 2011, they explicitly wanted to encourage "a fusion of Tahrir with the acampadas of Spain" (Adbusters, 2011). The Spanish Indignados contributed to popularizing the call to occupy Wall Street on Twitter, Facebook, and a number of blogs as early as July 2011, thus creating an early link between the two movements (González-Bailón and Wang, 2015, 98).

15M and Occupy merged forces in the organization of the 15O global day to commemorate six months from the beginning of the May 15 Occupation of Puerta del Sol. Unlike subsequent mobilizations, such as the ones against ACTA or TTIP/CETA that had an explicitly European character, the 15O protests were thought of explicitly as global and not necessarily as European. More than 1,000 cities in 82 countries registered events as part of the Global Day of Action (15oct, 2011). As part of the preparation for the protest, Take the Square published a "Guide for citizen participation" encouraging activists to post all information, photos, and descriptions of their local protests in the same database for citizen journalism to facilitate reporting of the event. Activists across the world were invited not only to follow the official Twitter and Facebook accounts of the movement but also to post on Twitter about events using hashtags following the same format: "#live15O and the code of the letters for each city +15O, for example: #mad15O or #nyc15O" (Alicekhatiba, 2011). There were also dedicated live streams that activists could join to watch events from other parts of the world (ibid.). The website also featured kits on how to use media like Mumble (Mumble DRY, 2011), more conceptual kits with instructions on how to occupy squares, and kits on how to ensure that local 15O events would be a success (Alicekhatiba, 2011). All these efforts show clearly that 15M activists used media not only to diffuse protest but also to diffuse knowledge *about* alternative media use as a key component of protest. The attempts to standardize and coordinate the message global protests sent was the result of having to deal with tensions between very different movement cultures across countries and within countries and of trying to find the balance between giving everyone a voice, employing individual modes of participation, and coming up with a unified media message (Mattoni, 2019).

The impressive work that went into preparing the 15O protests shows that the 15M movement activists saw themselves explicitly as diffusers of protest. By this point, diffusion was not accidental or a side project but a primary goal for activists. Spanish 15M activists acted consciously and enthusiastically to produce knowledge about procedures, tech platforms, and tactics that could be useful in other parts of the world. This enthusiasm was exceptional compared to the situation in other Southern European countries that took part in the protests. While left-wing social movements in Italy had been rather sceptical towards the benefits of digital tech for activism, the Greeks had been above all practical, using digital tech whenever necessary. Compared to them, the Spanish enthusiasm for experimentation with different media tools and practices has been exceptional, leading to the emergence of a new form of doing politics, that is, techno-politics (Treré et al., 2017).

At the same time, 15M attempts to diffuse protests experienced varying degrees of success in different contexts. The online spread of protest tactics and information seemed to be most successful in cases where there had already been some connections between activist scenes before. First, while around 1,000 cities had expressed their intention to protest on October 15, 2011, the cities where protests actually had more than 1,000 participants were substantially fewer, and indeed mainly situated in Europe and North America, with almost no events on other continents. The biggest protests in Europe were in Madrid with 500,000 participants, Valencia – 100,000, Barcelona – 60,000, Rome 300,000, Berlin – 10,000, Frankfurt and London – 5,000, and Athens – 4,000. The London protests were the beginning of what was going to become Occupy London. Protest arrived in Britain mostly through the US and less from its Mediterranean

European neighbours, once again showing the importance of pre-existing connections between protest players, this time facilitated by sharing the same language and cultural space.

Overall, the Global Protest of October 15 clearly had two hubs – a European one including Spain, Italy, and Greece (thanks to the original impetus and enthusiasm of Spanish activists) and a US one (thanks to Occupy activists). Research on the digital connections and flow of information between these two hubs during the preparation of the next Global Day of action on May 12, 2012, shows that even after the eventful October 15, 2011, protest, most information still flowed within the 15M movement and within Occupy and not between them. Despite enthusiastic attempts for bridging discourses and players, there were deep structural holes between Occupy and Los Indignados and only a few brokers connecting them (González-Bailón and Wang, 2015).

In terms of protest diffusion within Europe, the most spectacular aspect of the October 15 protest was that finally Italians went out to the streets. After months of discussions on why Italy doesn't mobilize, October 15 triggered a massive organizational effort in the country with a lot of negotiations and careful alliance building between different types of players: a mix of left-wing social movements and collectives, majoritarian and minoritarian trade unions, and various political parties on the left (Coordinamento, 2011). Due to the long time that passed between the Spanish mobilization in May and the Italian one in October, the label "Indignados" diffused in Italy before there was a group ready to identify itself as such. There was a disconnect between the label and the players who had to recognize it as theirs. Italian media first used the label "Indignados" to describe Spanish and Greek protests. After a while, though, mainstream media started using the label to describe a small group of activists camping in Piazza San Giovanni in Rome and then to describe student activists, trade unions, and others. These local Italian players also increasingly started accepting the term and self-describing in this way, even though they had been active long before the Spanish Indignados appeared (Zamponi, 2012, 411). After the success of the Spanish and Greek peaceful square occupations, the name "Indignados" became a symbol for the whole generation whose lives were strongly affected by the crisis. The way in which mainstream media hyped the label in a sense inspired activists to adopt it. Thus, a foreign term was assigned to local activists by media in order to make them newsworthy, while local activists appropriated the label precisely because it was so successful. The diffusion of the label was a negotiated process, a virtuous cycle in which both mainstream media and activists had only to gain from using it.

The Italian fate of the "Indignados" label, however, was not to be a successful one. While an impressive number of people turned to the streets on October 15 – between 200,000 and 300,000 marched in Rome according to different accounts – the day was marked by violence and riots initiated by the Black Block. The violence by provocateurs marked not only this day but also the

Italian anti-austerity movement for years to come, since the different groups that had come together to form an alliance remained split in their response to the riots and it was difficult to rebuild trust (Zamponi, 2012). Rather than initiating an occupation or a new intense period of mobilization in Italy, October 15, 2011, remained a traumatic moment of the anti-austerity movement. It was only a month later after these protests and after the G20 summit in Cannes that Berlusconi was removed from his post and replaced by the technocrat Mario Monti, leading to a dramatic drop in protests for the whole coming year (Andretta, 2018, 106).

Overall, October 15 marked the high point of Indignados-type anti-austerity protests diffused by bottom-up activists. Activists from Madrid and Barcelona that had gathered in the thousands could live stream on their phones about how the protests and occupations developed in other countries (Rodríguez Piña and Seco, 2011). Nevertheless, digital media practices were only one part of the story. Mainstream media with a global audience such as The Guardian, Reuters, and Al Jazeera also followed the protests with live blogs and rolling coverage, and a search in Factiva reveals that from October 14 to October 16 only there were more than 5,900 articles mentioning Occupy or Indignados in the world press. But not only did the coverage span a lot of countries. The way mainstream media reported on the protests was overall favourable (unlike subsequent reporting on left-wing populist parties) and also very much focused on the international character of the movement, emphasizing that protests were taking place simultaneously in multiple countries (Horn, 2011; Rodríguez Piña and Seco, 2011). Again, the reality on the ground points to a more nuanced understanding of the meaning of "global diffusion" of protest, since events took place mainly in Europe and the United States.

March to Brussels (and beyond)

As seen, information on upcoming and past protest events, including on relevant Facebook groups and hashtags, was actively spread by mainstream media journalists (Waldram, 2011). Bottom-up protesters also actively diffused information on their protests: slogans, strategies, and instructions on how to use specific digital media platforms such as N1 or Mumble. But in order to "act on" this information and go to the streets, activists needed something more than information – they needed strong local organizations and activists ready to "adopt" the message. Direct personal connections between activists from different countries definitely helped in this process of adoption. Within Europe, Indignados-style protests seemed to diffuse best between countries whose activists had been in contact before and had exchanged ideas and information but also built trust and solidarity. A quick look at the places of live meetings and events of Take the Square – in places such as Athens, Milan, Lisbon, Coimbra, and Porto (Take the Square Events, 2011) shows that there is a considerable overlap between countries where there were in-person events and countries with large Indignados protests. Protest was diffused not only online via digital and mainstream media, but also, and maybe even more importantly, offline through meetings where ideas, and also food, music, and living space were shared.

Indeed, a disproportionate amount of attention has been paid on the role of digital media for spreading protest in 2011. Mainstream media, academic researchers, and most importantly activists themselves have strongly focused on the role of social media platforms, live streaming, online voice conversations, etc. (Gerbaudo, 2012, 2013). Yet, the preparation of the global October 15 event also included another type of often overlooked diffusion – groups of activists from all corners of Spain marched to Madrid (Figure 2.2) and then all the way to Brussels, the heart of Europe, to organize Agora Brussels – an event to discuss ideas and proposals for democratic deepening. The March to Brussels picked up activists from France and Italy on the way and met with activists from the UK, Germany, and the Netherlands in Brussels, allowing for a common space to emerge. Marchers often kept digital "diaries" of their travels that show the seamless way in which political theatre performances and confrontation with the police were integrated into everyday life, as can be seen in the following extract from one such blog post from October 14, 2011:

> This is our free space. People entering here can liberate themselves from the straight jacket of society, and be who they want to be.
>
> Yesterday the German march arrived, and today the bikers from Holland came peddling in. They were received with a joyful happening animated by the clowns. Nothing political, just a human embrace.
>
> The Germans only did a week of marching, and still I heard one of them complaining that his feet hurt. "Woosy", I couldn't help but thinking, "we, the Spanish indignados, we do a week of marching before breakfast!"
>
> . . .
>
> The good news today was that the officer who ruthlessly kicked Marianne in the face, twice, and banged her head against the floor when she was handcuffed, has been arrested thanks to our people filming the aggression. We are urban guerrillas. And our cameras are our weapons.
>
> In the afternoon a pleasant autumn sun came out and I went to see a piece of theatrical action. It was about the "one percent" being put on trial, and the common people being called to the witness stand. It was performed next to the palace of justice, with a panoramic view over Brussels. We enjoyed it, as did our public, which consisted mainly of two police officers who were visibly amused.
>
> *(Revolução, 2011)*

After protesting and meeting activists from all over Europe in Brussels, some marchers decided to continue and go all the way to Greece. While occupations

FIGURE 2.2 Indignados March

Source: © Nemo/Wikimedia Commons/CC0 1.0 Universal (CC0 1.0) Public Domain Dedication

were a distinctly national event, these marches went beyond national borders and created long-lasting connections between citizens of different European countries. Of course, the marchers used digital technologies actively, live blogging from their march, posting future stops on Facebook, and popularizing their cause. But what the marches show is that the use of digital media for diffusion is always embedded in particular physical settings, and sometimes old-style walking can be a mechanism of diffusion of ideas as effective and potentially more long lasting than Twitter posts. In fact, diffusion of ideas was not simply a by-product of the march but at the core of its very conceptualization. Activists deliberately stopped in as many as towns and cities as possible to organize discussions, spread ideas, and make friends. In their own words:

> We make this march to animate people to take the public space and meet, to talk about politics and decide for their own lives. We make this march to propose and learn, to inspire and to be enriched, to speak and listen, to give and receive. We want to reach Rome and Athens to bring a message of hope and unity. Most of all, we want to participate in the Global Agoras in order to coordinate at international level, to prepare projects in common, to confront together the problems and create a just society for everybody.
>
> We walk for dignity. Together we can reach the Utopia.
>
> *(Marches to Brussels, 2011)*

Looked at from the perspective of protest diffusion, the Indignados marches throughout Europe in a way encapsulate all the strengths and weaknesses of diffusion driven by bottom-up activists. They were spontaneous and bottom-up. There was no overarching organization dictating the narrative of protesters, their use of particular statements or media. The marchers produced their own content and did everything possible to engage others with their enthusiasm and their cause. They managed to do this with varying success but little by little came to a halt as tiredness grew and enthusiasm diminished. Crucially, bottom-up activists who participated in these movements had little or no financial resources beyond their own time to dedicate to the movement, and thousands of protesters did dedicate hours, days, and months of their lives not only to protest but also to all the different forms of neighbourhood assemblies, online discussions, and working groups that followed the peak of street activism (Portos, 2019).

Bottom-up diffusion led by activists was voluntary, was often chaotically coordinated, and counted on human-to-human interactions, both online and offline, with all their joys and annoyances. Sometimes it spread like wildfire, when thousands of people joined an event on Facebook. Sometimes it was slow-paced but left a mark for a lifetime, as with the marchers who walked to Brussels and beyond to spread their ideas but also to listen to others in small and big cities on a continent with no borders – for capital but sometimes also for people.

Trade Unions Against Austerity

Anti-austerity protests were diffused not only by mainstream media and bottom-up activists (both in person and via digital media) but also by trade unions. By February 2011, when the call for the Portuguese Geração à Rasca movement was first launched, there had been four general strikes in Greece, a massive general strike in Portugal, one of the biggest in the country's history, a large manifestation against austerity in Italy, and protests against pension reform in Spain – all organized to a large extent by trade unions. Beyond these national actions, the European trade union organization ETUC had called four European action days from 2009 to 2011 (Pedrina, 2011).

Nevertheless, most national unions felt comfortable operating at the national level and had neither the resources nor the ambition to try to spread protest. Trade unions operate in a situation in which cross-border action has been made increasingly difficult by the system of economic governance of the EU that nationalizes social conflict and often sets states against states with the aim of achieving nation-specific targets (Erne, 2017). Unions in various member states have very different structural positions in the European single market and thus often have in fact conflicting interests. Indeed, while unions across the EU, including German ones, expressed solidarity with the struggles of Southern European workers facing dramatic austerity measures, they rarely went beyond such declarative measures: "Opposition to austerity tended to be a secondary priority for German and French unions. In Germany, the tone of opposition was moderated to maintain decent relations with the Merkel Government, whereas French unions often abdicated the issue to European confederations" (Prosser, 2020, 12).

When it comes to spreading protests and attempting to organize truly transnational actions, Spanish unions, similarly to Spanish bottom-up activists, stood out as particularly active. During the 12th Congress of the European Trade Union Confederation Congress from May 16 to May 19, 2011, in Athens, the Spanish unions Comisiones Obreras, known better as CCOO (Workers' Commissions), and the Unión General de Trabajadores UGT (General Union of Workers) proposed to examine the possibility of coordinating European strikes, including a European general strike (Prosser, 2020, 9). This proposal was made in a context of an important division on the issue of strategy – some unions believed that the most adequate way to address market challenges posed to democracy and equality was to "fall back" to the national level and try to save whatever was possible of the social state, as the "EU is on the way to neoliberal damnation" (Pedrina, 2011). On the other side were the advocates of the "offensive strategy" such as the Spanish CCOO and UGT trying to Europeanize social struggles and create a common front (ibid.).

Appetite for diffusion and coordination depended strongly on the national strength and opportunities of trade unions. Due to the disadvantaged position of Spain within the Eurozone but also because of their increasing weakness in the Spanish political context, Spanish unions had a clear interest in engaging in pan-European action (Prosser, 2020). These practical considerations were complemented by a genuine ideological support for more European integration and a belief that social Europe is possible (Pedrina, 2011). But while the delegates at the ETUC 2011 meeting did support the Spanish unions' proposal for coordinated action, they did so "without conviction" (ibid.).

German unions had little motivation to urge their members to protest in support of Southern labourers, but even the trade unions from countries that did have reason to coordinate did not engage full-heartedly in the mobilization process. The 24-hour general strike during the European Day of Action was to take place on November 14, 2012. Meanwhile, however, in Greece a Troika-friendly government brought to Parliament a renewed bailout agreement. Unions were pressured by their members to strike immediately and thus they called a 48-hour general strike for November 6 and 7 (Vogiatzoglou, 2015, 221). Nevertheless, the strike had a lower turnout than usual and passed uneventfully. The new bailout agreement was accepted and Greek trade unions realized that calling for mass participation in the European Day of Action on the 14th would be met with indifference at best, scorn at worst (ibid.). Thus, they did not publicize the event sufficiently and very few people turned up. In Italy the CGIL trade union (Italian Confederation of Labour) saw in the European Day of Action a good opportunity to mobilize without seeming to mount opposition to the technocratic Monti government, supported by CGIL's allied PD (Democratic Party). The day of action came at a point in which a controversial reform in high school governing bodies was passed and in Italy the main protesters were in fact not the unions but high school and university students and other activists that clashed with the police, prompting a statement by CGIL condemning the violence (Vogiatzoglou, 2015, 221–222). Thus, even within Southern European countries that supported more transnational action, attempts at joint action were challenged by national specific circumstances and alliances.

Despite such organizational problems when it came to having joint transnational events, trade unions were among the major protest organizers at the national level in each of the Southern European countries throughout the crisis. They were a crucial and leading actor in Portugal (Accornero and Ramos Pinto, 2015; Baumgarten, 2013; Carvalho, 2019) and played a major role in Spain (Carvalho, 2019), in Greece (Kanellopoulos et al., 2017; Kousis and Karakioulafi, 2013), and in Italy, where 45% of the total protest events between 2009 and 2014 included trade unions (Andretta, 2018). It is important to mention that trade unions in any of these countries rarely acted as a single unified player, with important distinctions, for example, between minority trade unions usually engaging in more provocative and disruptive actions and majority trade unions that had much cozier relations with established social democratic (and other) parties. As the crisis progressed, however, old alliances were challenged – for example in Italy, CGIL that had been traditionally in close ties with Partito Democratico and didn't protest while they were in power felt increasingly betrayed and several times went to the streets to protest the reforms introduced by the Renzi government (Andretta, 2018).

Overall, trade union action against austerity in the aftermath of the 2008 economic crisis has been considerable and impressive, as single-country protest event analyses have shown. Nevertheless, trade union action throughout the period mentioned failed to mobilize people's and, crucially, media's imagination in any way comparable to the fascination with the Indignados- and Occupy-style protests. The symbol of mobilizations throughout the crisis were not trade union flags but the Guy Fawkes mask associated with the hacktivist collective Anonymous. Why has this been the case? First, it seems that trade unions failed at the new media game. While most of them did engage in opening Twitter, Facebook, and YouTube accounts, their primary way of communication with media and the public throughout the crisis remained press releases. Whether the use of digital media leads to democratization is a complex question whose answer is far from straightforward (Rone, 2020). But by failing to engage substantially and creatively with digital technologies in this period and counting predominantly on the good old media strategies, trade unions neglected the performative dimensions of digital media use that would have allowed them to present themselves as a reformed, new type of democratic actor different from the political and business elites.

The reasons for such an approach can be many – from lack of resources to well-founded scepticism of the potential of new media. What is more, purely practically, trade unions have other mechanisms to mobilize their constituents and thus do not need to rely on Facebook events and online mobilization and diffusion, for example. Finally, looking at umbrella organizations in the UK and Germany more specifically, it seems that their main strategy has been lobbying, and they have counted much less on access to media and influencing public opinion (Junk, 2019). In fact, much more research is needed on trade union media practices, and more particularly on the media practices of Southern European trade unions during the crisis. Despite their dedicated and intense activity, unions in the period failed to create a sense of solidarity in the public that would perceive them as more than special interest actors (Culpepper and Regan, 2014). Mainstream media certainly played a key role in fuelling such perceptions throughout the crisis. While there is no systematic research on mainstream media representation of unions, existing research from Ireland on opinion and editorial commentary in the print media during the final quarter of 2009 revealed that a staggering 90% of press coverage was anti-union (Culpepper and Regan, 2014, 735).

All in all, union-led protests failed to stop austerity policies (at least, in the short term), but so did bottom-up-driven protests. Furthemore, trade unions largely failed to diffuse protest and organize joint actions but neither were bottom-up movements successful in protest diffusion beyond Southern Europe. Considering that both types of action were ineffective in a narrow policy and legal sense, the privileging of bottom-up protests over trade union ones in academic research seems to have to do more with their novelty and inventive digital media practices than with their success.

Movement Parties

Ultimately, it was not through protest politics itself but through the way protest politics transformed electoral politics that the massive anti-austerity movement started to make a difference in terms of government policies. The birth of so-called movement parties (della Porta et al., 2017; Gerbaudo, 2018) such as Podemos in Spain and Syriza in Greece marked the beginning of a new phase of anti-austerity struggles in which protest energy was redirected towards the electoral arena. Several of the parties emerging from protest movements made active use of digital technologies to encourage discussion and voting. Yet their promise to disintermediate politics often led to privileging a small group of party elites counting above all on plebiscitarian voting (Gerbaudo, 2018). Such problematic examples pointed to the need to increase intraparty democracy and focus more on truly deliberative forms of participation, going beyond simple plebiscites (Wolkenstein, 2019).

Beyond the electorally successful attempts of "translating" movements into parties, numerous others failed along the way: despite fierce criticism of party politics during the decade after the economic crisis, 295 new political parties were registered in Spain between 2009 and 2010 alone, and this number nearly doubled in the period of countrywide protests that occurred between 2011 and 2012 (Tormey and Feenstra, 2015).

What is more, not only were new parties created but often already existing parties transformed themselves in the aftermath of the eventful protests. In Barcelona, for example, the Joves d'esquerra Verda (JEV) (Green Left Youth), the youth wing of Iniciativa per Catalunya Verds (Initiative of Catalonia Greens) were active participants in the Indignados protests and the subsequent working groups aiming to offer an economic alternative to austerity. A good example of the multiple synergies and developments around the Indignados protests is the story of Jesús Hernández, the social policy and labour representative of JEV, who was later to move on to work in Brussels as an aide to MEP Ernest Urtasun from Initiative of Catalonia Greens and Catalunya en Comú. The Iniciativa per Catalunya Verds, as one of the parties that united to form Catalunya en Comú, had a long past and roots in the Partit Socialista Unificat de Catalunya (Unified Socialist Party of Catalonia). Even before Indignados protesters from all around Spain took to the streets, the JEV had started focusing on labour and social policies in the search of common ground with trade unions. Party members such as Jesús Hernández thus brought their expertise to the squares and to subsequent discussions on how to embrace cities and regions as important loci for more democratic decision-making on issues ranging from housing to public services.

As Catalunya en Comú became more established and sent Ernest Urtasun as an MEP to Brussels, Hernández followed on to discover the challenges but also the opportunities of working in a more institutionalized setting (interview with Jesús Hernández). While the team had little success in pushing forward concrete economic proposals, working at the European level allowed them to participate in broader initiatives and diffuse many of the ideas and political innovations of Catalunya en Comú in other countries and contexts. Key transnational events in which Urtasun participated, such as Municipalize Europe and the European Commons Assembly, were a key way to diffuse ideas emphasizing the importance of engagement with politics at the local level. In general, sending MEPs to the European Parliament allowed radical left and Green parties to diffuse ideas more broadly and form alliances across borders. While radical parties in Southern Europe did not diffuse protest strictly, they were crucial actors in the diffusion of ideas and political innovations that followed the 2011 protest eruption and in turn informed subsequent protests such as the one against TTIP and CETA.

Ideas on the Move

Movement parties after the 2011 anti-austerity protests were also important because they synthesized movement-produced knowledge with theories from the field of social and political science. It is not a coincidence, for example, that Pablo Iglesias, the leader of Podemos, as well as multiple other members of the party, came from academic circles. Iglesias, in particular, actively popularized thinkers such as Žižek, Butler, and Badieu in Spanish political discourse (Fernández, 2020). In aiming to institutionalize a left populist movement both Iglesias and his fellow Podemos politician and colleague from Universidad Complutense de Madrid, Íñigo Errejón, followed key works by Ernesto Laclau and Chantal Mouffe, even if they formed different political strategies on the basis of them (Chazel and Fernández Vázquez, 2020).

But academic thinkers were translated and "operationalized" into the Spanish debate not only by political parties. Many activists had direct access to key works in political thought thanks to a boom in publishing and translation that accompanied the Indignados movement (Fernández, 2020). The very notion of commons, for example, so crucial for movements such as Catalunya en Comú was introduced in Spain thanks to considerable translation work before it was further developed in new and creative ways. The diffusion of ideas predated protests and was further fuelled by them. A number of new publishing houses and edited series contributed to the forging of a new intellectual tradition in Spain, consciously different from the established Spanish Cultura de la Transición ("Culture of the Transition") period and speaking directly to contemporary activists' experience (Fernández, 2020, 3). Some of the essay series of the radical publishing house Traficantes de Sueños, for example, had more than 98% of their texts in translation from a foreign language (ibid., 6). At the same time, local Spanish authors such as Manuel Castells were also extremely influential in driving belief in digital technologies as a tool for political change. Castells's ideas were implemented in practice by Spanish activists and diffused throughout the globe thanks to the active efforts of the Indignados to diffuse protest, protest frames, and knowledge about specific media.

Indeed, the left-wing populism in the period after the economic crisis can be thought of as a synthesis of the political theories of hegemony by Ernesto Laclau and Chantal Mouffe and of the multitude by Michael Hardt and Toni Negri respectively, the sociological analysis of digital media by authors such as Manuel Castells, and the political economy theories developed by authors such as Joseph Stiglitz, Paul Krugman, and Wolfgang Streeck, whose book *Buying Time* was a crucial reference for Greek politicians and protesters alike during the 2015 referendum crisis. The fusion between analysis and practice has been clear not only in the leadership of the Spanish Podemos but also in the actions of another important academic analyst of the Greek crisis – economics professor Yanis Varoufakis who became a minister of finance for Syriza from January to July 2015. Intellectuals such as Varoufakis had easy access to mainstream media in Greece and in the West, provoking enthusiastic coverage due to his extravagant personality and engaging a transnational public in a wider dialogue on the conflicts between democracy, on the one hand, and the Troika, on the other.

During the post-2008 economic cycle, there has been a profound and to some extent inevitable blurring between academic analysis, political activism, and media activism in the lives of many intellectuals. To take just one instance, Costas Douzinas, who published prolifically in support of the Greek referendum in outlets such as *Open Democracy* and *The Guardian* has been not only a member of the Greek Parliament for Piraeus but also a professor of law and founder of the Birkbeck School of Law and the Department of Law of the University of Cyprus. Articles by him such as "Referendum and Democracy: Putting the Demos on Stage" (Douzinas, 2014a) or "Syriza Can Be the Future of Greece, and of Europe Too" (Douzinas, 2014b) are neither simply intellectual analyses nor political interventions. They are both. In Italy, key social movement scholars such as Paolo Gerbaudo have been increasingly active in using their analysis to inform social movements on the left not only on key theoretical ideas but also on how to avoid the traps of techno-fetishism in order to mobilize better. All in all, the border between movements, parties, trade unions, and intellectuals on the left has been highly permeable, with key players often "wearing several hats" at the same time and diffusing radical ideas with words as much as with political action.

This process of diffusion, as it probably has become clear by now, was very much facilitated by digital media. But it took place also on the pages of mainstream media and in the format of books. What is more, while many digital media enthusiasts professed the end of traditional media such as television and newspapers, the success of parties such as Podemos could not be explained without taking into account the ways in which they combined old and new media logics in a skilfully conceived media strategy (Casero-Ripollés et al., 2016). Podemos promoted discussions on the online party forum on Reddit and created its own alternative "TV" programme – La Tuerca – which hosted progressive voices from around the country, including the already mentioned Catalonian Green politician Ernest Urtasun. Yet, contrary to the nominal ideal of horizontality and giving equal voice to everyone, Podemos also consciously promoted Pablo Iglesias as a figure on mainstream TV in order to increase the party's recognisability (ibid.). Similarly, traditional media such as *The Guardian* had an important role in promoting radical figures such as Varoufakis and building transnational support for the Greek government, despite largely hostile mainstream media coverage of Syriza within Greece.

In sum, bottom-up activists, trade unions, political parties, intellectuals, and mainstream media actively diffused information, analyses, slogans, and resources to inform a meaningful opposition to austerity – first in the form of protest and later in the form of thinking of institutional alternatives. The diffusion of protest often had not only European but in fact also global ambitions. Yet, at least within Europe, the 2011 wave of protests diffused mainly among Southern European countries – Greece, Italy, Spain, and Portugal. Mass street protests against austerity followed in France only in 2016 with Nuit Debout (Gerbaudo, 2017). The ambitions for coordinated European action of Spanish trade unions quickly encountered the lack of enthusiasm of trade unions in other EU countries taking part in an economic governance regime that increasingly nationalizes social conflict. And while political parties such as Podemos and Syriza hoped to diffuse left-wing populism across Europe, the humiliating capitulation of Syriza after the 2015 referendum led many to abandon hopes of a European "left wave".

Most analyses of the post-crisis cycle of contention focus on the retreat to the national state in terms of protest frames and repertoires of contention and even in symbolic gestures, such as the increased use of national flags. What this chapter has tried to show is that although that was true, of course, we should not underestimate the conscious efforts of a number of political players to diffuse protest, protest frames, and ideas. The march of activists from all corners of Spain to Brussels and beyond is probably the clearest example of such a conscious effort of diffusion.

To be sure, two important points have to be made with regard to protest diffusion. First, in comparison to the subsequent protests against ACTA, TTIP, and CETA, Brussels-based NGOs played a very small role in the diffusion of protest against austerity. This had important consequences for the process of diffusion which was much less centralized, in terms of both players and (digital) media strategies. There was no common centralized platform, message, or narrative of protest in various countries. The situation was very different in protests against ACTA, TTIP, and CETA, where NGOs lobbied members of the European Parliament and had to speak a common, often apolitical, language based on expertise.

Second, the 2011 anti-austerity protests largely failed to diffuse in Eastern European countries such as Bulgaria, Romania, Latvia, and Lithuania despite the fact that these countries had also implemented tough austerity measures, in some cases even tougher than those imposed on certain Southern European countries. While in countries such as Bulgaria and Romania, there were massive protests, they focused primarily on corruption and demands for more democracy, but completely missed the left-wing critique against austerity. This curious and counter-intuitive absence is striking, and I discuss it in detail in the next section of this chapter.

2.4. The Curious Absence of Anti-Austerity Protests in Eastern Europe

> In every other Eurogroup, once the floor was opened for statements by the ministers, the same ritual occurred. First, Dr Schäuble's cheerleading team of Eastern European ministers would compete with one another as to who could out-Schäuble Schäuble. Then ministers representing previously bailed-out countries such as Ireland, Spain, Portugal and Cyprus – Schäuble's model prisoners – would add their Schäuble-compatible twopenn'orth before, finally, Wolfgang himself would step in to put the finishing touches to a narrative that had been under his thumb throughout.
>
> *(Varoufakis, 2017)*

In Homer's epics *The Odyssey* and *The Iliad*, the goddess Hera is consistently described as "cow-eyed", while Dawn is "rose-fingered" and Achilles is "swift-footed". Following the Homeric use of constant epithets, Greek finance minister Yanis Varoufakis consistently describes Eastern European finance ministers as "cheerleading" in his memoir *Adults in the Room*. That is their constant epithet. Varoufakis's insider account of the Eurogroup meetings is particularly interesting since it shows how while some governments, mainly the Southern European ones, were domestically accusing the EU of imposing austerity measures, during the Eurogroup meetings their finance ministers were hawkish supporters of such measures. Had Greece succeeded in its resistance to austerity, the swift adoption of austerity measures by other Southern European governments would have seemed too easy, too non-responsive to their own electorate, and therefore Greece had to be subdued.

The case of Eastern European finance ministers, however, is even more interesting. While Spain or Portugal would engage in double-speak, transferring blame to the EU at home and supporting Schäuble in Brussels, Eastern European countries such as Latvia, Lithuania, and Slovakia (who joined the Euro in January 2014, 2015 and 2009 respectively) readily accepted austerity measures and didn't try to shift the blame to the EU domestically to any comparable extent. Eastern European countries were the poster boys, the happy martyrs of austerity. Their finance ministers wanted to go hard on Tsipras (Virostkova, 2015) not only because in this way Greece wouldn't set a precedent but also because they did fully subscribe to the neoliberal ideology of supply-side reforms and austerity. This is what made them the perfect "cheerleaders". The main reason why finance ministers from Bulgaria and Romania could not take part in the cheerleading choir in the 2015 Greek tragedy confrontation is that Bulgaria and Romania were not part of the Eurozone but still had their own currency.

In Southern Europe, the transition to democracy was followed by austerity. In Eastern Europe, there had been no democracy without austerity (Gagyi, 2015). Austerity measures had been well known to Eastern European societies that become laboratories of neoliberal reforms in the 1990s. In the period of transition to democracy, Marxism and left-wing political thought had been thoroughly discredited in Eastern Europe in the 1990s. Their place was filled by the liberal pensée unique spread by a number of new think tanks created with the aim of promoting democracy, free markets, and individual freedom at the expense of the "bad" state seen as a wasteful oppressive force.

In countries such as Bulgaria, for example, citizens have consistently approved cuts in state expenditures, especially when it comes to "welfare" and "social security" – terms that have been conflated in political and media discourse (Grigorova, 2018). Anti-communist narratives from the 1990s of the inefficient state combined with suspicions of administrative corruption and accusations towards ethnic minorities for being "welfare cheats" were employed to secure wide support for programmes that retrench the welfare state (ibid.). But even in such a pro-austerity context, the palpable destruction of everyday life security and standard of living led citizens of countries such as Bulgaria and Romania to indignation. On the other hand, in the Baltic states Latvia and Lithuania there was a notorious absence of mass protests even in the midst of the post-economic-crisis protest cycle.

Romania had experienced a large teachers and transport strike already in the middle of 2010. Yet, the country remained relatively calm during the eventful year of 2011 that shook the European South. The next big protests in Romania followed in January 2012 when the Palestinian-born doctor Raed Arafat, founder of the Romanian Mobile Emergency Service for Resuscitation and Extrication (SMURD), resigned from his position as subsecretary in the Ministry of Health due to government plans to privatize parts of the emergency services (Margarit, 2016a, 2018). The protest in defence of Arafat gathered around 2,000 people who confronted the police by throwing Molotov cocktails; in the ensuing clashes around 29 people were injured (Euractiv, 2012). Protesters in Romania went to the streets not only for economic reasons but also to demand a new framework of communication with politicians who showed themselves as completely non-responsive (interview with Vintilă Mihăilescu, Mitev, 2012)

In February 2012, both Romanian and Bulgarian citizens went to the streets for protests against the Anti-Counterfeiting Trade Agreement (ACTA) that was perceived as a threat to civil liberties online. I will explore in more detail the spread of protests against ACTA in the next chapter. For now it suffices to say that these were the biggest protests in Bulgaria since the 1990s and mobilized unprecedented citizen rage among young protesters who went to the streets with the Bulgarian flag and Anonymous masks to defend Internet freedom. They were thus at least formally within the repertoire of the movements of the squares (Gerbaudo, 2017), even if they were in fact protesting with a very specific and narrow demand: Internet freedom. There were also a number of big anti-ACTA protests in Romania not only in the capital Bucharest but also in other cities, including the student centre Cluj Napoca, followed by other single-issue protests throughout the year. The first year after the 2008 economic crisis, in which both Romania and Bulgaria saw massive mobilizations with tens of thousands of people on the streets, was 2013, two years after the events that shook Spain and the whole of Southern Europe.

The Bulgarian 2013 Protests

In January and February 2013, thousands of Bulgarians went to the streets to protest against high electricity and hot water bills and against monopolies, understood not only as the monopolies of foreign electricity companies but also as political monopolies in a general climate of corruption and lack of representation (Gueorguieva, 2017; Rone, 2017). This first winter wave of discontent in Bulgaria spread through over 30 cities and included road blockades, marches with protesters carrying national flags, protest performances of people burning symbolically their electricity bills, as well as arson with protesters burning the cars of foreign electricity distribution companies.

Fire became the underlying theme of the protests, as this form of mass public discontent was complemented by a much more personal and dramatic form of protest – self-immolation. On February 20, 2013, the alpinist and photographer Plamen Goranov set himself on fire in front of the municipality of Varna, a big Bulgarian port city, in protest against the oligarchic capture of the city. A series of self-immolations followed. People of all ages, unemployed and marginalized, resorted to the desperate act of self-immolation, often within the confines of their own homes, leaving nothing but a note. In contrast to the highly mediatized street protests against monopolies, organized through online Facebook pages and groups and consistently covered on mainstream Bulgarian TV, self-immolations were most often done by socially excluded citizens with little public visibility. After a sharp rise in the number of self-immolations, reporting stopped due to fears it might inspire further cases.

In a sense, Bulgarian self-immolations were the exact opposite of the Spanish Indignados protests. While the Indignados gathered together and occupied squares in a carnival of democratic experimentation and digital innovation, self-immolations most often took place in the houses of the protesters with increasingly less media attention drawn to them. With the exception of Plamen Goranov, whose brave act was done on a public square and widely discussed and commemorated in documentaries and feature films, the subsequent almost 30 self-immolations were much less discussed. Meanwhile, mass public street protests in Bulgaria continued. On February 18, Minister of Finance Simeon Dyankov resigned, and after violent clashes between protesters and the police on February 19, the 140th anniversary of the execution of Bulgarian revolutionary Vasil Levski, on February 20, Bulgarian Prime Minister Boyko Borisov resigned as well. On March 3, Plamen Goranov died from his wounds in the hospital and on March 6 the mayor of the city of Varna also resigned.

The winter 2013 protests in Bulgaria were not formulated explicitly as protests against austerity. They were rather protests against monopolies, corruption, and minority rule (minorities understood here as elites but also ethnic minorities that have been consistently portrayed as "welfare cheats"). Among the main demands were the nationalization of power distribution companies, electoral law reforms, more "citizen/expert rule", "no mediators", and "Bulgaria for Bulgarians" (Rone, 2017, 150). In a sense, what these winter protests demanded was a mix of technocracy, since politicians were perceived as corrupt, and more citizen participation. Demands for nationalization had to do more with nationalism and the sense of being exploited by foreigners rather than with any type of socialist vision. Overall, the demands of the winter protests offered a synthesis between nationalism and the ideology of civil society that was imported by NGOs in the 1990s and was often expressed in the rather trivial phrase, "what the country needs is more civil society". This type of "citizen nationalism" was meant for ethnic Bulgarians and not for minorities, be they elites or ethnically Turkish or Roma Bulgarian citizens (Nikolova et al., 2014). Even though these protests were clearly triggered by the dramatic consequences of austerity policies in Bulgaria that dated all the way back to the 1990s, they lacked any reference to left-wing anti-austerity critique but focused as usual on corruption (Vajsova, 2017). Thus, there was a fundamental disconnect between the protest wave that shook the South and the winter 2013 protests in Bulgaria.

The winter wave of protests in Bulgaria was followed by a summer wave of protests against the new coalition government of the Bulgarian Socialist Party and the Movement for Rights and Freedoms. The #DANSwithme protests of the summer were triggered by the appointment of the media mogul with a shady reputation Delyan Peevski as the head of the State Agency for National Security – DANS. Unlike the winter protests that spread across the whole country, the summer #DANSwithme protests were very much concentrated in Sofia. In the first weeks of the protest, there was a multitude of protesters from different political backgrounds, including left-wing activists and anarchists. Throughout the protests, for more than two months there was an evening assembly at the central city spot Orlov Most (Eagles Bridge). The assemblies practiced prefiguratively direct democracy and were clearly influenced by the example of the Indignados and Occupy. Yet, as the events evolved the multitude of protesters found it increasingly difficult to speak with one voice (Gueorguieva, 2017).

By and by, the summer protests started bringing back anti-communist slogans from the 1990s and consolidated as right-wing liberal protests against corruption. The summer protests shared with the Spanish Indignados a critique of corruption and a fascination with digital technologies, expressed in the intense use of hashtags, Facebook groups, and live streams (Pavlov, 2019) from a wide variety of protest performances, including collective dancing and a re-staging of French revolutionary paintings. Similarly to the Indignados protest, the summer protests in Sofia also persisted in time and became a place for recurrent meetings, discussion, and the formation of active citizen groups. One of the groups that consolidated during the protests was a collective of students, including many of the organizers of the anti-ACTA protests from 2012, that went on to occupy Sofia University in autumn 2013 (Dinev, 2016). The Bulgarian summer protests differed from the Southern European ones in the complete absence of an economic critique of austerity. The main demands of the protests were the resignation of the left-wing government and more morality in politics, instead of corruption. Furthermore, while political discussions and assemblies at the neighbourhood level had been crucial in Spain, they were largely absent from the Bulgarian case.

Interestingly, the hacktivist collective Anonymous in Bulgaria was very much against the summer protests, accusing protesters of being liberal "sorosoids" or "sorostutes" – neologisms invented to describe liberal NGOs with foreign funding. Similarly to mainstream media, controlled by Delyan Peevski (whose appointment caused the whole wave of summer protest to begin with), Anonymous in the Bulgarian context were on the side of the left-wing coalition government and were potentially co-opted by the very oligarchic circles protesters opposed (Rone, 2016). Yet, rather than being an isolated case, the discourse of Anonymous in the Bulgarian context expressed a growing tension in Bulgarian society between a growing right-wing conservative consensus and the right-wing liberal discourse of NGOs supported by Sofia's middle class.

All in all, while Bulgaria in 2013 saw an unprecedented rise of citizen activity and protest, it is difficult to describe either the winter protests or the summer ones as anti-austerity. The January–February 2013 protests were the closest Bulgaria got to protesting austerity and its consequences, yet citizen demands were formulated in an overtly nationalist key and focused mainly on monopolies and corruption. They were protests against austerity that did not perceive themselves as such and thus cannot be described as such. The summer protests and the student occupation, on the other hand, were firmly embedded in the liberal anti-corruption, pro-civil society rhetoric that could be traced back all the way to the 1990s and that was increasingly countered by the nationalist conservative discourse of the oligarchic media machine.

It is indicative that in Bulgarian, the very word "austerity" has been extremely uncommon in public discourse. A Factiva search shows that the direct Bulgarian translation of "austerity" – "остеритет" has been mentioned in total 32 times in Bulgarian media, all concentrated between 2015 and 2020. The more figurative translation of "austerity" – "затягане на коланите" (tightening of the belts) – has been used only 184 times from 2002 to 2020. In comparison, the word "*austeridad*" in Spanish has been used by Spanish media 239,917 times in the period 1994 to 2020. Even if we take the shorter period from 2002 to 2020, the mentions of the word in the Spanish press are 232,926. Clearly, discussions of austerity have been almost completely absent from the Bulgarian public sphere despite the fact that the policies of austerity have been there since the 1990s and intensified after the 2008 economic crisis. Not only were there no discussions on austerity, but the very language which would allow such discussions to happen was missing. How can this paradox be explained?

First, the protest tradition in Bulgaria has had two main pillars: anti-left-wing protests from the 1990s and environmental protests that were the first type of social movement to emerge in communist Bulgaria. In general, as in many other Eastern European countries, in Bulgaria it is right-wing citizens that are more likely to protest since they were the ones in opposition to the left-wing communist regime (Borbáth and Gessler, 2020). This is a very different historical heritage from the one in Southern Europe, where left-wing citizens have been historically in opposition to right-wing dictatorships (ibid.). In addition, as already mentioned, in the 1990s a number of liberal right-wing NGOs entered Bulgarian public life promoting a very specific type of "civil society" that focused more on identity politics than on economics. Whenever they focused on economic topics it was usually to promote free market (neo-)liberal ideas. There was a deep paradigm shift in university education as well – while most humanities departments in Western Europe are dominated by left-wing intellectuals, sociology, political science, history, and a number of other key disciplines in Sofia University, for example, have been predominantly right-wing for a long time. In addition, trade unions in the country have had a notoriously low level of public support and legitimacy. The main (at least nominally) left-wing newspaper in the country – *Duma* – has had a falling distribution rate and sales, and most mainstream media newspapers and TV stations have been controlled by a narrow circle of oligarchs promoting a mixture of nationalist and sensationalist content (Rone, 2016). Thus, there were simply no players in Bulgaria to "adopt" the anti-austerity frames diffused by Spanish activists. Where the Southern European movements did resonate was in their critique of elite corruption and demands for more "real democracy now". When it comes to economics, Eastern European protests went down a very different path from Southern European ones. Yet the 2013 protests turned out to be eventful, as they were associated with the import and adoption of left-wing discourse and key frames to make sense of reality.

Left in Translation: Left-Wing Frames Diffuse to the East

Some of the key players to "import" left-wing claims and frames of analysis were in fact Bulgarian students from Western universities who returned home after the crisis with a renewed interest in Marx and left-wing class analysis. These intellectuals had access to international left-wing media such as *Open Democracy* and *The Guardian* where they popularized the Bulgarian protests and made them known to a wider transnational public (Ivancheva, 2013; Tsoneva and Medarov, 2013). A number of researchers from the Novi Levi Perspektivi collective (New Left Perspectives) were actively researching the 2013 protests and as participant observers in the protests started discussions among protesters themselves about new, more left-wing ways of conceiving their causes. Collectives such as Diversia (formed by student occupiers such as Ivaylo Dinev and active protesters such as Stanislav Dodov and Neda Genova), Novi Levi Perspekitivi (formed by a number of PhD researchers with experience from foreign universities, including Jana Tsoneva, Georgi Medarov, Madlen Nikolova, Tsvetelina Hristova, and Ognyan Kasabov, among others), and finally Solidarna Bulgaria (Solidary Bulgaria) that focused strongly on labour struggles and was, in a sense, the most "locally-rooted" left-wing collective, were crucial for formulating a left-wing analysis of social struggle and for subsequently organizing a number of left-wing protests in defence of women's rights and against TTIP and CETA. The small number of participants in these initiatives (even if one also counts the various anarchist groups and autonomous workers' syndicates in Bulgaria) means that they all know each other and often work together to diffuse a different language and a critique of social exploitation. Nevertheless, all these players are mostly still very marginal within public discourse, and second, they gained traction only after the 2013 protests. In retrospect, the 2013 protest themselves remained thus very much right-wing dominated.

What all this points to is that the diffusion of left-wing protests to Bulgaria happened not directly by Indignados-style activists but much more indirectly – through a combination of the import of Marxist thought by foreign-educated Bulgarian PhDs and a rekindled labour union action at home. It was only at the intersection of these two forces that the seeds of a new type of social action could appear. Intellectuals thus again proved a crucial player in citizen mobilizations, very much similar to what was observed in Southern Europe. At the same time, left-wing protests in Bulgaria since 2013 have struggled to gather protesters in numbers comparable to either the winter or the summer wave of protests in 2013. The diffusion of discourses and struggles is a painful and slow process, especially when done by activists lacking resources and access to mainstream media. In the captured media environment of Bulgaria, left-wing discourse couldn't reach more people without the creation of media such as Baricada that has been steadily gaining popularity in recent years. In fact, Baricada has been an East-East project, with a sister website in Romania. Another East-East media collaboration, serving as a hub for sharing perspectives, has been the LeftEast blog publishing relevant, often academic, analyses from around the region. It was also on LeftEast that some of the few analyses of the Romanian protests focusing on austerity appeared.

The Romanian Autumn

The year 2013 had been dramatic not only in Bulgaria but also in neighbouring Romania, where massive protests erupted over the controversial gold mining project at the natural and archaeological reserve Roşia Montană. The Roşia Montană Mining Project was initiated by a subsidiary of the Canadian Company Gabriel Resources that planned to extract almost 250 tons of gold with the Romanian state-owned company Minvest SA Deva. The companies won the license back in the year 2000, without bidding, but it took them more than a decade to obtain all the necessary permissions. Throughout this decade, many local residents, students, priests, and academics from Romania, as well as environmental organizations from the country and abroad, mobilized and created a strong network to oppose the mine, the use of cyanide, and forced relocations of local citizens (10ISDS Stories, 2019). It is this dense activist network that provided the backbone of mobilization once the project became publicized in July 2013 as part of an ambitious investment programme of the Romanian government (Odobescu and Ciorniciuc, 2013).

On September 1, 2013, citizens from all over the country took to the streets to protest against the destruction of the national heritage site. The protests became a weekly event with marches every Sunday and continued up to February 2014.

According to some, this protracted protest action was inspired to some extent by the summer wave of protests in Bulgaria that also continued for months:

> Widely covered by the Romanian mainstream media (e.g. "Proteste Bulgaria" 2013; every national television and journal paid attention to the events), the events revealed the endurance of the protesters during seven months and most certainly inspired the Romanian protesters to be persistent in their demands (as some protesters affirmed on the Facebook pages).
>
> *(Margarit, 2016b)*

The Romanian protests against the Roşia Montană project, dubbed by international media the "Romanian Autumn", were in many senses similar to the summer wave of protests in Bulgaria. They were framed as protests against government corruption and were very much driven by civil society – in the Romanian case in the form of environmental NGOs well embedded in transnational networks (Anghel, 2013). The Romanian Autumn also faced a negative campaign by mainstream media that not only discredited them but in the beginning simply refused to report on them at all (Ciobanu, 2013), most probably due to the substantial money the Canadian Gabriel Resources had paid for TV advertising (Barbu, 2013). Thus, Romanian Autumn protesters had to rely largely on digital media such as Facebook, YouTube, and Zoom to popularize their cause. In addition, similarly to Southern European protesters and in fact to their Bulgarian neighbours, Roşia Montană activists popularized their cause on the pages of left-wing media such as *The Guardian* and *Open Democracy*.

But again, while the media practices of Romanian protesters approximated those of their Southern European counterparts, the discourse of the protests was very different. While in Portugal one could attend anti-austerity protests with suggestive names such as *Que se Lixe a Troika!* (Screw the Troika!), in subsequent protests in Romania activists were strongly pro-European, blaming their own corrupt government and framing their discontent in slogans such as *Vrem o ţară ca afară!* (We want a country like abroad!) that saw in the EU not a constraint in democracy but the only player who could lead Romania to it (Gubernat and Rammelt, 2020). This strong entanglement between anti-government, anti-corruption, and pro-European message in protesters' rhetoric, even when they were in fact protecting the commons, is what clearly sets them apart from Southern Europe and brings them closer to Bulgarian protesters.

Despite the incidence of mass protests in both Romania and Bulgaria within the cycle of contention after the crisis, these protests were not perceived by the majority of their participants as anti-austerity ones. While sharing with Southern European protests demands for democratic deepening and anti-corruption messages, protests in Bulgaria and Romania both lacked a systematic left-wing critique of post-crisis economic policies. In both countries, there were no strong local left-wing players that could adopt the message diffused by the Indignados, regardless of whether it came through digital media or mainstream media. What is more, it seems that personal contacts between activists from the East and the South have been less frequent and established than personal contacts between activists from the South. There were also no strong contacts between activists from Romania and Bulgaria, despite the closeness of the two countries.

Still, in comparison to countries such as Latvia and Lithuania, Bulgaria and Romania at least had mass street protests. On the contrary, the Eastern European Baltic countries were marked by the notorious absence of any substantial protest against austerity measures. This remarkable lack of contention in the face of tough austerity measures has not failed to attract researchers' attention. Several different explanations have been put forward by researchers. First, close ethnographic work in the unemployment office in Riga in the aftermath of the crisis has revealed the multiple mechanisms through which welfare policies disciplined the population by framing the precariousness and poverty as the results of individual responsibility within a particular moral discourse of individual freedom (as opposed to communist oppression) (Ozoliņa, 2019). This type of moral discourse has fit in the long-term project of promoting neoliberal policies complemented with nationalism in the transition period (Bohle and Greskovits, 2012). A third potential reason for the lack of protest has been tough protest policing in countries such as Lithuania, for example, that did experience some protests and street riots in 2008 as the first austerity measures. The criminalization of protest and the increasingly tough measures of policing citizen discontent against austerity have gone hand in hand with a growing trend towards authoritarian rule in postsocialist Lithuania (Juska and Woolfson, 2012). Nevertheless, there have been signs of growing unrest in the police labour force itself giving some hopes for the possibility of protests in Lithuania that go beyond the usual nationalist tropes (ibid.). Finally, emigration has been suggested as a major "pressure valve" allowing young people unsatisfied with the economy of their country to simply move away. Austerity in Lithuania, for example, not only fragmented the labour market but also stimulated extraordinarily high levels of emigration. These processes have been described as "the formation of a new austeriat" (Juska and Woolfson, 2015). It is indicative that most Baltic researchers that even ask the question why there haven't been protests in their countries are in fact writing from Western universities. Thus, again in the Baltic context, it is foreign-educated intellectuals who dare to question austerity.

Shrinking Countries, Rising Emigration

Emigration has been an important and widespread phenomenon of the postcrisis years that has hit both Europe's Southern and Eastern peripheries. Arguably, the East has suffered more. Bulgaria, Lithuania, and Latvia in fact have been the top three fastest shrinking countries in the whole world, followed by a number of other Eastern and Southern European countries, due to a mixture of high emigration, low birth, and high mortality rates (Kiersz, 2020). Emigration in the aftermath of the 2008 economic crisis has served as a form of alleviating social pressures. Following the classic Hirschmanian paradigm, in the conditions of free movement within the EU, citizens from the East and the South have chosen "exit" instead of "voice" (Hirschman, 1970, 1993). Yet, as seen in the cases of Eastern European countries, at least when it comes to politically active citizens, they have continued to be engaged in domestic politics even when moving abroad and have often brought back and introduced more critical and alternative viewpoints acting as key agents of diffusion (Rone and Junes, 2020). What is more, the extensive use of digital media has allowed many of these exiled activists to contribute to public discussions on Facebook or even to create online magazines such as the left-wing *Diversia* in Bulgaria (ibid.).

But while emigrant activists can be key for diffusing ideas, their political influence often remains marginal. Even when forming coalitions with local players such as trade unions, activists find it hard to reach the general public in the absence of access to mainstream national media. This is a crucial point. Despite the techno-enthusiasm of the post-economic-crisis protests about digital technologies, the story of all major protests in Europe and beyond is very much a story of mainstream media coverage of digital practices in a hybrid media system (Chadwick, 2013). It was the combination of digital media tools and mainstream media attention and exposure that propelled to unprecedented visibility movements such as Indignados. In the absence of prominent left-wing print mainstream media in countries such as Bulgaria, newly appearing left-wing players have found it very difficult to reach a larger audience, especially the general population reading newspapers and watching TV controlled by national oligarchs. Emigration might help diffuse ideas and discourses, but they are always at risk of remaining marginal (Rone and Junes, 2020).

2.5. Conclusions: Go East! Go West! Forge New Connections

Summing up the discussion so far, the European South and East have implemented very similar austerity measures in the post-crisis period. Yet, protesters in the South politicized austerity measures from a left-wing perspective and were highly critical of the Troika's non-democratic actions. In the East, countries such as Latvia or Lithuania saw very low levels of anti-austerity protest, while protesters in Romania and Bulgaria took to the streets en masse, but focused mainly on issues of corruption and government incompetence and saw in the EU a corrective to non-trustworthy local governments. There were certainly instances of South-South diffusion led most often not only by bottom-up protesters but also by mainstream media, trade unions, intellectuals, and political parties. The diffusion between the South and the East however was not substantial. There was not much diffusion of protest between Bulgaria and Romania either, apart from one facilitated by mainstream Romanian media reporting on the Bulgarian protests.

While protesters in both EU peripheries embraced digital technologies and opposed corruption, discourses in the East differed from Southern ones when it came to the critique of economic policy. The reason for this was the lack of local left-wing players in the East who could adopt frames critical of austerity. On the contrary, Eastern protesters generally fell back into right-wing liberal narratives from the 1990s, showing how important intellectual work is in order to frame any type of protest. At the same time, the 2013 protests allowed a number of left-wing actors, mainly academics educated abroad, to form new organizations. Local left-wing media such as Baricada appeared in Bulgaria and Romania and have since consistently tried to change public discourse and introduce topics such as workers' rights, inequality, and austerity. In fact, as a researcher I have occasionally contributed materials on worker exploitation and the rise of the far right in the Bulgarian Baricada or Diversia. Yet, the rise of progressive media has been arduous and has taken place manily at the fringes of Eastern European societies that have moved more and more from right-wing liberalism to right-wing conservatism.

So what is to be done? Exploring the connections between protests in the South and the East, there are several key takeaways for activists who want to diffuse protest. First, you cannot do it alone. Despite widespread mistrust towards trade unions and political parties, for example, empirical research on the cycle of anti-austerity protests in Southern Europe has shown that they were most successful in mobilizing and diffusing their messages wherever there was confluence and cooperation between bottom-up activists, trade unions, radical political parties, and intellectuals. The claim that the protests were organized completely spontaneously by citizens who had zero political experience has been shown to be a myth (Flesher Fominaya, 2015). There was, of course, an element of spontaneity, but in Spain, where the protest cycle was the longest and particularly transformative, spontaneity combined with long and dedicated activist work allowing many new coalitions and synergies to form.

That is not to say that all allies are good allies. The formation of protest coalitions often brings more headaches than solutions. As seen in the Italian protests from October 15, 2011, sometimes the actions of even a small group of activists can deeply polarize the coalition and break trust for years to come. In addition, participants in the same movement might actively conspire against each other and play dirty tricks using all the affordances of digital technologies to create fake profiles, manipulate votes, and steal passwords of social accounts (Rone, 2019). At the same time, accepting the need for forming coalitions is a key first step away from politically non-feasible illusions of protest that is self-sufficient, spontaneous and sustainable over the long term. There have been many legitimate and important reasons why social movement activists after 2008 wanted to do it "their way", dispensing with older forms of mediation. Trade unions had indeed dramatically lost legitimacy, and radical parties in Spain such as Izquierda Unida were also involved in massive corruption schemes together with mainstream parties. Nevertheless, it is impossible to believe that all trade unions and all political parties in all EU countries are corrupt. Certainly, activists could identify at home and abroad players that they agree with and could help them spread their message without having to compromise their identity and integrity. As the enthusiastic and dedicated campaign of Los Indignados to spread the occupation of squares showed, activists seem to reach mainly other activists from countries that have already established protests scenes and personal connections with the diffusers. Trade unions that form part of European-wide umbrella organizations, on the other hand, have the potential to reach also workers from other parts of the continent, providing an important additional channel for protest diffusion.

In turn, trade unions in particular have a lot to learn from activists' innovative use of digital media platforms in order to be closer to their base. The experiments of the Spanish Indignados with Free and Open Source Software (FOSS) platforms away from the commercial Facebook and Twitter can be a good way to provide alternative forms of worker communication. A crucial element of success for any such strategy is to increase the usability of FOSS platforms.

Second, players from both EU's South and East should try to reach out and forge new connections with each other. At the level of intellectual work, reaching out and connecting the East and the South would mean more comparative research on EU's Eastern and Southern peripheries, focusing not only on social movements but also on questions of political economy and public policy. A number of topics are relevant for both peripheries of Europe, emigration being the most pressing and immediately obvious one. In addition, social network research focusing on flows of labour and capital between the East and the West can reveal important new avenues for building solidarity movements. Research on Southern European politics rarely speaks to research on Eastern European politics, separated in completely different disciplinary silos. Outlining common problems and transformations facing the two regions is an important step for creating the basis of future common causes.

In addition, there has been remarkably little cooperation and exchange of information between Southern and Eastern European trade unions. Deep structural reasons account for this lack of cooperation, due to the fact that Western and Eastern European workers have been led to believe they have very different interests in a common EU market. Yet, an attempt to form a united front would help workers identify many common interests and struggles. A stronger union movement in the East that pressures local capitalists to provide higher wages can very much serve in the interest of Southern workers facing social dumping. There is no doubt that any East–South trade union dialogue would be very hard, especially considering years of neoliberal economic policies in the East. Yet, this doesn't mean that it shouldn't be attempted.

Furthermore, Southern activists could expand their routes and search contacts with left-wing activists in the East that have started appearing after the crisis. The Indignados March to Brussels that continued to Greece could have also easily continued to Sofia, considering how close the two countries are geographically. Italian, Spanish, and Greek activists could attempt more joint actions with the newly emerging left-wing Eastern European organizations, providing important know-how on organization, mobilization, and media use. Paradoxically, most of the organizational know-how and funding of the new Bulgarian left have come not from the protests of the South but through German left-wing organizations such as Rosa Luxembourg Foundation. Yet, Southern activists have a lot of practical experience that might be very useful in the East. The experience of the Mareas in Spain, thinking of ways to improve education and healthcare, for example, could inspire similar initiatives in the East, tackling the topic of austerity not in an abstract way but through concrete proposals of how to improve vital social sectors. Similarly, the importance of neighbourhood solidarity practices cannot be overestimated and is something largely absent in East European countries. The ideas and practices of strong Southern municipalist movements could also bring transformative insights to the role of citizens deciding on how their cities and neighbourhoods should be run. Finally, the initiatives springing out of the 2011 Indignados movement also have a lot to offer as experience in terms of how to use innovative digital practices to tackle corruption (Mattoni, 2017). Engaging with fellow activists in the East could include not only online and live seminars but also common activities, lecture series, discussions, and debates in which transmitters and adopters can negotiate what is being transmitted. Such types of exchanges clearly have to predate the diffusion of protest itself to guarantee that there will be players interested in adopting protest. In the absence of such an effort to reach out and build connections, it might be safe to assume that Southern left-wing protests will continue finding it difficult to diffuse in the East.

Similarly and equally importantly, activists in Eastern countries need to cooperate more and build connections that could later allow them to participate in common protest waves, taking place at the same time and having similar targets. Different Eastern European countries have a lot to teach not only each other but also Southern activists about long-forgotten left-wing traditions and the pitfalls of actually existing socialism. The close geographical proximity between countries such as Romania and Bulgaria means that activists could also engage more easily in direct contact, visiting each other for lectures, seminars, and discussions of common strategy, striving towards what has been recently termed a "Bulgarian-Romanian mutual empowerment" (Mitev, in print). Complementing these direct contacts with digital media connections and more translation work could allow Eastern European activists to go beyond ideas of their particular country's exceptionalism and note the commonalities between their political fights.

Overall, for diffusion of protest to happen across countries, digital media are not enough. Both diffusers and adopters need to reach out and make an effort that takes time, resources, and nerves. The diffusion of protest and ideas is neither automatic nor easy. It is a political act of faith – a gamble that might miserably fail. Yet the stakes are so high that it is a gamble worth taking.

References

10ISDS Stories (2019): Suing to Force Through a Toxic Goldmine, Gabriel Resources vs Romania. *10 ISDS Stories*. Retrieved from https://corporateeurope.org/sites/default/files/2019-06/Gabriel%20Resources%20vs%20Romania.pdf.

15MPedia (2020a): *Juventud Sin Futuro*. Retrieved from https://15mpedia.org/wiki/Juventud_Sin_Futuro.

15MPedia (2020b): *No Les Votes*. Retrieved from https://15mpedia.org/wiki/No_les_votes.

15MPedia (2020c): *Plataforma de coordinación de grupos pro-movilización ciudadana*. Retrieved from https://15mpedia.org/wiki/Plataforma_de_coordinaci%C3%B3n_de_grupos_pro-movilizaci%C3%B3n_ciudadana.

15oct (2011): *October 15th United for #GlobalChange More Than 1,000 Cities – 82 Countries*. Retrieved from https://15oct.takethesquare.net/.

Acornero, Guya (2018): The 'Mediation' of the Portuguese Anti-Austerity Protest Cycle: Media Coverage and Its Impact. In: Tao Papaioannou and Suman Gupta (eds.), *Media Representations of Anti-Austerity Protests in the EU: Grievances, Identities and Agency*. Abingdon: Routledge, 188–206.

Accornero, Guya and Pedro Ramos Pinto (2015): 'Mild Mannered'? Protest and Mobilisation in Portugal Under Austerity, 2010–2013. *West European Politics*, 38:3, 491–515.

Adbusters (2011): *#OccupyWallStreet: A Shift in Revolutionary Tactics*, 13 July. Retrieved from www.adbusters.org/blogs/adbusters-blog/occupywallstreet.html.

Alicekhatiba (2011): Guia de Participacion Ciudadana Para el #15oct #oct15 #15o #o15. *Take the Square*. Retrieved from https://web.archive.org/web/20111228093537/, http://takethesquare.net/es/2011/10/14/guia-de-participacion-ciudadana-para-el-15oct-oct15-15o-o15/.

Andretta, Massimiliano (2018): Protest in Italy in Times of Crisis: A Cross-Government Comparison. *South European Society and Politics*, 23:1, 97–114.

Anghel, Ionut (2013). Not so Local as It May Seem. In: Elena Zamfir and Filomena Maggino (coords.). *The European Culture for Human Rights: The Right to Happiness*. Cambridge: Cambridge Scholars Publishing, 95–106.

Ban, Cornel (2016): *Ruling Ideas: How Global Neoliberalism Goes Local*. Oxford: Oxford University Press.

Barbu, Petre (2013): Televiziunile pe Care Roşia Montana Gold Corporation a Consumat Publicitate. *Forbes*. Retrieved from www.forbes.ro/televiziunile-pe-care-rosia-montana-gold-corporation-a-consumat-publicitate_0_8710-10149.

Barnes, Lucy and Timothy Hicks (2020): Are Policy Analogies Persuasive? The Household Budget Analogy and Public Support for Austerity. *SocArXiv*, 13 May. Doi:10.31235/osf.io/7qa2b.

Baumgarten, Britta (2013): Geração à Rasca and Beyond: Mobilizations in Portugal After 12 March 2011. *Current Sociology*, 61:4, 457–473.

Baumgarten, Britta and Rubén Díez García (2017): More Than a Copy Paste: The Spread of Spanish Frames and Events to Portugal. *Journal of Civil Society*, 13:3, 247–266.

BBC (2011): Italy Crisis: Silvio Berlusconi Resigns as PM. *BBC News*. Retrieved from https://www.bbc.com/news/world-europe-15708729.

Beattie, Jason (2015): Greek Prime Minister Alexis Tsipras 'Beaten Like a Dog and Crucified' by EU Sanctions. *The Mirror*. Retrieved from www.mirror.co.uk/news/world-news/greek-prime-minister-alexis-tsipras-6059935.

Beissinger, Mark and Gwendolyn Sasse (2014): An End to Patience? The 2008 Global Financial Crisis and Political Protest in Eastern Europe. In: Larry Bartels and Nancy Bermeo (eds.), *Mass Politics in Tough Times: Opinions, Votes and Protest in the Great Recession*. Oxford: Oxford University Press.

Bickerton, Christopher (2016): *The European Union: A Citizen's Guide*. New York: Penguin, Random House.

Blyth, Mark (2013): *Austerity the History of a Dangerous Idea*. Oxford: Oxford University Press.

Bohle, Dorothee and Béla Greskovits (2012): *Capitalist Diversity on Europe's Periphery*. Ithaca and London: Cornell University Press.

Borbáth, Endre and Theresa Gessler (2020): Different Worlds of Contention? Protest in Northwestern, Southern and Eastern Europe. *European Journal of Political Research*, 59.

Carolina (2011): Cómo cocinar una revolución no-violenta (v1.0). *Take the Square*. Retrieved from https://web.archive.org/web/20120417145259/http://takethesquare.net/es/2011/08/18/como-cocinar-una-revolucion-no-violenta/.

Carvalho, Tiago (2019): *Contesting Austerity: A Comparative Approach to the Cycles of Protest in Portugal and Spain Under the Great Recession (2008–2015)*. PhD Thesis, Department of Sociology, University of Cambridge, Cambridge.

Casero-Ripollés, A., R.A. Feenstra and S. Tormey (2016): Old and New Media Logics in an Electoral Campaign: The Case of Podemos and the Two-Way Street Mediatization of Politics. *The International Journal of Press/Politics*, 21:3, 378–397.

Castañeda, Ernesto (2012): The Indignados of Spain: A Precedent to Occupy Wall Street. *Social Movement Studies*, 11:3–4, 309–319.

Chadwick, Andrew (2013): *The Hybrid Media System: Politics and Power*. Oxford: Oxford University Press.

Chan, Joseph M. and Chin-Chuan Lee (1984). The Journalistic Paradigm on Civil Protests: A Case Study of Hong Kong. In: Andrew Arno and Wimal Dissanayake (eds.), *The News Media in National and International Conflict*. Boulder: Westview, 183–202.

Chazel, Laura and Guillermo Fernández Vázquez (2020): Podemos, at the Origins of the Internal Conflicts Around the 'Populist Hypothesis': A Comparison of the Theoretical Production, Public Speeches and Militant Trajectories of Pablo Iglesias and Íñigo Errejón. *European Politics and Society*, 21:1, 1–16.

Ciobanu, Claudia (2013): The Revolution Begins with Rosia Montana. *Open Democracy*. Retrieved from www.opendemocracy.net/en/can-europe-make-it/revolution-begins-with-rosia-montana/.

Connolly, Kate and Ian Traynor (2008): Hungary Receives Rescue Package, with Strings Attached. *The Guardian*. Retrieved from www.theguardian.com/business/2008/oct/29/hungary-economy-imf-eu-world-bank.

Coordinamento (2011): *Coordinamento 15 ottobre*. Retrieved from https://15ottobre.wordpress.com/coordinamento-15-ottobre/.

Crespy, Amandine and P. Vanheuverzwijn (2019): What 'Brussels' Means by Structural Reforms: Empty Signifier or Constructive Ambiguity? *Comparative European Politics*, 17, 92–111.

Crouch, Colin (2009): Privatized Keynesianism: An Unacknowledged Policy Regime. *The British Journal of Politics and International Relations*, 11, 382–389.

Culpepper, Pepper D. and Aidan Regan (2014): Why Don't Governments Need Trade Unions Anymore? The Death of Social Pacts in Ireland and Italy. *Socio-Economic Review*, 12:4, 723–745, October. Doi:10.1093/ser/mwt028.

de la Porte, C. and E. Heins (2015): A New Era of European Integration? Governance of Labour Market and Social Policy Since the Sovereign Debt Crisis. *Comparative European Politics*, 13:1, 8–28.

della Porta, Donatella and Alice Mattoni (2014): *Spreading Protest: Social Movements in Times of Crisis*. Essex: ECPR Press.

della Porta, Donatella et al. (2017): *Movement Parties Against Austerity*. London: Polity Press.

Díez García, Rubén (2017): The 'Indignados' in Space and Time: Transnational Networks and Historical Roots. *Global Society*, 31:1, 43–64.

Dinev, Ivaylo (2016): Mahaloto na Zimniya Protest: Zimata na 2013 г. *Bŭlgarska Etnologiq*, 1, 51–70.

Douzinas, Costas (2014a): Referendum and Democracy: Putting the Demos on Stage. *Open Democracy*. Retrieved from www.opendemocracy.net/en/can-europe-make-it/referendum-and-democracy-putting-demos-on-stage/.

Douzinas, Costas (2014b): Syriza Can Be the Future for Greece, and for Europe too. *The Guardian*. Retrieved from www.theguardian.com/commentisfree/2014/jun/03/syriza-future-greece-europe-radical-left.

DW (2017): Dijsselbloem in Hot Water After Eurozone Nations Booze and Women Charges. *Deutsche Welle*. Retrieved from www.dw.com/en/dijsselbloem-in-hot-water-after-eurozone-nations-booze-and-women-charges/a-38069620.

Erne, Roland (2017): How to Analyse a Supranational Regime That Nationalises Social Conflict? The European Crisis, Labour Politics and Methodological Nationalism. In: E. Nanopoulos and F. Vergis (eds.), *The Crisis Behind the Euro-Crisis: The Euro-Crisis as Systemic Multi-Dimensional Crisis of the EU*. Cambridge: Cambridge University Press.

Euractiv (2012): Healthcare Bill Sparks Violent Protests in Romania. *Euractiv*. Retrieved from www.euractiv.com/section/healthy-citizens/news/healthcare-bill-sparks-violent-protests-in-romania/.

Ferra, Ioanna (2020): *Digital Media and the Greek Crisis: Cyberconflicts, Discourses and Networks*. London: Emerald Publishing.

Flesher Fominaya, Cristina (2015): Debunking Spontaneity: Spain's 15-M/Indignados as Autonomous Movement. *Social Movement Studies*, 14:2, 142–163.

Fruela, Fernández (2020): Tool-Box, Tradition, and Capital: Political Uses of Translation in Contemporary Spanish Politics. *Translation Studies*. Doi:10.1080/14781700.2020.1731589.

Gagyi, Agnes (2015): Social Movement Studies for East Central Europe? The Challenge of a Time-Space Bias on Postwar Western Societies, Intersections. *East European Journal of Society and Politics*, 1:3, 16–36.

Gazzari, Matteo (2011): 'Ora tocca a noi' la festa dei giovani Non+ disposti a tutto. Retrieved from https://firenze.repubblica.it/cronaca/2011/07/14/news/ora_tocca_a_noi_torna no_i_giovani_non_disposti_a_tutto-19118685/.

Gerbaudo, Paolo (2012): *Tweets and the Streets. Social Media and Contemporary Activism*. London: Pluto Press.

Gerbaudo, Paolo (2013): Protest Diffusion and Cultural Resonance in the 2011 Protest Wave. *The International Spectator: Italian Journal of International Affairs*, 48:4, 86–101.

Gerbaudo, Paolo (2017): *The Mask and the Flag: Populism, Citizenism and Global Protest.* London: Hurst and Company.

Gerbaudo, Paolo (2018): *The Digital Party: Political Organization and Online Democracy.* London: Pluto Press.

González-Bailón, Sandra and Ning Wang (2015): Networked Discontent: The Anatomy of Protest Campaigns in Social Media. *Social Networks*, 44, 95–104.

Grigorova, Vanya (2018): 'The People' Against Welfare Payments: Or the Art of Making Those in Need Ask for More Restrictions Against Themselves. [Народът срещу социалните помощи]. *KOI*. Retrieved from http://solidbul.eu/?p=7695.

Gubernat, Ruxandra and Henry P. Rammelt (2020): 'Vrem o ţară ca afară!': How Contention in Romania Redefines State-Building Through a Pro-European Discourse. *East European Politics and Societies*. Doi:10.1177/0888325419897987.

Gueorguieva, Valentina (2017): *Mnozhestva na nesŭglasnite.* Sofia: Sv Kliment Ohridski.

Hänska, Max and Stefan Bauchowitz (2018). #ThisIsACoup: The Emergence of an Anti-Austerity Hashtag Across Europe's Twittersphere. In: L. Basu, S. Schiffere and S. Knowles (eds.), *The Media and Austerity: Comparative Perspectives.* London: Routledge, 248–261.

Harvey, David (2005): *A Brief History of Neoliberalism.* Oxford: Oxford University Press.

Himanen, Pekka (2012): Crisis, Identity and the Welfare State. In: Manuel Castells, João Caraça and Gustavo Cardoso (eds.), *Aftermath: The Cultures of the Economic Crisis.* Oxford: Oxford University Press, 154–176.

Hirschman, Albert (1970): *Exit, Voice, and Loyalty: Responses to Decline in Firms, Organizations, and States.* Cambridge: Harvard University Press.

Hirschman, Albert (1993): Exit, Voice, and the Fate of the German Democratic Republic: An Essay in Conceptual History. *World Politics*, 45:2, 173–202.

Horn, Heather (2011): How World Media Is Covering Occupy Wall Street. *The Atlantic.* Retrieved from www.theatlantic.com/international/archive/2011/10/how-world-media-is-covering-occupy-wall-street/246677/.

Horvath, Julius (2009 [2008]): Hungarian Financial Crisis. *Case Network E-Briefs.* Retrieved from www.files.ethz.ch/isn/137987/01_2009.pdf.

Iniesta, Maite (2011): El 15-M vuelve al lugar donde empezó todo. *El Publico.* Retrieved from www.publico.es/espana/15-m-vuelve-al-lugar.html.

Ivancheva, Maria (2013): The Bulgarian Winter of Protests. *Open Democracy.* Retrieved from www.opendemocracy.net/en/bulgarian-winter-of-protests/.

Joint Statement (2011): *Joint Statement by Puerta del Sol Economics Working Group and Syntagma the citizens of Puerta del Sol and Syntagma Square Express Our Indignation and Invite All the 'Indignados' in All the Squares Around the World to Join Us.* Retrieved from http://takethesquare.net/2011/09/03/joint-statement-by-puerta-del-sol-economics-working-group-and-syntagma/.

Jornal de Notícias (2011): 'Geração à rasca' é referência para Espanha. *Jornal de Notícias.* Retrieved from www.jn.pt/mundo/geracao-a-rasca-e-referencia-para-espanha-18573 58.html.

Junk, Wiebke Marie (2019): Representation Beyond People: Lobbying Access of Umbrella Associations to Legislatures and the Media. *Governance*, 32:2, 313–330.

Juska, Arunas and Charles Woolfson (2012): Policing Political Protest in Lithuania. *Crime, Law and Social Change*, 57, 403–424.

Juska, Arunas and Charles Woolfson (2015): Austerity, Labour Market Segmentation and Emigration: The Case of Lithuania. *Industrial Relations Journal*, 46:3, 236–253.

Kanellopoulos, Kostas, Konstantinos Kostopoulos, Dimitris Papanikolopoulos and Vasileios Rongas (2017): Competing Modes of Coordination in the Greek Anti-Austerity Campaign, 2010–2012. *Social Movement Studies*, 16:1, 101–118.

Kiersz, Andy (2020): The 20 Countries Facing Population Collapse. *Business Insider*. Retrieved from www.businessinsider.com/the-fastest-shrinking-countries-in-the-world-declining-populations?r=US&IR=T.

Kousis, Maria and Christina Karakioulafi (2013): *Labour Unions Confronting Unprecedented Austerity in Greece, 2010–2013*. Paper for panel P301, Southern European Labour Contention: New and Old Repertoires, Social Alliances, and Party Relations, ECPR General Conference, Bordeaux, 4–8 September.

Kickert, Walter and Edoardo Ongaro (2019): Influence of the EU (and the IMF) on Domestic Cutback Management: A Nine-Country Comparative Analysis. *Public Management Review*, 21:9, 1348–1367.

Marches to Brussels (2011): Retrieved from https://marchestobrussels.takethesquare.net.

Margarit, Diana (2016a): The Days We Don't Give in: The Romanian Social Movements Between 2012 and 2015. *East Blog*. Retrieved from http://eastblog.univie.ac.at/2016/01/13/the-days-we-dont-give-inthe-romanian-social-movements-between-2012-and-2015/.

Margarit, Diana (2016b): Civic Disenchantment and Political Distress: The Case of the Romanian Autumn. *East European Politics*, 32:1, 46–63.

Margarit, Diana (2018): Ideology and Social Movements: A Comparative Analysis of the 2013 Protests in Bulgaria, Hungary and Romania. In: Adam Fagan and Petr Kopecky (eds.), *The Routledge Handbook of East European Politics*. London: Routledge.

Mattoni, Alice (2017): From Data Extraction to Data Leaking: Data-Activism in Italian and Spanish Anti-Corruption Campaigns. *Partecipazione e Conflitto*, 10:3, 723–746.

Mattoni, Alice (2019): Making the Syntagma Square Protests Visible: Cultures of Participation and Activists' Communication in Greek Anti-Austerity Protests. *Information, Communication & Society*, 14.

Meloni, Walter Paternesi (2017): *Austerity & Competitiveness in the Eurozone: A Misleading Linkage*. Departmental Working Papers of Economics. Rome: Department of Economics, University Roma Tre.

Milanovic, Branko (2016): *Global Inequality: A New Approach for the Age of Globalization*. Cambridge: Harvard University Press.

Mitev, Vladimir (2012): *Превърнахте ни в бедняци, но не ни обявявайте за мързеливци – Интервю на Владимир Митев с Винтила Михайлеску [You Made Us Poor, but Don't Accuse Us of Being Lazy – Interview of Vladimir Mitev with Vintilă Mihăilescu]*. Retrieved from http://solidbul.eu/?p=667&fbclid=IwAR0n98ACwklx_PG5VNXhJLvUvu7F0BdcOGd5_pa_cH0W80eLqm0NLpgfg1o.

Mitev, Vladimir (in print): *Distant Neighbours: Bulgarian-Romanian Relations and the Need for Mutual People's Empowerment*.

Morlino, Leonardo and Cecilia Emma Sottilotta (2019): Southern Europe and the Eurozone Crisis Negotiations: Preference Formation and Contested Issues. *South European Society and Politics*, 24:1, 1–28.

Mumble DRY (2011): *Movimento 15M, El Lugar donde puedes hablar y ser escuchad@*. Retrieved from http://mumble.democraciarealya.es/.

Nachtwey, Oliver (2018): *Germany's Hidden Crisis: Social Decline in the Heart of Europe*. London: Verso.

New York Times (2009): *Romania Seeks Bailout from EU and IMF*. Retrieved from www.nytimes.com/2009/03/10/business/worldbusiness/10iht-bailout.4.20738820.html.

Nikolova, Madlen, Jana Tsoneva and Georgi Medarov (2014): *Politics Without Politics: 'Us' and 'Them' in the Protests and the Crisis of Representation*. Sofia: Foundation Media Democracy.

Odobescu, Vlad and Radu Ciorniciuc (2013): There's Something Rotten in Bucharest: Protests Turn Political in Romania. *The World*. Retrieved from www.pri.org/stories/2013-09-27/theres-something-rotten-bucharest-protests-turn-political-romania.

Oikonomakis, Leonidas and Jérôme E. Roos (2016). A Global Movement for Real Democracy?: The Resonance of Anti-Austerity Protest from Spain and Greece to Occupy Wall Street. In: Marcos Ancelovici et al. (eds.), *Street Politics in the Age of Austerity: From the Indignados to Occupy*. Amsterdam: Amsterdam University Press, 227–250.

Ozoliņa, Liene (2019): Embracing Austerity? An Ethnographic Perspective on the Latvian Public's Acceptance of Austerity Politics. *Journal of Baltic Studies*, 50:4, 515–531.

Pavlov, Konstantin (2019): *Rolyata na Internet Technologiite I sotsialnite mrezhi za grazhdanskoto uchastie v Bulgaria*. PhD Thesis, Sofia University, St. Kliment Ohridski, Sofia.

Pedrina, Vasco (2011): *The Euro Crisis and the European Trade Union Movement*. Retrieved from http://column.global-labour-university.org/2011/01/euro-crisis-and-european-trade-union.html.

Portos, M. (2019): Keeping Dissent Alive Under the Great Recession: No-Radicalisation and Protest in Spain After the Eventful 15M/Indignados Campaign. *Acta Politica*, 54, 45–74.

Prosser, Thomas (2020): How Do Social Movements Behave Within EMU? The Case of Trade Union Reaction to EU Austerity. *Journal of European Integration*. Doi:10.1080/07036337.2020.1730345.

Regan, Aidan (2014): What Explains Ireland's Fragile Recovery from the Crisis? The Politics of Comparative Institutional Advantage. *CESifo Forum*, 15:2, 26–31.

Regan, Aidan (2017): The Imbalance of Capitalisms in the Eurozone: Can the North and South of Europe Converge? *Comparative European Politics*, 15, 969–990.

Revolução (2011): *Great Day's Eve, Revolução*. Retrieved from https://spanishrevolution11.wordpress.com/2011/10/14/great-days-eve/.

Rodríguez Piña, Gloria and Raquel Seco (2011): Los indignados regresan en masa a Sol, epicentro de su protesta. *El País*. Retrieved from https://elpais.com/politica/2011/10/15/actualidad/1318683837_874343.html.

Rone, Julia (2016): The People Formerly Known as the Oligarchy: The Co-Optation of Citizen Journalism. In: Mona Baker and Bolette Blaagaard (eds.), *Citizen Media and Public Spaces*. London: Routledge, 208–224.

Rone, Julia (2017): Left in Translation: The Curious Absence of an Austerity Narrative in the Bulgarian 2013 Protests. In: Donatella della Porta (ed.), *The Global Diffusion of Protest: Riding the Protest Wave in the Neoliberal Crisis*. Amsterdam: Amsterdam University Press.

Rone, Julia (2019): Fake Profiles, Trolls, and Digital Paranoia: Digital Media Practices in Breaking the Indignados Movement. *Social Movement Studies*, 1–17.

Rone, Julia (2020): Democracy in the Era of Social Media: Why the Deus Ex Machina Will Not Work This Time. *Europe in the Brave New World: Transform Europe 2020 Yearbook*. Retrieved from https://www.researchgate.net/publication/341489210_Democracy_in_the_era_of_social_media_why_the_deus_ex_machina_will_not_work_this_time.

Rone, Julia and Tom Junes (2020): Voice After Exit? Bulgarian Civic Activists Between Protest and Emigration. *East European Politics and Societies*. Doi:10.1177/0888325420902246.

Rosas, Antonio (2014): Protesting in a Cultural Frame: How Social Media Was Used by Portuguese 'Geração à Rasca' Activists and the M12M Movement. In: Solu Ashu (ed.),

Handbook of Research on Political Activism in the Information Age. Hershey: IGI Global, 296–318.

Scharpf, Fritz (2016): *Forced Structural Convergence in the Eurozone – Or a Differentiated European Monetary Community*. MPIfG Discussion Paper 16/15. Köln: Max-Planck-Institut für Gesellschaftsforschung.

Simiti, Marilena (2014): *Rage and Protest: The Case of the Greek Indignant Movement*. London: GreeSE, Hellenic Observatory Papers on Greece and Southeast Europe 82, Hellenic Observatory, LSE.

Singh, Abhijeet (2018): 10 Years of Lehman Brothers' Bankruptcy: A Timeline of Decade-Old Crisis at Defunct Wall Street Giant. *Financial Express*. Retrieved from www.financialexpress.com/market/10-years-of-lehman-brothers-bankruptcy-a-timeline-of-decade-old-crisis-at-defunct-wall-street-giant/1313066/.

Statistical Data Warehouse (2020): *Government Interest Expenditure (as % of GDP)*. Retrieved from https://sdw.ecb.europa.eu/quickview.do;jsessionid=0654A1246E0ABF2A9894 05747CCE23AD?SERIES_KEY=325.GFS.Q.N.IT.W0.S13.S1.C.D.D41._Z._Z._T. XDC_R_B1GQ_CY._Z.S.V.CY._T.

Streeck, Wolfgang (2013): *The Politics of Public Debt, the Debt State, the Politics of Public Debt, Neoliberalism, Capitalist Development, and the Restructuring of the State*. MPIfG Discussion Paper 13/7. Cologne: Max Planck Institute for the Study of Societies.

Streeck, Wolfgang (2014): *Buying Time: The Delayed Crisis of Global Capitalism*. London: Verso.

Take the Square (2011): *Take the Square*. Retrieved from https://web.archive.org/web/20120113213724/http://takethesquare.net/es/.

Take the Square Events (2011): *Take the Square: Tag Meeting*. Retrieved from https://take thesquare.net/tag/meeting/.

Todor, Arpad (2014): Romania's Austerity Policies in the European Context. *Romanian Journal of Society and Politics*, 9:1, 25–42.

Tormey, Simon and Ramón A. Feenstra (2015): Reinventing the Political Party in Spain: The Case of 15M and the Spanish Mobilisations. *Policy Studies*, 36:6, 590–606.

Trading Economics (2020): *Hungary Households Debt to GDP*. Retrieved from https://tradingeconomics.com/hungary/households-debt-to-gdp.

Treré, Emiliano, Sandra Jeppesen and Alice Mattoni (2017): Comparing Digital Protest Media Imaginaries: Anti-Austerity Movements in Spain, Italy & Greece. *Triple C: Communication, Capitalism and Critique*, 15:2.

Tsoneva, Jana and Georgi Medarov (2013): 'Resign!' – Bulgaria's Protesters Need a Better Slogan Than That. *The Guardian*. Retrieved from www.theguardian.com/commentisfree/2013/nov/27/bulgaria-student-protesters-resign.

United for Global Change #15oct (2011): Retrieved from https://web.archive.org/web/20120107072638/www.facebook.com/15octobernet.

Vajsova, Lea (2017): Sŭdebna vlast ili konspiracija? Vŭznikvaneto na grazhdanina-sledovatel v konteksta na centriranata okolo pravova dŭrzhava i borba s korupciqta politka. *Kritika I Humanizŭm*, 48, 257–278.

Varoufakis, Yanis (2017): *Adults in the Room: My Battle with Europe's Deep Establishment*. London: Penguin Books.

Verney, Susannah and Anna Bosco (2013): Living Parallel Lives: Italy and Greece in an Age of Austerity. *South European Society and Politics*, 18:4, 397–426.

Virostkova, Lucia (2015): Slovakia Takes Hard Look at Greek Talks. *EUObserver*. Retrieved from https://euobserver.com/beyond-brussels/129086.

Vogiatzoglou, Markus (2015): Workers' Transnational Networks in Times of Austerity: Italy and Greece. *Transfer: European Review of Labour and Research*, 21:2, 215–228.

Waldram, Hannah (2011): Occupy Together: How the Global Movement Is Spreading Via Social Media. *The Guardian*. Retrieved from www.theguardian.com/news/blog/2011/oct/14/occupy-england-protests-gather-momentum-via-facebook.

Wolkenstein, Fabio (2019): *Rethinking Party Reform*. Oxford: Oxford University Press.

Zamponi, Lorenzo (2012): 'Why Don't Italians Occupy?' Hypotheses on a Failed Mobilisation. *Social Movement Studies*, 11:3–4, 1–11.

Zuckerman, Gabriel (2015): *The Hidden Wealth of Nations*. Chicago: University of Chicago Press.

3

ACTA LA VISTA BABY

The Diffusion of Protest Against the Anti-Counterfeiting Trade Agreement

3.1. What ACTA Is and Why It Is Important to Study the Diffusion of Protest Against It

The anti-austerity protests in the aftermath of the financial crisis that we discussed in the previous part of this book have been widely researched. But there is one transnational mobilization that is rarely mentioned in the context of this wave of contention, even though it took place at its peak – in early 2012 – and informed to a considerable extent the subsequent EU mobilizations against the Transatlantic Trade and Investment Partnership (TTIP) with the US and against the Comprehensive Economic Trade Agreement (CETA) with Canada that I discuss in the next chapter. The mobilization in question is the campaign against the Anti-Counterfeiting Trade Agreement (ACTA), and it shook Eastern Europe, Germany, and Austria in the early months of 2012. This chapter focuses closely on the anti-ACTA protests and tries to explain their curious pattern of diffusion.

The stated goal of ACTA (2011) was to provide an international framework to improve the enforcement of intellectual property rights (IPR) laws. The three primary components of the agreement were international cooperation, enforcement practices, and the establishment of a new international benchmark for legal frameworks on IPR enforcement (ACTA Fact Sheet, 2008). Some of the agreement's provisions, especially the possible requirement for Internet service providers to monitor their users' communications, were perceived as a threat to Internet freedom but also to privacy as a fundamental right within the EU. Furthermore, the negotiation process of ACTA was perceived as deeply undemocratic. Trade policy has been one of the few exclusive EU competences, and in order to democratize negotiations the Lisbon Treaty gave more powers to the European Parliament. Many members of the European Parliament, however, didn't even have access to the negotiation texts. The agreement had been scarcely discussed, and Kader Arif, the European Parliament's rapporteur on ACTA, resigned denouncing the negotiations for the treaty as a "masquerade". In the grand scheme of things, ACTA was probably less important for the EU than comprehensive trade agreements such as TTIP or CETA. It also seemed very technical and niche. Nevertheless, it was ACTA that became the first trade agreement to be strongly politicized in the EU, provoking a mass civil society campaign that ultimately led to its demise.

While the anti-ACTA campaign did not include occupation of squares but only the more traditional protest marches, it shared many important features with other protests in the wave of contention, including the adoption of the Anonymous mask and the national flag as crucial symbols (Gerbaudo, 2017), the demand for more democratic decision-making, and most importantly the belief in the Internet and digital technologies as a tool for empowerment that could contribute to a more horizontal democratic society (Beyer, 2014; Jarvis, 2014; Juris, 2012; McCarthy, 2015). The big difference is that for anti-ACTA protesters, the Internet was more than a tool – it became a cause in itself. While NGOs framed their opposition to ACTA in terms of human rights, bottom-up protesters went to the streets to defend Internet freedom, interpreted most often as the freedom of sharing culture (and files) online and the freedom of expressing oneself.

I took part in the anti-ACTA protest in Sofia (February 11, 2012) and filmed it as part of a research project. Once I joined the march, I could not help feeling that something unprecedented, at least for the Bulgarian context, was happening. The temperature was −10 degrees Celsius, protesters with Guy Fawkes masks were marching on the streets, and I had not seen such crowds in front of the Bulgarian Parliament for more than a decade. On the same day, protests against ACTA took place also in Berlin, Hamburg, Munich, Vienna, and many other European cities. But the wave of discontent had already started weeks earlier in Poland.

On January 26, Poland signed ACTA in Tokyo, together with other 21 EU member states and the EU itself (Bryant, 2012). At this point, there were already thousands of Polish citizens protesting on the streets, while a group of Polish lawmakers put on Guy Fawkes masks during a session of their Parliament to symbolically oppose the signature (Myslewski, 2012).

As mainstream media, Brussels-based NGOs, the Pirate Party, and the hacktivist collective Anonymous publicized the issue, protesters in a number of countries took to the streets. As the map in Figure 3.1 shows, the protest in Sofia I attended was just one among many others in a truly transnational mobilization.

Understanding the mobilization against ACTA is important, as it was one of only a few successful examples of trans-European protest taking place simultaneously in several EU member states (della Porta and Caiani, 2009; della Porta and Parks, 2015; Teune, 2010). It also came to be the first trade agreement to be reviewed by the European Parliament, providing an example of a trans-European

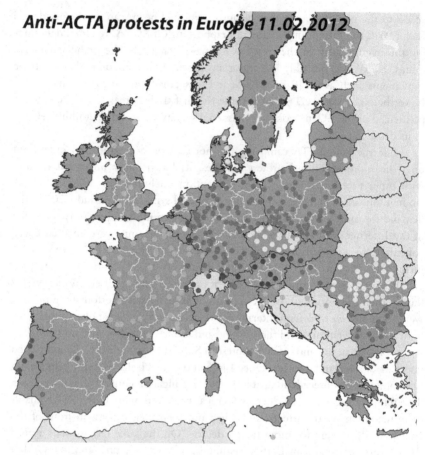

FIGURE 3.1   Planned protests against ACTA for February 11, 2012

Source: © Stanqo/Wikimedia Commons/Public Domain

public debate (Losey, 2013, 50). What is more, it was the first agreement to be rejected by the European Parliament after its powers were extended by the Lisbon Treaty, which came into force in 2009. On July 4, 2012, 478 MEPs voted against ACTA, 39 in favour, and 165 abstained (European Parliament, 2012). The legally informed, persistent, and innovative campaigning by transnational NGOs, many of which were based in Brussels, successfully combined with spontaneous protests of thousands of people in many EU countries to create a remarkable instance of citizen involvement in EU politics. No longer an obscure technical issue, intellectual property rights became the apple of contention of European politics. Nevertheless, a careful in-depth analysis of the multiple players who diffused protest and the way they navigated complex media arenas is still missing.

While several authors have examined ACTA in the context of long-term struggles against stringent IP rules (Benkler et al., 2015; Lee, 2013; Horten, 2013), a key novelty and contribution of this chapter is that it examines the anti-ACTA mobilization with a specific focus on protest diffusion. Most anti-ACTA protesters earnestly believed that the Internet could help spread protest and bring about democracy. But the analysis of these particular protests in defence of Internet freedom shows that while digital media are extremely important, we should put "digital media in their place" in order to understand their true significance for protest diffusion. Digital media were widely available across the EU, but protests against ACTA spread only in particular countries and in a far from uniform manner. Instead of counting on digital media alone, key players also took into account the role of mainstream media and feedback loops in an increasingly hybrid media system. Before focusing on the players and their media practices, however, I briefly discuss why a seemingly technical agreement against counterfeiting provoked such strong resistance.

3.2. The Politicization of IP

What Is in a Name?

In order to understand why many people perceived ACTA as a threat to Internet freedom, it is important to provide a short introduction to what the agreement is and what were the main motives to push for it. The first substantial problem with ACTA lies in its very name: Anti-*Counterfeiting* Trade Agreement. The terms "counterfeit" and "counterfeiters" are used in a rather loose and instrumental way in the title and throughout the agreement and can often be misleading: especially when applied to cases that are *not* examples of counterfeiting. A typical example of a counterfeit good might be a bag with a fake label "Gucci", sold on the streets, that was actually not produced by "Gucci". The proponents of ACTA also gave scary examples of counterfeit toys that might be dangerous for children, or even counterfeit medicines (ACTA Fact Sheet, 2008, 1). But while there are few doubts when it comes to counterfeit toys or bags, the question of counterfeit medicines is more tricky and controversial. Doctors Without Borders, for example, insist that the very term "counterfeit medicines" is highly misleading as it lumps together legitimate quality generic medicines with substandard medicines (that do not meet quality standards – might contain too much or too little of the active ingredients, might be contaminated, etc.) or even fake medicines (deliberately and fraudulently mislabelled, giving false information on where it was made or by whom) (Access Campaign, 2009). Kader Arif, the lead ACTA negotiator in the European Parliament, emphasized,

> [G]eneric medicines are not counterfeited medicines; they are not the fake version of a drug; they are a generic version of a drug, produced either

because the patent on the original drug has expired, or because a country has to put in place public health policies.

(Arthur and Agencies, 2012)

In fact, many countries such as India and South Africa have used compulsory licensing – allowing the production of medicines whose patents have not expired in exchange for a set fee for the license paid to the owner of the patent. This possibility has been foreseen in the TRIPs agreement (Agreement on Trade-Related Aspects of Intellectual Property Rights) and is crucial for developing countries which cannot afford to pay for highly expensive patented HIV drugs, for example.

ACTA ignored these cases of legitimate use of generic medicines. Furthermore, the agreement also had provisions extending to the digital environment and addressing copyright infringements. Online infringement of copyright, however, is very different from "counterfeit" and is difficult to address from a technical perspective (Adams and Brown, 2009). In order to know whether users are infringing copyright, Internet service providers must monitor users' communications, which might lead to serious breaches of privacy. Attempts to prevent copyright infringement online can easily lead to digital surveillance, which in turn raises fears of censorship, chilling effects, and deterioration of democratic dialogue. In fact, it was precisely ACTA's attempt to tackle copyright infringement in the digital environment that provoked mass discontent and protest. What is more, the highly intrusive measures that ACTA requires were negotiated in secrecy and outside democratic control, in a way very similar to the negotiation and imposition of austerity measures discussed in the previous chapter.

Why did the EU pursue such a controversial agreement? The EU Commission gives a straightforward, no-nonsense answer to this:

> The competitiveness of the EU economy depends on large part of economic activities that need IPR protection, i.e. high quality products and brands (trademarks, geographical indications), innovative industries (patents) or entertainment (copyright). Large-scale abuse of these rights by counterfeiters who free-ride on the innovative and quality-enhancing efforts undertaken by the EU industry has a devastating impact on growth and employment.
>
> *(ACTA Fact Sheet, 2008)*

Thus, there is a clear economic logic of protecting competitive advantage behind negotiating ACTA. The EU and its developed countries basically wanted to protect their advantages by "kicking away the ladder" for developing countries and not allowing them to infringe copyright the same way they once had done (Chang, 2002). The fact that intellectual property has ascended from the sidelines to the centre of discussion in G8 documents in the last decades reflects "the changing perception of IP, shifting from a technical specialist issue to a general political issue of great importance" (Haunss, 2013, 18; see also Farrand, 2014).

Connecting IP to Trade: Forum Shifting and Contestations Over IP

But how could developed countries historically convince developing countries to sign intellectual property treaties that were clearly against the interest of those countries? One of the pivotal events that changed the international framework of IP regulation was the establishment of a connection between IP and trade. Once these two areas were connected, developed countries could effectively pressure developing countries into accepting IP protection laws. The inclusion of TRIPS in GATT (General Agreement on Tariffs and Trade) was the culmination of a programme of intense lobbying by the US, supported by the EU, Japan, and other developed countries. Rules on IP protection were imposed externally on countries from the developing world that did not benefit from strict protection of patents or industrial design, for example, as they had to develop and catch up. The only reason why many developing countries accepted the TRIPS agreement is because its ratification was a compulsory requirement for World Trade Organization membership and any country that wanted to gain access to the markets opened by the WTO had to take TRIPS as well, or leave everything (Hoekman and Kostecki, 1995; Martin, 2015). Once they had signed TRIPS, states could be challenged for IP infringement through the WTO dispute settlement mechanism.

One of the most controversial aspects of TRIPS, which became the apple of contention later on during the Doha Round of negotiations of the WTO (the round begun in 2001 and negotiations broke down in 2008), was the already mentioned question of access to medicines. The problem was often understood as an inadequate balance of interests between the pharmaceutical companies of the developed world and public health in the developing world. Some authors go as far as claiming that the IPRs initiative of the developed countries goes against human rights and is responsible for many additional deaths of the global poor by cutting them from life-saving medicines for the AIDS/HIV virus, for example (Pogge, 2005). Unsurprisingly, developing countries such as Brazil and India coordinated their opposition to stringent IP protection rules during the Doha negotiations. In response, the EU and the US adopted the strategy of "forum shifting": trying to bypass the WTO and the World Intellectual Property Organization (WIPO), considered ineffective, and pushing forward TRIPS-plus intellectual property restrictions (Sell, 2009; Rossini, 2012). The Anti-Counterfeiting Trade Agreement that the EU signed was precisely such an attempt at forum shifting (Haggart, 2014; Roffe and Seuba, 2015, 21). Considering that the agreement was meant to protect EU commercial interests, it is remarkable that it met such strong resistance in the EU.

The first big protests against ACTA had taken place in Mexico in 2010 (Haggart, 2014). In 2012, in the midst of the cycle of contention following the economic crisis, it was EU citizens' turn to take to the streets. The profoundly non-democratic way in which the agreement was negotiated together with the potential for Internet surveillance caused a major backlash that fit in the general mood of discontent with the political system shaking the European Union. Yet, protests against ACTA spread far from evenly.

3.3. The Diffusion of Protests Against ACTA: The Main Players and Their Media Practices

Several Unsuccessful Attempts to Explain the Successful Diffusion of Anti-ACTA Protests

On January 24, 2012, many Polish websites participated in a blackout for an hour in protest against ACTA. The media action was followed by mass popular protests of people who self-organized on Facebook and went in the thousands to the streets to protest against ACTA. More than 15,000 people took to the streets in Krakow, 5,000 in Wroclaw, and thousands more in Poznan, Lublin, Sieradz, and Warsaw. In fact, Poland was the only country where the street protests preceded the signing of ACTA (January 26). Protests followed in several EU countries: several hundred protested in Paris and Brussels on January 28. On February 4, around 3,000 people went to the streets in Slovenia, mainly in Ljubljana and Maribor, and around 1,000 in each of the cities of Stockholm, Prague, and Bratislava. Finally, on the coordinated European day of protest – February 11, 2012 – protests spread in Germany (10,000 Berlin; 20,000 Munich; 1,000 in Frankfurt, Nuremberg, Augsburg, Leipzig, and Hanover), Austria (4,000 in Vienna; 3,000 in Graz), Bulgaria (7,000), Romania (3,000 in Cluj-Napoca, 300 in Bucharest), Estonia (1,500 in Tallinn), and others. Overall, protests against ACTA diffused successfully in the East, West, and North of Europe, especially in the East, but not at all in the South. What could explain such a curious pattern of protest diffusion? Before moving on to answer this question, I present several unsuccessful attempts to explain protest diffusion and show that structural or "independent variable"-based explanations fail to account for the pattern of diffusion observed. It is only then that I focus on why protest diffused successfully where it did.

To begin with, the high salience of ACTA in Eastern Europe has been often attributed to the heritage of communism. In the context of Poland, for example, commentators have claimed that the country's communist past has led to an increased appreciation of freedom of speech online and a readiness to protest against any attempt at censorship (Tarkowski, 2012). While relevant when it comes to Eastern Europe, this argument cannot explain why both East and West Germany, Austria, and Sweden mobilized strongly against ACTA.

An alternative explanation for the strong mobilization against ACTA in Eastern Europe focuses not so much on anti-censorship and defence of free speech as on defence of file sharing as a main reason to protest against ACTA. In the context of Eastern European countries, there is a strong case to be made for economic reasons to defend file sharing. As Karaganis (2011) and co-authors show in their report on media piracy in emerging economies, one of the main reasons for widespread digital piracy online is that people in emerging economies simply cannot afford to buy many of the cultural products of major content industries due to their high prices. Second, some of the countries in Eastern Europe are considered small markets, and many cultural products are not imported there and available to buy. As a result, cultures of circulation and sharing of cultural content develop. What is more, a major reason for public support for piracy might be found in the failure of the state to provide a suitable cultural infrastructure: a good example in this regard is the mass closing of cinemas in Bulgaria after 1989, which often left whole cities without a single cinema (Rone, 2014). Considering these factors, it is not surprising that so many people in Eastern Europe took to the streets to protest against ACTA and protect their "right" to download and share files. But again, while such types of explanations for file sharing work perfectly for Eastern Europe, they cannot explain the widespread protests against ACTA in countries such as Germany, Austria, and Sweden that are not known for dire economic conditions or deficient public infrastructure.

Explaining piracy as a political cause in Sweden, Jonas Anderson (2011) makes the exact opposite point: digital piracy cannot be explained with material deprivation but rather with the recent shift to post-materialism in advanced capitalist economies. While such a theory might be relevant for the case of Sweden, it nevertheless has less explanatory power in the case of Bulgaria, for example, where as seen in the previous chapter, only one year after the anti-ACTA mobilization people went to the streets because they could not pay their electricity bills.

But what about actual, empirically observed, levels of digital piracy? A possible hypothesis could be that the population of countries where digital piracy is widespread felt most affected and threatened by ACTA and thus went to the streets. Indeed, many of the countries with large protests against ACTA are among the top 10 in terms of percentage of population engaged in piracy (TorrentFreak, 2016). However, Spain and Greece also rank very high in terms of piracy, and yet there was almost no mobilization against ACTA in these countries (ibid.). And on the contrary, Austria and Germany, which both have low levels of piracy, have been two of the countries with the largest protests against ACTA. Thus, levels of digital piracy alone, regardless of whether people engage in it for materialist or post-materialist reasons, cannot explain the diffusion of anti-ACTA protests.

Neither can we explain the mobilization against ACTA with the standard conflicts of interest between developing and developed countries when it comes to investment in research and development or intellectual property infringements. We could hypothesize that countries that invest more in research and development might push for more restrictive intellectual property protection, while countries that invest less would be more defiant and fight against strict intellectual property regimes, or at least not enforce them too stringently. The fact that anti-ACTA protests were so big in Eastern Europe where the record of research and development investment has been particularly low seems to suggest such a hypothesis. In practice, however, we notice that countries such as Sweden, Austria, and Germany, whose levels of investment in research and development are among the highest in the EU (R&D, 2013), also witnessed significant resistance towards stringent intellectual property regimes. Similarly, when it comes to TTIP and CETA that I discuss in the next chapter, Germany has been both the biggest winner of international trade and the country with some of the largest mobilizations against it.

Finally, a classic social movement theory explanation of the diffusion of anti-ACTA protests would focus on the political opportunity structures and show that anti-ACTA protests diffused only where the political opportunity structure (POS) understood as comprising three broad sets of properties of the political system: formal institutional structure, its informal procedures and prevailing strategies with regard to challengers, and the configuration of power relevant for the confrontation with the challengers (Kriesi, 1991) was favourable. Yet, Austria, Bulgaria, Germany, Denmark, and Poland – the countries with some of the largest protests – had more differences than similarities in their POSs and in the elite responses to challengers demanding more Internet freedom and the "right" to share files.

To sum up, the diffusion of anti-ACTA protests cannot be explained by the heritage of communism alone, nor by the price of cultural goods and failing cultural infrastructure in post-socialist countries, post-materialist ideology in advanced capital economies, levels of digital piracy, the strength of pro-ACTA lobbyists, the levels of investment in research and development, or POS. What is more, many of the explanations considered so far are mutually contradictory and hard to generalize for all cases.

Instead, following the players and arenas paradigm, I propose a different explanation: protests against ACTA diffused mainly in countries that had players who had previously mobilized on the issue of Internet freedom. In addition, protests against ACTA seemed to diffuse mainly in countries that had *not* previously mobilized against austerity, showing that not only the existence of relevant players but also timing is crucial for explaining diffusion. As I will discuss in more detail later in the chapter, Spain had many actors that could have engaged with ACTA, but they were already dedicated to the more general anti-austerity protests.

In the Beginning There Were SOPA and PIPA . . .

The anti-ACTA protests erupted across the EU at the beginning of 2012. Yet, the first round of negotiations on ACTA had already started in Geneva back in

June 2008. The negotiations were shrouded in secrecy, and most of the information on the negotiators' positions and the extent of agreement between parties
came from leaked documents published on WikiLeaks. Digital rights organizations such as the US's Electronic Frontier Foundation (EFF) and the EU's La
Quadrature du Net (LQDN) and European Digital Rights (EDRi) followed
ACTA closely from the very beginning (interviews with Jérémie Zimmermann
and Joe McNamee). Numerous expert analyses were also published by academics on both sides of the Atlantic, for example a series of research papers by the
Washington College of Law's Program on Information Justice and Intellectual
Property (PIJIP), the opinion of Brown and Korff (2009) on the compatibility
of ACTA with the ECHR and the EU Charter of Fundamental Rights, and the
Opinion of the European Data Protection Supervisor on ACTA (2010, 2012).
What is more, the Canadian academic Michael Geist provided timely and suc-
cinct analyses of the developments with ACTA in his regular blog posts. News
websites specializing in technology, such as Techdirt and ArsTechnica, were also
crucial in informing about the latest controversies around the negotiations. What
is more, these intellectuals and media drew on a long tradition of critical thinking
in the sphere of intellectual property rights that we can trace back to the early
years of the free software community and the movement for open culture, both
of which originated in the US before spreading throughout the world (Lessig,
2004; Stallman, 2015, 2017).

Nevertheless, the general public, i.e. people who are neither legal experts nor
tech geeks, became informed of the agreement and its potential consequences
only in January 2012. This happened largely due to chance and coincidence in
timing. In January 2012, the major US campaign against the US Stop Online
Piracy Act (SOPA) and the Protect IP Act (PIPA) bills took place: its most
spectacular moment was the January 18th blackout of 115,000 websites in the
US, among which were the English Wikipedia, Craigslist, Cheezburger, Boing
Boing, Cyanide & Happiness, Internet Archive, Marxists Internet Archive, Tumblr, Twitter, WordPress, and many others (Lee, 2013, 103). Google joined the
protest by placing a censor bar over their logo, urging people to "tell Congress:
please don't censor the web!" and providing information on SOPA and PIPA.
The global reach of US companies allowed information on the campaign to diffuse rapidly across the world. On January 19, the US seized the domain names
and closed the sites associated with Megaupload, the torrent tracker owned by the
notorious Kim Dotcom.

Poland Rises Up

On the same day, in Poland there was a meeting organized by Igor Ostrowski, the
deputy minister of the newly created Ministry of Administration and Digitization.
The meeting of the "Dialogue Group" (an ad hoc group of businesses, NGOs,
and other stakeholders that was formed in 2010 to advise the Polish government

on laws that could affect the Internet) was held in the conference room of the prime minister's office and took a dramatic turn when Ostrowski revealed that Poland was planning to sign ACTA on the 26th of January and there was no point in discussing it. The problem was that the NGOs had received an explicit promise a year ago that, until their concerns about the deal were answered, the government would cease all talks on ACTA (Wozniak, 2012). Then, out of the blue, the government announced that it would sign the bill, which made civil organizations furious and triggered them to immediately start campaigning against the signature. One of the reasons why the campaign against ACTA started in Poland was that the country already had well-established and connected NGOs in the sphere of digital rights who had entered into dialogue with the Ministry of Administration and Digitization. The sense of a breach of trust when these organizations learned about the government's decision triggered them to quickly organize and disseminate information about ACTA in Poland and beyond. From this moment on, the connection between SOPA and PIPA in the US and ACTA in Poland was not difficult to make.

On January 21 and 22, Anonymous hacked several Polish government websites as a sign of protest. A message from the Twitter user @AnonymousWiki after the sites went down read: "Dear Polish government, we will continue to disrupt and interfere with your government official websites until the 26th. Do not pass ACTA." The same user later posted: "We have dox files and leaked documentations on many Poland officials, if ACTA is passed, we will release these documents" (BBC News, 2012). The hacktivist stunt gained widespread media coverage and made the tension between Internet freedom and intellectual property highly salient for the general public.

On January 24, many Polish websites participated in a blackout for an hour, but the culmination of all this were the popular protests of people who self-organized on Facebook and went in the thousands to the streets to protest against ACTA. The bottom-up movement not only organized via digital media, but also produced numerous videos from the protests, blog comments, and informational materials that then were taken up by mainstream media. The salience of the issue was increased even further when lawmakers for the liberal Palikot's Movement put on Anonymous masks in Parliament to show their dissatisfaction, while the largest opposition party, the right-wing Law and Justice Party, called for a referendum on the matter (Arthur and Agencies, 2012).

A search in Google trends shows that the peak of Google searches on ACTA was from January 22 to 28. This peak of public attention was made possible by the expertise and quick reaction of NGOs. Still, NGOs alone could not have attracted so much attention to the issue in the absence of SOPA and PIPA as precedents in the US, the action on part of Anonymous who defaced websites, online media that participated in the blackout, bottom-up protesters who used digital media to mobilize street protests (Mercea and Funk, 2016), politicians who put on masks in the Parliament, and mainstream media that reported on all this asking NGOs for advice and know-how. Of course, these different actors were not always cooperating smoothly. In fact, the Polish anti-ACTA campaign had rather complicated internal dynamics. To begin with, there was tension between Anonymous and the NGOs. The latter thought that the hacktivist attacks of Anonymous subverted the anti-ACTA campaign from within, making it look like a protest in defence of downloading free porn, while in fact there were serious human rights issues at stake (Lee, 2013, 127–128). Referring to the Anonymous attacks of his government websites, Donald Tusk even insisted that he would not back down from signing ACTA and give in to "blackmail" (Masnick, 2012). In his account of the events around ACTA, Edward Lee narrates how Marcin "Sirmacik" Karpezo, a free culture activist and member of Poland's Free and Open Source Software Foundation, along with Tehora, a grad student specializing in econometrics and computer science, reached out to a foreign contact with connections to Anonymous to negotiate and try to convince them to stop their attacks as they were actually counterproductive to the movement (Lee, 2013, 128). Anonymous published a temporary cease-fire agreement threatening, however, that if the "peaceful" means do not succeed, they will return with much harsher attacks (ibid.). Thus, while hacktivist media practices in Poland were originally successful and welcome, they were far from uncontroversial.

What is more, bottom-up protesters often had unconventional answers when asked why they protest that were not always based on facts of expertise. That is why NGOs organized a seminar for all bottom-up protest organizers to make sure they are on the same page and to provide expertise-based frames (interview with Jedrzej Niklas). In any case, disagreements about the appropriate frames and tactics did not weaken the movement as it had already gathered impressive momentum. Even more importantly, Polish protests inspired action and diffused also in other EU member states.

The Diffusion of Anti-ACTA Mobilization Across the EU: The Cases of Bulgaria and Germany

As this description of the beginnings of the anti-ACTA campaign in the previous paragraphs has shown, initial mobilization was driven by a variety of players, including intellectuals, US digital media companies protesting against the US SOPA and PIPA acts, transnational and Polish NGOs, online Polish media who participated in the Polish blackouts, the Anonymous hacktivists, and of course other bottom-up protesters who flooded the streets. Not only were activists using digital media to spread their message, but digital companies also took a political stance that pushed a lot of people towards activism. Far from being neutral intermediaries, Google, Twitter, and the rest assumed an activist role in the US SOPA and PIPA debates and thus also became important players in the EU context, due to their global reach.

The action of these global media players in the US context raised the salience of bills related to intellectual property and allowed European NGOs to frame ACTA as the "new SOPA". Journalists in the English-language press started publishing papers with suggestive titles such as "If you thought SOPA was bad, just wait until you meet ACTA"(Kain, 2012) or "SOPA stopped for now, anti-censorship activists turn to ACTA" (Clark Esteves, 2012). English-language media and publications in English by transnational NGOs raised the salience of the issue internationally. But then, whether local players would organize in response depended to a large extent on whether there were previously existing protest traditions and players engaging with the issue to begin with. As we don't have space in the current chapter to explore how the anti-ACTA mobilization played out in each EU member state, in the following paragraphs we will focus on how the mobilization played out in two other countries that followed the example of Poland and had large protests against ACTA – Bulgaria and Germany.

What is particularly interesting about Bulgaria and Germany is that both had massive mobilizations against ACTA and yet in these countries the type of players that engaged in mobilization were quite different. What is more, various types of players had a different appetite for trying to diffuse protest beyond their country's borders.

In Bulgaria, the largest protest against ACTA took place on February 11, 2012. Unlike Poland, in Bulgaria there wasn't at the time a strong and well-developed NGO sector concerning digital rights. Thus, the mobilization against ACTA was led by a group of students previously engaged in demonstrations for more accessible high education (interviews with Ivaylo Dinev and "Charlie Parker"), who met the fervent support of, on the one hand, bloggers and intellectuals, and on the other hand, the file-sharing community that had already protested several times against the closing of torrent trackers in previous years. Some of these students went on in 2013 to organize the student occupation of Sofia University.

Among the most active bloggers who published on ACTA in 2012 were political commentators Komitata (who later went on to defend a PhD on the use of digital media in the Bulgarian 2013 protests) and Boyan Yurukov (based in Brussels), lawyer Emil Georgiev, and media law expert and Sofia University professor Nelly Ognyanova. These bloggers and intellectuals served as key intermediaries who analyzed the agreements on the basis of foreign expertise and publications in both media and NGO sites. The other crucial, and rather unexpected, player who supported the mobilization against ACTA and promoted contacting members of European Parliament was the illegal torrent tracker Zamunda. Activism by pirate websites has a long history in Bulgaria. Back in 2006, there was a major campaign of the Bulgarian Ministry of Culture called "Piracy Steals" ("Пиратството ограбва") that was met with a serious backlash (Spassov, 2011). In 2006 and 2007, the Bulgarian police targeted the major illegal torrent trackers in the country – first Arena and then Zamunda – confiscated their servers, and charged their owners with copyright infringement and spreading pornographic content. In 2010 the police raided for the second time the premises of the torrent trackers, provoking massive public discontent. Already in 2007, the administrators of the illegal torrent tracker Zamunda organized a protest attended by several hundred youngsters in defence of the torrent tracker and the "right" to download (Dnevnik, 2007). In 2008 two campaigns took place in defence of Internet freedom. The first one was called "Stop the Monitoring of the Internet". The second campaign – a protest march of between 100 and 200 people – was called "Freedom and Not Fear" (Spassov, 2011, 313). The "Freedom and Not Fear" march was attended by a colourful mixture of nationalists, anarchists, and Greens. Considering this contentious history of online file-sharing sites, it becomes more understandable why in 2012 the illegal torrent tracker Zamunda was again a highly active player encouraging protest against ACTA. The popular torrent tracker with millions of visitors published long comments on the agreement and even urged users to contact Bulgarian members of the European Parliament. The emails and phones of MEPs were posted on the title page of the tracker in order to make contacting them and lobbying against ACTA easier. File sharing became a cause that united students, bloggers, and illegal websites in a political battle in which nationalist and liberal human rights frames were merged in defence of piracy (Rone, 2013) but also of Internet freedom in a more general sense.

Anti-ACTA campaigners in Bulgaria tried to keep away all political party actors who wanted to use the momentum of the movement in order to gain popularity. Bulgaria did not have a Pirate Party at the time, but there was no lack of parties eager to own the issue – both the Bulgarian Socialist Party, back then in opposition, and the nationalist party Ataka issued statements and published videos to oppose the agreement (BNT, 2012). Political parties voicing their concerns on the issue, even when protesters refused any association with them, increased ACTA's visibility in mainstream media news and contributed to a number of debates on the issue, including on morning TV shows.

In Bulgaria, the hacktivist collective Anonymous supported the protests but did not have a principal role in them (interviews with Ivaylo Dinev and "Charlie Parker"). Unlike what could be observed in Poland, Bulgarian student protesters did not have any conflicts with the Anonymous collective and readily borrowed their identity markers in order to popularize the protest. For instance, one night, the organizers put Anonymous masks on the faces of a sculpture composition on the monument of the Soviet Army in Sofia. Overall, the mobilization against ACTA in Bulgaria was mostly bottom-up driven, led by student protesters who got their expertise from local bloggers and intellectuals but also from international NGOs and media. It was a clear case of adopter-driven protest diffusion with little attempts by either Polish NGOs or transnational NGOs to stage events or trigger mobilization in Bulgaria in particular. What made diffusion possible in the Bulgarian case was the already high level of politicization of file sharing and Internet freedom as topics, which meant that organizers were already politicized and had previous experience with mobilization. These actors recognized the anti-ACTA issue as "theirs" and moved to organize protest.

The situation was similar in Germany where the biggest protests also took place on February 11. In Germany, however, the main actors driving the mobilization were not only students but also the German Pirate Party and its local branches. The German Pirate Party was founded in 2006. In 2011 and 2012 the Pirates had a series of electoral victories but in the following years, mainly due to internal scandals, they lost much of their support (Meiritz and Reinbold, 2013). Nevertheless, 2012 was still a strong year for the Pirates. Just a year before, in 2011, they had received 8.9% of the votes in Berlin's state elections. The party was on the rise, and ACTA was a natural cause for it to focus on. A key activist in the anti-ACTA protests was Sebastian Radtke, described by *The Daily Dot* as the "most effective freedom fighter no one in the U.S. has ever heard of" (Collier, 2012). Radtke joined the Pirates in 2011, and after he realized the party did not have a campaign to oppose the agreement, he partnered with another Pirate – Thomas Gaul – and declared a Europe-wide protest:

> He set up a Wiki page to help others to organize locally, enlisted pirates across the continent, and spent two weeks utterly devoted to the protests, which included "~10.000 emails" and "2–4 hours every day" on the phone.
>
> *(ibid.)*

Thus, it was the German Pirates that in fact coordinated the whole bottom-up campaign across the European Union. The group also was responsible for setting up the wiki.stoppacta-protest.info website which was meant to help protest organizers in different countries. There was also a centralized wiki which had all the protest details for all countries in one place. The activist organization Access Now also set up a parallel page where they published all Facebook events (Lee, 2013, 138).

The German Pirate Party distributed flyers that were free to download online and created videos and banners that websites could embed (Piraten Partei ACTA, 2019). What is more, the Pirates did not focus only on digital media. The importance they placed on mainstream media coverage becomes clear when we see the meticulous way that they kept track of every time the issue was discussed and collected links to media materials (Piraten Partei Medien, 2019). Most importantly, even though protests in Germany were dominated by bottom-up activists, they had no problems protesting alongside political actors that were perceived as critical of the establishment. Claudia Roth, the Green Party leader in Germany, and board member Malte Spitz saw in the mass protests a "fulminant signal against ACTA and for living democracy in the digital age". What is more, the German anti-ACTA demonstrations were not only openly supported by the left and the Pirate Party but also co-organized by them (BZ, 2012).

The German Pirates were also active transmitters of protest across Europe, providing protesters across the continent with centralized information on similar events, expertise, and solidarity. What the German Pirates did was to provide the digital infrastructure, the skeleton for organization, and then the initiative depended on the adopters in the other countries. In this sense, the Pirates as a political party acted very much as enablers of protest. The organizational platform they provided was taken up by local players in countries in which Internet freedom had been previously politicized.

NGOs also participated in the German campaign but to a lesser extent in comparison with Polish NGOs. In the German context, the NGO Digitale Gesellschaft, founded in 2010 and a member of the European Digital Rights Initiative, organized a successful campaign for producing postcards, stickers, and info-flyers with anti-ACTA messages that were chosen from multiple suggestions made by opponents of the agreement as a response to a call for catchy slogans. Digitale Gesellschaft also organized a crowd-sourcing campaign to raise the money needed to print all the materials and managed to collect 15,000 euro for the goal. Some of the key messages on stickers were: "Leave our Internet alone or we will take your fax machines", "If they put us in jail because we download music, then I insist that they separate us by genre", "Whoever gives up freedom to gain security, will ultimately lose both", "Reform instead of Cement", "Culture means Remix", "Copy freedom without losses" (Digitale Gesellshaft, 2012).

Finally, Anonymous were highly active in the German mobilization against ACTA and urged for protests against the agreement already on November 5, 2011, Guy Fawkes Day. On the blog of Anonymous Hamburg, one can find the speech of individual activists of the Chaos Computer Club, the Pirate Party, and Anonymous itself (Internet-Tsunamis, 2016). One of the interesting challenges to Anonymous was how to participate in the protests as a collective while at the same time *not* revealing their identity, i.e. remaining anonymous. The solution to this question in Germany, but also in Bulgaria and Poland, was the Anonymous Guy Fawkes mask that allowed all kinds of players to join the protests, putting differences behind them and uniting under a common symbol. The Anonymous collective was well connected transnationally and actively diffused calls for action and information on the agreement.

The efforts of German players to diffuse protest transnationally were complemented by the efforts of major European NGOs in the sphere of digital rights such as La Quadrature du Net or the European Digital Rights Network – EDRi – which made sure that actors across Europe would use more or less similar frames, based on appropriate legal expertise.

The Role of NGOs

As already mentioned, intellectuals and NGOs had been analyzing ACTA and publishing on the dangers associated with the agreement since 2008. Yet, popular protests took off only in the small window of opportunity between the end of January 2012 and the end of February 2012. Similarly, the hacktivist attacks of Anonymous concentrated their actions mainly in the period after the closing of Megaupload and around the popular protests. Media attention also followed closely this boom of bottom-up activist initiative. In a sense, different players operated on different time scales. The NGOs' production of expertise and lobbying had not only long preceded the boom in protests and in media salience, but also continued until the July 2012 session of the European Parliament, long after the big protests and mainstream media attention had faded.

The role of NGOs was particularly important since they provided the legitimacy of the whole campaign by producing their own legal expertise and translating academic knowledge in an accessible language on their websites for protesters and the public to read. While the European Commission was actively insisting that myths and misinformation dominate the campaign against ACTA (EU Commission, 2012), NGOs tried to make sure in every possible way that expertise was widely available and people protested with the right arguments. Joe McNamee, the executive director of the European Digital Rights Initiative, recalled a particular meeting with proponents of ACTA in the European Parliament who insisted that protesters on the streets were ignorant, were fed with misinformation, or had no idea what they were protesting about. At this point McNamee invited the politician who said this to go to the website of EDRi and check whether there was a single fact there that was not true (interview with Joe McNamee). This was an especially clever move: it is obvious that the demands of the protesters were not as elaborate and legally accurate as those of EDRi. However, by associating themselves with the protests, EDRi provided them with the legitimacy of expertise while at the same time gaining legitimacy themselves from this unprecedented awakening of citizen energy in Europe. While anti-ACTA protests came as a surprise to NGOs (Parks, 2013, 2015), the NGOs quickly figured out how to use the momentum of the protests. As McNamee remarked, "politics lives from momentum, as sport" (interview with Joe McNamee).

NGOs did not organize popular protests. What is more they didn't expect them. But they reacted swiftly and skilfully. Jérémie Zimmermann from the French La Quadrature du Net (LQDN) explained that once it became clear that people were organizing for a protest, LQDN took it as their primary task to produce leaflets, videos, and all types of visual materials for protesters to use so that they could know and explain what exactly they were protesting about (interview with Jérémie Zimmermann). Zimmermann was particularly enthusiastic about the video *What Is ACTA?* (whose German translation managed to get more than 3.6 million views in 2012). *What Is ACTA?* was made by a professional animator who contacted the group and offered his help for the cause. After days of editing work, tens of versions (some versions differed from each other with no more than a second of silence), and a long debate on the textual contents and the graphic design, the video was uploaded online: it was re-embedded and reposted multiple times, translated in multiple languages, and seen millions of times. The use of video format turned out to be a successful, easily understandable, and compelling way of providing information.

What is more, NGOs became the go-to expert for most mainstream media. The Polish NGO Panoptykon was overwhelmed by media attention and questions during the anti-ACTA campaign (interview with Jedrzej Niklas). The group had to respond quickly to the expectations both on part of EDRi, its umbrella organization, and the general public in Poland, which counted on Panoptykon to provide expertise on the topic. The sudden catapulting to such a key intermediary position could be explained with the long-term efforts of the energetic, expert, and proactive team of the foundation, but it was also a product of chance and of the convergence of different expectations at the same time. This intense experience of communicating with the public on TV, media, and numerous online outlets also increased the reputation of the organization and led to its establishment as an authority in the field. Media practices sometimes achieve much more than their immediate goal and have important outcomes for the players' own standing, experience, and organizational confidence.

The unexpected diffusion of street protests largely coordinated by the German Pirates was matched by a carefully controlled and crafted information and lobbying campaign, led by large transnationally connected NGOs. Not only did NGOs use their contacts in the European Parliament in order to gain allies and sway the opinion of deputies against ACTA; in all their published materials LQDN and EDRi also urged citizens in general to get involved and to contact their MEPs, to write to them and call them with questions on ACTA. NGOs channelled and transformed citizen anger through innovative citizen practices in ways that were particularly effective when working with EU institutions.

LQDN was particularly active in this respect, devising tools such as the Pi Phone that allowed citizens to contact MEPs for free and provided them a script with straight-to-the-point questions to ask in a polite way. What is more, LQDN organized as well the inventive "Brussels Safari", in which civil activists from all over Europe gathered in the EU Parliament and tried to "hunt down" particular deputies and have conversations with them. And while such "exotic" innovations did not spread beyond Brussels, simpler practices, such as writing emails to MEPs, that were encouraged by both EDRi and LQDN, diffused successfully and gained wide popularity. As already mentioned, in Bulgaria, in the absence of a Pirate Party or strong NGO coalitions, the appeal to people to write to MEPs was published by several bloggers and on the front page of the illegal torrent tracker Zamunda.net. Regardless of how and where citizens found out about the initiative, the results were overwhelming. Everyone working at the European Parliament at the time commented on the sheer impression made by hundreds of emails and phone calls a day (interviews with Mattias Bjarnemalm and Bendert Zevenbergen). Paradoxically, despite the presence of tens of thousands people on the streets, it was the email campaign that affected MEPs in the most immediate way and made them consider ACTA.

The Depoliticization of Protest Claims Against ACTA

A crucial aspect of the intervention by NGOs was the way they framed ACTA as an *apolitical* cause in all their materials and lobbying efforts. It was emphasized multiple times in my interviews with NGO representatives that the mobilization against ACTA went beyond left and right and had to remain an issue not "owned" by any single political faction or party. Jérémie Zimmermann, for example, noted that the battle against ACTA was not an issue that naturally belonged to any single party. He claimed that this was a major advantage in organizing the opposition as it allowed NGOs and experts to strategically make parties outcompete each other with arguments such as "the liberals adopted this issue, you can't allow them to become associated with it, you should do something about it as well". The practice on the ground, as we saw, was quite complicated. Many political parties took part in the mobilization against ACTA, be they "natural allies" such as the Pirate Party or other parties with strong positions on the issue, including radical left parties, Green parties, left-wing populist movements such as Palikot in Poland, and even nationalist parties as the Bulgarian Ataka.

More importantly, bottom-up protesters' claims against ACTA were highly politically charged. Activists in Eastern Europe pointed to the price of cultural products and often interpreted "Internet freedom" as the freedom to download cultural products. In Poland the fight against ACTA was sometimes compared to the fight against Nazism or communism. In Bulgaria, Internet users called ACTA "the Ottoman Empire of the Internet". During the Bulgarian anti-ACTA protests, there was a protestor holding a flag with the mask of the hacktivist group Anonymous on its obverse side and the slogan "Freedom or Death" on its reverse side. "Freedom or Death" is a key historical phrase from the 19th-century struggles for national liberation, which has been recently rediscovered by the radical right in the country. During the anti-ACTA protests, this romantic nationalist vision of freedom became entangled with Internet freedom in a common frame. In Germany, too, anti-ACTA protestors often had arguments that pointed to Stasi and compared the requirements for Internet service providers to monitor communications to censorship during the communist period. What is more, protesters in all countries referred to broader political problems of inequality and in some cases even discussed ACTA in relation to the Occupy protests. Mattias Bjarnemalm, the Internet policy advisor of the Greens in the European Parliament, suggested in an interview that the protests against ACTA in Eastern Europe were largely protests against national governments and ACTA became a symbol that concentrated popular rage against bad quality of life and corruption. Such an observation fits well with the fact that, for example, in Bulgaria, the organizers of the protests against ACTA later on became organizers of the anti-government university occupation in 2013.

NGOs carefully countered these political overtones and avoided all political rhetoric in their communication materials. Some of the most frequent statements NGOs made with regard to the agreement were related primarily to the procedural problems with ACTA, such as "negotiated behind closed doors", "undemocratic", and "influenced by lobbies". NGOs also often made economic claims pointing out that ACTA might stifle economic growth, innovation, and trade. Another important group of arguments referred to the negative impact of ACTA on developing countries and the obstacles it poses to access to medicines.

NGOs managed to successfully impose these set of frames thanks to both their reputation as experts and the transnational connections they had. I analyzed activists' documents from the campaign against ACTA in Bulgaria, Germany, and Poland to trace who quoted whom and in what direction information diffused. On the graph in Figure 3.2, the positioning of the nodes point to their modularity class, while the size of the nodes corresponds to the indegree of the actors, i.e. who are the ones most often referred to/quoted.

The analysis of patterns of frame diffusion in the mobilization against ACTA reveals that there was a strong transnational diffusion of information in the mobilization. What is more, there was a clear pattern of political claims diffusion from the centre to the periphery, i.e. from big NGOs with transnational connections to national NGOs, bloggers, and "ordinary" activists. Different political players from one nation, let's say Bulgarians or Poles, tended to quote mainly actors with the same nationality (and correspondingly, language) or transnationally connected NGOs. Actors from one nation, however, would very rarely quote actors from another nation. For example, Bulgarian bloggers or protesters would almost never quote the frames of Polish bloggers and protesters or vice versa. This is what explains the modularity we can see in the graph where one can clearly distinguish between clusters of Bulgarian actors, Polish actors, and German actors, all quoting the NGOs in the very centre. The transnational diffusion of claims about ACTA thus happened clearly with the mediation of NGOs. This also meant that the depoliticized frames preferred by NGOs dominated the debate and protesters could not push forward their more political messages.

All in all, the main players who drove the diffusion of protests against ACTA in the EU were big digital media in the US that participated in the blackouts against SOPA and PIPA and thus raised the salience of the issue; Polish NGOs; street protesters; Anonymous who defaced websites, marched, created videos, and made ACTA a topic in the European political debate; the German Pirate Party that created wikis, collected and disseminated information online and in mainstream media, and encouraged the organization of transnational protests; and finally Brussels-based NGOs that through publishing expert analyses pushed for the spread of particular depoliticized claims on why the agreement was problematic. These were the actors that actively pushed for the

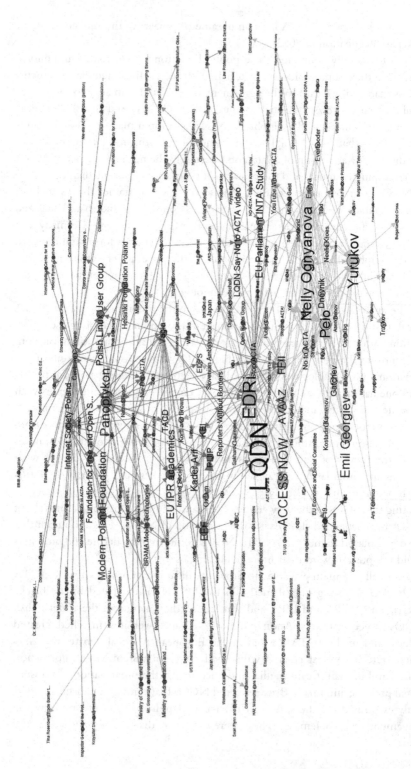

FIGURE 3.2 Directional map of who quoted whom in the mobilization against ACTA

transnational diffusion of protest. But we should not underestimate the importance of local players, including bottom-up protesters, intellectuals, NGOs, media, and political parties, who acted as avid adopters and in turn mobilized local protesters.

It is precisely the presence and strategic agency of these local players already interested in the politicization of Internet freedom that explain why protest managed to spread in these particular countries that otherwise have so widely diverging POSs, political cultures, and economic profiles. Each of the players involved in the diffusion process had their own preferences to media practices, protest frames, and repertoires, and they often clashed. Bottom-up protesters put forward more politicized frames, while NGOs preferred more apolitical ones. Hacktivists engaged in defacing websites, while NGOs found this unacceptable. This shows that protest diffusion is a highly political agentic process in which different players have their own strategy and try to push for their own message.

The mobilization against ACTA became a key formative experience for the German Pirate Party but also for national and Brussels-based transnational NGOs that later cooperated in the organization of the pan-European campaign against TTIP and CETA. The anti-TTIP and CETA campaign was more centralized from the very beginning with clear messages to be diffused through common digital platforms. Before we proceed to analyze this campaign in the next chapter, however, I will briefly analyze in the next section why the protests against ACTA failed in some European countries and, ultimately, what practical takeaways activists can get from the diffusion of protests against ACTA.

3.4. This Protest Is Not Available in Your Country: Why Spain Did Not Protest Against ACTA

So far I have explained protest diffusion with the presence and strategic media practices of players active on Internet issues. Considering this, countries such as Cyprus and Luxembourg that had low levels of Internet politicization to begin with and few players active on the issue could not have anti-ACTA protests and are clear cases of failed diffusion. But what about a more difficult case such as Spain, where there were highly active players focusing on Internet freedom but still no anti-ACTA protests? How can one explain failed diffusion in this case? A crucial factor explaining why protests against ACTA did not diffuse in Spain seems to be timing. In the same way Indignados-style occupations could not diffuse to Italy in 2011 because Italian activists were already at a different stage of mobilization (Zamponi, 2012), anti-ACTA protests couldn't diffuse in Spain in 2012 because Spanish free and open source software activists were already strongly engaged in systemic anti-austerity protests. Thus, is not only the particular constellation of players in a country that matters but also whether these players are ready to mobilize in the current moment or already moving on from previous mobilizations.

As mentioned in the previous chapter, one of the most important events in the run up to the Indignados protests was the No les Votes campaign, started by several influential tech-activists, lawyers, and bloggers in Spain as a protest against Ley Sinde – a controversial law that aimed at curbing illegal downloading on the Internet. Ley Sinde was strongly criticized in Spain for reasons similar to the ones pointed out against ACTA a year later in many European countries: lack of public debate, prioritization of private interests, and threats to fundamental rights. Ley Sinde was not a stand-alone law but a provision of the Sustainable Economy Bill proposed by Zapatero's government in order to modernize the Spanish economy in several different spheres, stimulating competitiveness, environmental sustainability, innovation, professional specialization, and emerging sectors (El País, 2011). The Sustainable Economy Bill was explicitly prepared as a response to the economic crisis and as a proactive move for boosting the Spanish economy (Expansión, 2009) and was embraced by both the right-wing Partido Popular (PP) and the left-wing Partido Socialista Obrero Español (PSOE).

After criticism was voiced, the Ley Sinde provision was taken out of the Sustainable Economy Act and subjected to revisions. Initiated as a reaction to the approval of Ley Sinde, the No les Votes ("Don't vote for them") campaign urged citizens not to vote for PP, PSOE, and the Catalan nationalist Convergència i Unió (CiU) at the municipal elections of May 22. Contrary to many of the accusations against the campaign, it did not urge people *not to vote at all* but simply not to vote for any of the parties that approved Ley Sinde. The first manifesto of No les Votes paid exclusive attention to Ley Sinde and accused PSOE, PP, and CiU of negotiating together to pass the law and of failing their main obligations towards citizens (15MPedia, 2020).

The intertwining of resistance towards Ley Sinde and towards the traditional parties in Spain, the move from protest on an Internet issue to protest against the political system as such, can be clearly seen in several comments of users to the blog post in which Enrique Dans (2011), a popular blogger and one of the initiators of the campaign No les Votes, explained what it is all about. The user *KikeMb*, for example, states:

> #005 KikeMb – 16 febrero 2011–20:40 So it is that Ley Sinde is the drop that spilled the cup, the cup of patience, my patience. Thank you for this initiative in which I trust completely as a warning and punishment for the political class that does not do anything for its citizens.
>
> *(Dans, 2011)*

No les Votes was only one campaign among several. As we already saw in the chapter on protests against austerity, organizations such as Juventud sin Futuro, Democracia Real Ya, and Plataforma de Afectados Por La Hipoteca created a common front to oppose austerity. What united all these groups was not only the message against austerity but also their belief in the emancipatory potential of digital technologies (Treré et al., 2017).

Considering this extent of politicization of Internet issues and the prominence of the belief in the emancipatory power of the Internet in campaigns preceding Los Indignados, the lack of diffusion of protest against ACTA is all the more striking. Nevertheless, if one takes into account the literature on protest cycles with its emphasis on different stages of contention (emergence, coalescence, formalization, and decline), the history of Los Indignados movement shows clearly that by January 2012 when ACTA became an issue in other parts of Europe, the protest cycle in Spain had moved beyond emergence and coalescence and had entered a stage of formalization. Players interested in Internet freedom had been already long engaged in fighting a broader battle against austerity and had started to form organizations for this goal. No les Votes, a campaign initiated in February 2011 to oppose Ley Sinde, for example, transformed from a campaign on Internet issues to a campaign for systemic political change – the second updated version of the No Les Votes' manifesto paid less attention to Ley Sinde and more attention to corruption, the electoral law, and the importance of searching for political alternatives. Thus, even though Internet freedom was highly politicized, ACTA as a single-issue protest diffusing across Europe in January 2012 could not find enthusiastic local adopters in Spain. In fact, ACTA failed to provoke any substantial street protests in all of the Southern European countries that had experienced anti-austerity mobilizations in 2011.

It is not a coincidence that most countries that had major protests against ACTA in 2012 – Bulgaria, Poland, Germany, Austria, Romania, etc. – had not yet experienced a major protest against austerity. Protesting against ACTA allowed the youth in these countries to express its outrage and solidarity with other global protests. The criticism towards the non-democratic nature of the agreement also echoed critiques of the non-democratic nature of austerity measures in the South. Yet, anti-ACTA protests were single-issue protests and especially in Eastern European countries were driven by a mix of nationalist and right-wing liberal discourse. The situation was different in Germany and Austria where it was left-wing parties and the Pirates that opposed the agreement. The common ground between both Eastern and Western protesters against ACTA was the techno-fetishist belief in the power of Internet to bring freedom and democracy. It was this belief in digital technologies that had diffused from the Indignados and Occupy protests in 2011 to the anti-ACTA protests in 2012.

To sum up, the protests against ACTA did not happen in Spain because key Spanish players had already fought against their Ley Sinde and because they had integrated the cause of Internet freedom and the belief in digital technologies in mass scale anti-systemic demonstrations. Refining my initial hypothesis, I must note that what is important for protest to diffuse is not only the presence of players that have previous mobilization experience with a particular cause and are ready to promote it, but also that these players have not moved to new types of protests, with a higher degree of generality. The anti-ACTA mobilization came too late and had little potential to ignite political players in Spain. Thus, the right players were there but at the wrong time.

3.5. Takeaways for Activists: How to Follow Up on Issues and Avoid Depoliticization

When describing the success of the anti-ACTA campaign, Jérémie Zimmermann from LQDN mentioned that success usually has many fathers, while failure has none (interview with Jérémie Zimmermann). Everyone wants to claim their role when the outcome is successful. What is more, it is much more difficult to draw lessons from successful cases such as the anti-ACTA campaign, because the things that go wrong are less obvious when everything turns out well in the end

The diffusion of protest and the ultimate rejection of ACTA were the result of the sustained and combined efforts of "many fathers" – various players with different types of media practices. What is more, each type of player had distinct preferences and visions for what types of frames and forms of contention should be diffused. Looking at the mobilization from the perspective of bottom-up activists only, a number of problematic aspects could be improved if activists want to have more weight and power to define objectives and content in the diffusion process.

First, bottom-up activists organized only for a short period of time, around key international days of protests. They were very successful in January and February 2012 and much less successful in protest organization in the following months when media stopped reporting as actively and citizens lost interest in the issue. A potential reason for this might be that many of the bottom-up activists that protested against ACTA in countries such as Poland, Germany, and Bulgaria saw ACTA as a single issue and did not establish more long-term networks that would focus on Internet politics and develop knowledge and expertise on this. Activists' analyses of the agreement shared on organizational pages were most often borrowed from NGOs, who were the experts in the field. NGOs were also the ones that continued following the topic and pressured lawmakers in the EU, even after the protests had faded away.

The problem is that NGOs can do only so much without the legitimacy of popular protest. ACTA was rejected, but most of its provisions were still adopted in secret handshake deals between the European Commission and different types of macro-intermediaries such as Facebook, Google, Pay Pal, and eBay (Tusikov, 2017). As Joe McNamee, the executive director of the European Digital Rights Initiative, noted, most pro-IP lobbyists in fact hated ACTA since it provided activists with the perfect compact target to protest against. What happened after the rejection of the agreement could be interpreted as *forum shifting to the underground* (Tusikov, 2017). IP lobbyists and policy makers just made a series of informal agreements that in some cases went even further than ACTA. So in a sense, the mobilization against the agreement was a flash in the pan that managed to block this particular piece of legislation but not the general direction of the enforcement of IPRs.

A key lesson to be learned from this case is the necessity for activists to follow up on their causes and not lean completely on the work and expertise of other types of players. While the mobilization and diffusion of protest against ACTA happened on a variety of online platforms and very much thanks to mainstream media coverage as well, sustaining contact beyond the phase of street protests can be largely facilitated by digital media. What was missing in the case of ACTA was, for example, a long-term transnational mail list or bulletin that could allow activists to stay informed and alert and to form common identities (Kavada, 2015). What is more, most events, pages, and groups related to the protest were on Facebook, which meant that they could arbitrarily disappear, as some of them in fact did. Activists could have collaborated better with the free and open source community to create more sustainable platforms over which they had control.

Second, it was the German Pirates who set the wiki with all information on local protests, which was a good way to have a central overview of what was going on. And it was NGOs that produced and managed to impose the key claims on why ACTA is a bad agreement. Bottom-up protesters were above all adopters but not diffusers of protest and did not set the claims that dominated the debate. This is a main difference from the anti-austerity protests that we discussed in the previous chapter, where bottom-up activists were the key diffusers of protest. Thus, the second practical suggestion for activists is to be more proactive and engage in direct communication with protesters in other countries, inviting them over or engaging in a constructive dialogue beyond simple declarations of solidarity. Furthermore, following up on the takeaways from the previous chapter, it is important for activists not to close themselves off in their own geographic and cultural area when trying to diffuse their ideas or protest repertoires but to reach out to countries from different cultural areas.

Third and finally, the fact that bottom-up activists often "borrowed" ready analyses produced by NGOs and were in a sense "educated" into the proper arguments by them secured the coherence of the movement and its ultimate success. At the same time, bottom-up activists and NGOs are distinct types of players with different strategies, long-term goals, and ideologies even when they fight for the same goal. The dependence of bottom-up activists on NGOs in terms of framing the agreement meant that the types of frames that dominated the debate were the depoliticized frames preferred by NGOs. The problem is that while arguments such as "we want to download porn" given occasionally by street protesters were indeed not legitimate enough, there were also good arguments given by street protesters that remained underrepresented. The importance of economic circumstances for explaining piracy in Eastern Europe, for example, cannot be neglected. What is more, many countries have simply not been considered as big enough markets to export cultural products to them. These are important arguments in defence of file sharing that however have remained strongly neglected thanks to the prominence of Western intellectuals and NGOs when analyzing the problem and proposing solutions. What bottom-up activists could draw as practical idea from the case of protest diffusion against ACTA is to actually try to elaborate their own arguments and popularize them in both online and digital media to make themselves heard. The economic aspects of ACTA are extremely important, but they were largely neglected by NGOs focusing on human rights. Thus, bottom-up protesters had few allies when trying to popularize a discourse connecting ACTA to political problems such as poverty, inequality, and democratic failings.

Activists could promote such a discourse by setting up discussion groups (also transnational ones) both online and offline and deliberating on the issue to formulate and better express their own views. Common wikis and spaces for deliberation, not only organization, could also be useful. What is more, activists could invite NGOs to these deliberation spaces, engage them in debates, and potentially reach some common positions and interpretations. Overall, the depoliticization of the debate on ACTA was not necessary or inevitable, and if it took place, it was due mainly to the passivity of activists.

NGOs managed to achieve their key goal, which was to convince MEPs to reject ACTA. But in the absence of subsequent mobilization from below, and accordingly in the absence of funding and media attention, they could do little to stop the secret handshake deals that made the provisions of ACTA reality, even in the absence of ACTA. All this comes to show again that protest diffusion is a process driven by a variety of political players in complex media arenas. It is an agentic political process, and if activists position themselves well and are creative and consistent enough in their media practices, they can make a big difference. They could not only increase their relative weight in comparison to their allies but also secure a more lasting and stable success for the common cause they fight for.

References

15MPedia (2020): Manifesto "No les votes". *15MPedia*. Retrieved from https://15mpedia. org/wiki/Manifiesto_%C2%ABNo_les_votes%C2%BB.

About Stop TTIP (2016): Self-organized European Citizens' Initiative. Retrieved from https://web.archive.org/web/20160214175757/https://stop-ttip.org/about-stop-ttip/.

Access Campaign (2009): *Substandard and Counterfeit Medicines*. Retrieved from www. msfaccess.org/spotlight-on/substandard-counterfeit-medicines.

ACTA (2011): *Anti-Counterfeiting Trade Agreement, Final Text in English*. Retrieved from https://ustr.gov/acta.

ACTA Fact Sheet (2008): *The Anti-Counterfeiting Trade Agreement (ACTA): Fact Sheet*. Retrieved from http://trade.ec.europa.eu/doclib/docs/2008/october/tradoc_140836. 11.08.pdf.

Adams, Andrew and Ian Brown (2009): Keep Looking: The Answer to the Machine Is Elsewhere. *Computers and Law*, 19:6, 32–35.

Anderson, Jonas (2011): The Origins and Impact of Swedish Filesharing: A Case Study. *Journal of Peer Production*. Retrieved from http://peerproduction.net/issues/issue-0/ peer-reviewed-papers/the-origins-and-impacts-of-swedish-filesharing.

Arthur, Charles and Agencies (2012): ACTA Protests Break Out as EU States Sign Up to Treaty. *The Guardian*. Retrieved from www.theguardian.com/technology/2012/jan/27/acta-protests-eu-states-sign-treaty.

BBC News (2012): Polish Sites Hit in Acta Hack Attack. *BBC News*. Retrieved from www.bbc.com/news/technology-16686265.

Benkler, Yochai, Hal Roberts, Robert Faris, Alicia Solow-Niederman and Bruce Etling (2015): Social Mobilization and the Networked Public Sphere: Mapping the SOPA-PIPA Debate. *Political Communication*, 32:4, 594–624.

Beyer, Jessica (2014): The Emergence of a Freedom of Information Movement: Anonymous, WikiLeaks, the Pirate Party, and Iceland. *Journal of Computer-Mediated Communication*, 19, 141–154.

BNT (2012): BSP iska parlamentarna deklaracija sreshtu ACTA. *BNT*. Retrieved from http://news.bnt.bg/bg/a/70211-bsp_iska_parlamentarna_deklaracija_sreshtu_akta.

Brown, Ian and Douwe Korff (2009): Terrorism and the Proportionality of Internet Surveillance. *European Journal of Criminology*, 6:2, 119–134.

Bryant, Martin (2012): The EU and 22 Member States Sign the Controversial ACTA 'Internet Surveillance' Treaty. *The Next Web*. Retrieved from https://thenextweb.com/eu/2012/01/26/the-eu-and-22-member-states-sign-the-controversial-acta-internet-censorship-treaty/#.tnw_zawL8Qpu.

BZ (2012): Anti-ACTA-Demos: Tausende Menschen gehen auf die Straße. *Badische Zeitung*. Retrieved from www.badischezeitung.de/deutschland-1/anti-acta-demos-tausende-menschen-gehen-auf-die-strasse--55776806.html.

Chang, Ha-Joon (2002): *Kicking away the Ladder: Development Strategy in Historical Perspective*. London: Anthem Press.

Clark Estes, Adam (2012): SOPA Stopped for Now, Anti-Censorship Activists Turn to ACTA. *The Atlantic*. Retrieved from www.theatlantic.com/technology/archive/2012/01/sopa-stopped-now-anti-censorship-activists-turn-acta/332615/.

Collier, Kevin (2012): The Top Ten Most Influential Internet Rights Activists in 2012. *The Daily Dot*. Retrieved from www.dailydot.com/society/top-10-internet-rights-activists-2012/.

Dans, Enrique (2011): *Nolesvotes como movimiento ciudadano*. Retrieved from www.enriquedans.com/2011/02/nolesvotes-como-movimiento-ciudadano.html.

della Porta, Donatella and Manuela Caiani (2009): *Social Movements and Europeanization*. Oxford: Oxford University Press.

della Porta, Donatella and Louisa Parks (2015): Europeanisation and Social Movements: Before and After the Great Recession. *European Integration, Processes of Change and the National Experience*, 255–278.

Digitale Gesellshaft (2012): *How to Build an Anti-ACTA campaign*. Retrieved from https://digitalegesellschaft.de/2012/06/how-to-build-an-anti-acta-campaign/.

Dnevnik (2007): The Protest in Defence of the Torrent Trackers. *Dnevnik*. Retrieved from http://www.dnevnik.bg/bulgaria/2007/03/24/321980_protestut_v_zashtita_na_torent_trakerite/?ref=miniurl.

El País (2011): Las Claves de la Ley de Economía Sostenible. *El País*. Retrieved 28 April 2016, from http://economia.elpais.com/economia/2011/02/15/actualidad/1297758783_850215.html.

EU Commission (2012): *10 Myths About ACTA*. Retrieved from www.google.it/url?sa=t&rct=j&q=&esrc=s&source=web&cd=4&ved=0ahUKEwi9_6rr8ILNAhVCUhQKHVyIAqsQFgg1MAM&url=http%3A%2F%2Finfojustice.org%2Fwp-content%2Fuploads%2F2012%2F02%2FEU-10-Myths-About-Acta-January-2012.pdf&usg=AFQjCNE2KvqSvpUDrnnnbvvduqwUbmM6VQ&cad=rj.

Expansión (2009): *El Gobierno Aprobará La Ley de Economía Sostenible*. Retrieved from www.expansion.com/2009/11/22/economia-politica/1258894944.html.

European Parliament (2012): European Parliament Rejects ACTA. Retrieved 5 April 2016, from www.europarl.europa.eu/news/en/news-room/20120703IPR48247/European-Parliament-rejects-ACTA.

Farrand, Benjamin (2014): *Networks of Power in Digital Copyright Law and Policy: Political Salience, Expertise and the Legislative Process*. London: Routledge.

Gerbaudo, Paolo (2017): *The Mask and the Flag. Populism, Citizenism and Global Protest*. London: Hurst and Company.

Haggart, Blayne (2014): *Copyfight: The Global Politics of Digital Copyright Reform*. Toronto: University of Toronto Press.

Haunss, Sebastian (2013): *Conflicts in the Knowledge Society. The Contentious Politics of Intellectual Property*. Cambridge: Cambridge University Press.

Hoekman, Bernard and Michael Kostecki (1995): *The Political Economy of the World Trading System: From GATT to the WTO*. Oxford: Oxford University Press.

Horten, Monica (2013): *A Copyright Masquerade*. London: Zed Books.

Internet-Tsunamis (2016): Internet-Tsunamis: Politische Massen im digitalen Zeitalter. 3.4. *ACTA*. Retrieved from http://www.internet-tsunamis.de/3-4-acta/.

Jarvis, Jason (2014): Digital Image Politics: The Networked Rhetoric of Anonymous. *Global Discourse: An Interdisciplinary Journal of Current Affairs and Applied Contemporary Thought Publication*, 4:2–3, 1–24.

Juris, Jeffrey (2012): Reflections on #Occupy Everywhere: Social Media, Public Space, and Emerging Logics of Aggregation. *American Ethnologist*, 39:2, 259–279.

Kain, Erik (2012): If You Thought SOPA Was Bad, Just Wait Until You Meet ACTA. *Forbes*. Retrieved from www.forbes.com/sites/erikkain/2012/01/23/if-you-thought-sopa-was-bad-just-wait-until-you-meet-acta/#69c52a8d628f.

Karaganis, Joe (ed.) (2011): *Media Piracy in Emerging Economies*. Report of the Social Science Research Council. Retrieved from http://piracy.americanassembly.org/the-report/.

Kavada, Anastasia (2015): Creating the Collective: Social Media, the Occupy Movement and Its Constitution as a Collective Actor. *Information, Communication & Society*, 18:8, 872–886.

Kriesi, Hanspeter (1991): *The Political Opportunity Structure of New Social Movements: Its Impact on Their Mobilization*. FS III 91–103 Discussion Paper. Berlin: Wissenschaftszentrum Berlin für Sozialforschung.

Lee, (2013): *The Fight for the Future: How People Defeated Hollywood and Saved the Internet – for Now*. Retrieved from http://thefightforthefuture.com/.

Lessig, Lawrence (2004): Free Culture: How Big Media Uses Technology and the Law to Lock Down Culture and Control Creativity. *Journal of Cultural Economics*, 29:2, 148–152.

Losey, James (2013): *The Anti-Counterfeiting Trade Agreement and the Networked Public Sphere: How to Avoid a Convergent Crisis*. MA Thesis, Uppsala Universitet, Uppsala.

Martin, Lisa (ed.) (2015): *The Oxford Handbook of the Political Economy of International Trade*. New York: Oxford University Press.

Masnick, Mike (2012): People in Poland Come Out to Protest ACTA in Large Numbers; Polish Gov't Calls It 'Blackmail'. *Techdirt*. Retrieved from www.techdirt.com/articles/20120126/03543117549/people-poland-come-out-to-protest-acta-large-numbers-polish-govt-calls-it-blackmail.shtml.

McCarthy, Matthew (2015): Toward a Free Information Movement. *Sociological Forum*, 30:2, 439–458.

Meiritz, Annette and Fabian Reinbold (2013): Sinking Ship: Germany's Struggling Pirate Party. *Der Spiegel.* Retrieved from http://www.spiegel.de/international/germany/pirate-party-fails-to-capitalize-on-nsa-scandal-a-923303.html

Mercea, Dan and Andreas Funk (2016): The Social Media Overture of the Pan-European Stop-ACTA Protest: An Empirical Examination of Participatory Coordination in Connective Action. *Convergence,* 22:3, 287–312.

Myslewski, Rik (2012): Polish Lawmakers Don Guy Fawkes Masks to Protest ACTA. *The Register.* Retrieved from www.theregister.co.uk/2012/01/27/acta_protests_in_poland/.

Opinion of EDPS (2010): *Opinion of the European Data Protection Supervisor.* 2010/C 147/01. Retrieved from https://secure.edps.europa.eu/EDPSWEB/webdav/shared/Documents/Consultation/Opinions/2010/10-02-22_ACTA_EN.pdf.

Opinion of EDPS (2012): *Opinion of the European Data Protection Supervisor.* Retrieved from https://secure.edps.europa.eu/EDPSWEB/webdav/shared/Documents/Consultation/Opinions/2012/12-04-24_ACTA_EN.pdf.

Parks, Louisa (2013): *Political Process, Popular Protest and the EU: The Case of ACTA.* Paper Presented at the ESA Conference – Crisis, Critique and Change, Turin, 28–31 August.

Parks, Louisa (2015): *Social Movement Campaigns on EU Policy: In the Corridors and in the Streets.* London: Palgrave Macmillan.

Piraten Partei ACTA (2019): *ACTA.* Retrieved from https://wiki.piratenpartei.de/ACTA#Online-Werbemittel.

Piraten Partei Medien (2019): *ACTA/Medien.* Retrieved from https://wiki.piratenpartei.de/ACTA/Medien.

Pogge, Thomas (2005): Human Rights and Global Health: A Research Program. *Metaphilosophy,* 36, 182–209.

R&D (2013): Gross Domestic Expenditure on R&D, 2003–13 (% of GDP). *Eurostat.* Retrieved from http://ec.europa.eu/eurostat/statistics-explained/index.php/R_%26_D_expenditure.

Roffe, Pedro and Xavier Seuba (eds.) (2015): *The ACTA and the Plurilateral Enforcement Agenda: Genesis and Aftermath.* Cambridge: Cambridge University Press.

Rone, Julia (2014): My Own Private Public Library. *Seminar.net – International Journal of Media, Technology and Lifelong Learning,* 10:1. Retrieved 25 April 2016, from http://seminar.net/images/stories/vol10-issue1/rone%20my%20own%20private%20public%20library.pdf.

Rone, Julia (2017): Left in Translation: The Curious Absence of an Austerity Narrative in the Bulgarian 2013 Protests. In: Donatella della Porta (ed.), *The Global Diffusion of Protest: Riding the Protest Wave in the Neoliberal Crisis.* Amsterdam: Amsterdam University Press.

Rossini, Carolina (2012): *The Unsettling Trend of Forum Shifting in International Intellectual Property.* Retrieved from www.eff.org/de/deeplinks/2012/12/iip-forum-shifting-trend.

Sell, Susan (2009): *Cat and Mouse: Forum Shifting in the Battle Over Intellectual Property Enforcement.* Retrieved from www.researchgate.net/profile/Susan_Sell2/publication/228172149_Cat_and_Mouse_Industries'_States'_and_NGOs'_Forum_-_Shifting_in_the_Battle_Over_Intellectual_Property_Enforcement/links/55e49e1908ae2fac4722ec57.pdf.

Spassov, Orlin (2011): Мобилизиране сега: партии, граждански движения, нови медии. Дичев, Ивайло и Орлин Спасов (ред.) *Нови медии, нови мобилизации.* София: Отворено Общество, 284–327.

Stallman, Richard (2015): *Did You Say 'Intellectual Property': It's a Seductive Mirage.* Retrieved from www.gnu.org/philosophy/not-ipr.html.

Stallman, Richard (2017): *The GNU Project*. Retrieved from www.gnu.org/gnu/thegnu project.html.

Tarkowski, Alek (2012): Poland as a Case-Study in the History of Anti-ACTA Protests. *Centrum Cyfrowe*. Retrieved from http://centrumcyfrowe.pl/poland-as-a-case-study-in-the-history-of-the-anti-acta-protests/.

Teune, Simon (ed.) (2010): *The Transnational Condition. Protest Dynamics in an Entangled Europe*. New York: Berghahn Books.

TorrentFreak (2016): Europe Has the Highest Online Piracy Rates, by Far. *TorrentFreak*. Retrieved from https://torrentfreak.com/europe-has-the-highest-online-piracy-rates-by-far-160801/.

Treré, Emiliano, Sandra Jeppesen and Alice Mattoni (2017): Comparing Digital Protest Media Imaginaries: Anti-Austerity Movements in Spain, Italy & Greece. *Triple C: Communication, Capitalism and Critique*, 15:2.

Tusikov, Natasha (2017): *Chokepoints: Global Private Regulation on the Internet*. Oakland: University of California Press.

Wozniak, Michal "Rysiek" (2012): *RysioBrag: Subjectively on Anti-ACTA in Poland*. Retrieved from http://rys.io/en/70.

Zamponi, Lorenzo (2012): 'Why Don't Italians Occupy?' Hypotheses on a Failed Mobilisation. *Social Movement Studies*, 11:3–4, 1–11.

4

TTIP-ING OVER DEMOCRACY[1]

The Diffusion of Protests Against TTIP and CETA

4.1. TTIP and CETA: "A Symbolic and Practical Assertion of Western Renewal"?

In 2006, the EU's 2006 Global Europe communication established an offensive Free Trade Agreement Agenda which aimed to promote the interests of the EU's upstream market exporters, while neglecting the EU's remaining "pockets of protection" (Siles Brugge, 2013). One could expect this approach to change with the advent of the Great Recession when trade became an increasingly politicized issue with far right parties rising across Europe, yet the Commission remained firm in pursuing its free trade vision. This apparent paradox could be explained with the sway of neoliberal ideas among policy makers at the Directorate-General for Trade (DG Trade), who could conceptualize the way forward and out of the crisis only through more of the same policies, i.e. through further liberalization (ibid.). Neoliberal trade policy, perceived as a way to stimulate further internal and external liberalization, was "articulated as the panacea for further economic growth, which in theory perfectly links external objectives and policies with internal constraints and policies" (de Ville and Orbie, 2014, 159).

In the context of the Greek crisis, in 2010 then EU Commissioner Karel De Gucht claimed that the EU faced a double economic challenge:

> We have, on the one hand, to address our structural weaknesses on the supply side in order to increase our growth potential and, on the other hand . . . to consolidate our public finances . . . That is where trade and trade policy come in because trade is an engine of efficiency, and hence prosperity.
>
> *(De Gucht 2010, quoted in de Ville and Orbie, 2014, 159)*

In the aftermath of the 2008 economic crisis, pursuing austerity domestically in order to "address structural weaknesses on the supply side" and increase export competitiveness made logical sense only within a broader vision of economic recovery based on foreign trade and investment.

The Anti-Counterfeiting Trade Agreement was important in this respect as a way to secure European intellectual property abroad. Yet, the European Commission also had much more comprehensive and ambitious agreements in mind that could open for European companies the huge US market as well as the markets of a number of other developing and developed countries. After the stalemate at the Doha Round of the World Trade Organization multilateral negotiations in the year 2000, the EU started pursuing bilateral trade agreements to promote its deep trade agenda, focusing especially on the removal of non-tariff barriers (Leblond and Viju-Miljusevic, 2019, 1840). Non-tariff barriers, known also as "beyond-the-border" barriers, have been increasingly important, first because tariffs did become generally lower as a result of several successive GATT negotiation rounds, and second because trade in the 21st century faced three important and rather fundamental structural changes: the increased trade of services over borders (the so-called servicification of trade), the globalization of value chains, and the increased digitization of trade, including a rise in electronic commerce and data flows across borders (ibid., 1837–1838). These developments meant that if the EU and its member states wanted to trade successfully with third countries, they needed to guarantee not only the protection of their intellectual property but also the compatibility between European standards and regulations and foreign ones and the protection of European investment interests abroad.

It was in order to promote further trade liberalization, both abroad and at home, that the European Commission initiated negotiations for comprehensive trade agreements with the US, Canada, Vietnam, Japan, Singapore, and the Southern Common Market (Mercosur), among others. While most of these trade agreements passed unnoticed, the Transatlantic Trade and Investment Partnership with the US attracted wide public attention and provoked mass protests. Once TTIP was abandoned by Donald Trump, the momentum from the campaign against TTIP was used to oppose the Comprehensive Economic and Trade Agreement (CETA) with Canada. In this chapter, I explore in detail how protests against TTIP and CETA spread throughout Europe. Before doing this, however, some words are needed on how the European Commission justified the negotiations of TTIP and why activists and, increasingly, the general public opinion in several European countries were so concerned about it.

Economic and Geopolitical Motivations for TTIP

The mobilizations against TTIP came soon after ACTA was rejected by the European Parliament. The European Commission used many of the same negotiating practices that it had with ACTA, but it tried to be more careful and proactive in presenting TTIP. The Commission gave two main reasons for pursuing the agreement with the US: an economic one and a geopolitical one, which are actually closely intertwined. The main motive for the start of the TTIP negotiations was the desire to stimulate economic growth in the best way DG Trade considered it possible:

> the world financial crisis and the following period of sluggish growth have incentivized policy makers to look for new sources of growth. With little room to loosen fiscal and monetary policies further, it was believed that trade liberalization promises substantial benefits at relatively low costs.
>
> *(Felbermayr, 2016, 221)*

Of course, the fact that there was "little room to loosen fiscal and monetary policies further" reflected not so much an objective reality as the dominant ideology at the time. There was ample room to loosen fiscal policies, yet it was a political decision to not do this. External trade and further liberalization, instead of fiscal stimuli and domestic consumption, were seen as the engine of growth for an EU stuck in a recession.

But there was also a second, more geopolitical side to the negotiations of TTIP. The EU and the US have been each other's main trading partners in goods and services, and together they have the largest bilateral trade relationship in the world. Either the EU or the United States is the largest trade and investment partner for almost all other countries in the global economy. The two economies also provide each other with their most important sources of foreign direct investment (Gambini et al., 2015). With the rise of Brazil, Russia, India, China, and South Africa (BRICS), however, the share of global trade accounted for by the EU and the US has been falling with the prospect of China soon overtaking both and becoming the single most important trading power in the world. It is indicative that, during the first Obama administration, there was a perceived "pivot" in US policy towards Asia – both in the security realm, where US defence strategy increasingly focused on the South China Sea, and in trade and investment via the Trans-Pacific Partnership (TPP). Still, as the first European Council President Herman Van Rompuy claimed, "Americans realize that the pivot is not an alternative to Europe and NATO. On the contrary, a strong transatlantic relationship is a precondition for America's focus on Asia" (Egan and Nugent, 2015, 30). It was during the second Obama administration that the TTIP talks with the EU started, and it is clear that the EU was the side that had more to gain from TTIP, as the US (until the election of Donald Trump in 2016) was playing a game on two fronts, negotiating both TTIP with the EU and the TPP with Asian countries.

As proponents of TTIP noted, both the EU and the US initiated the negotiations on TTIP, in a context of daunting economic challenges, each of them trying to position itself and both trying to position themselves together in order to succeed in a world of intensified competition and diffuse economic power. What is more, by joining their forces the EU and the US hoped to avoid the prospects of becoming rule-takers to become rule-makers, instead creating a benchmark for global models and fighting against both protectionist measures and the lowering of labour, consumer, and environmental standards (Hamilton and Pelkmans, 2015, 3). To summarize, TTIP was supposed to not only bring much needed economic growth but also further the economic strength of the EU and the US in the face of the rising BRICS economies. What is more, the agreement was meant to ensure higher standards in a number of fields than those one could expect Asian countries led by China would set:

> TTIP can potentially serve as a symbolic and practical assertion of Western Renewal, vigour and commitment not only to each other but to high-rules based principles of international order. It is an initiative that can be assertive without being aggressive. It challenges fashionable notions about a "weakened west".
>
> *(Hamilton and Pelkmans, 2015, 9)*

The prominence of such arguments can be seen in the way they were repeated by key political actors. As late as December 2016, when it was almost certain the TTIP has died, the Federation of German Industries clearly expressed support both for TTIP and its sister agreement with Canada, CETA:

> "In the wake of the British referendum, it is more important than ever that we strengthen the EU and provide positive stimuli for growth," said BDI President Ulrich Grillo on Sunday in Berlin. . . "We Europeans will have a better chance of shaping the process of globalisation to include high standards if we tackle these issues shoulder to shoulder with the United States."
>
> *(BDI, 2016)*

The arguments in favour of starting the TTIP negotiations were undoubtedly strong and convincing. Yet, there were major problems with both of them. First, the economic benefits of TTIP were far from certain. The Commission had no solid empirical evidence that TTIP would induce growth. In addition, the way benefits would be distributed was also not clear, and there were major reasons to believe that the agreement might lead to substantial reallocation and displacement effects (Felbermayr, 2016, 232). Most of the models that the EU Commission had commissioned made overly optimistic predictions about the ability of the EU and the US to eliminate regulatory barriers for trade, thus starting their computations from wrong premises. These models also downplayed the potential deregulatory impact of the agreement. Thus, far from being a reliable exact-science guide to future outcomes, the models served the pro-liberalization agenda of the European Commission (de Ville and Siles-Brügge, 2015).

Most importantly, the economic studies quoted by the EU Commission glossed over the differences in impact that different forms of liberalization might have in the case of TTIP – for example, regulatory harmonization was more likely to lead to a potential "downgrading" of standards across the Atlantic than to mutual recognition. The difference between harmonization and mutual recognition is relevant also for assessing the grandiose claims about the EU and the US setting the rules for all other countries. This might be the case if there is a harmonization of rules and standards between the EU and the US, but this scenario was rejected as too complicated and politically unviable as it could lead to a "race to the bottom" in the process of harmonization. The mutual recognition of standards, however, was most probably going to be valid only bilaterally (de Ville and Siles-Brugge, 2016). To put it differently, the EU would have been able to export to the US goods produced with EU standards, but it was not certain that third countries that export their goods to EU and follow EU standards would be able to export to the US as well. The European Parliament report on TTIP's potential impact on developing countries noted that in order for developing countries to actually benefit from TTIP, there had to be "an explicit clause extending the mutual recognition/equivalence of standards to third countries". What is more, these countries had to be involved in the relevant discussions (Manrique Gil et al., 2015). Until the late stages of TTIP negotiations, there were still no explicit clauses extending the mutual equivalence of standards to third countries. Thus, the whole argument of the EU and the US setting higher standards for the rest of the world remained more of an empty rhetorical exercise than a viable scenario.

In short, the two main reasons given by the EU Commission for starting the TTIP negotiations were in certain respects problematic and too optimistic about the future. One could not be certain what the economic benefits of TTIP were (if any) and how were they to be distributed among the population. What is more, considering that most probably TTIP would have presupposed a mutual recognition regime, it couldn't have set global rules and standards. The only argument that remains was the one that focused on the importance of transatlantic partnership in the face of the rise of China. Nevertheless, the question of what price was to be paid for such partnership reverberated strongly and caused unprecedented politicization of trade, including mass street protests, in several EU countries.

What's Wrong With TTIP and CETA?

Over the years, EU's trade agreements rarely attracted public attention beyond NGOs' circles, since the EU was the bigger trading partner able to export its standards and focus on the interests of its own investors. Yet, when in July 2013 the EU started negotiations for TTIP – the major trade agreement with the US – NGOs in the EU rang the bell of alarm, and this time more people were ready to listen. Not only was this agreement negotiated in secrecy, similarly to the preceding Anti-Counterfeiting Trade Agreement rejected by the European Parliament in 2012, but there were also strong concerns about the inclusion in TTIP of the so-called investor-state dispute settlement (ISDS) mechanism that allowed investors to sue states in case their interests were aggrieved. Investor-state dispute settlements in general allow foreign investors to completely bypass national court systems and sue the hosting country for damages in private tribunals of arbitration. The EU has multiple trade agreements with ISDS clauses, but until TTIP the argument had always been that ISDS protected the interests of EU investors against arbitrary interventions by states where there was corruption, no rule of law, and potential dangers of arbitrary expropriation (ISDS Fact Sheet, 2013, 4). Following this logic, the question NGOs posed was: why did an EU-US agreement require ISDS, considering that both negotiating sides perceived themselves as strongholds of the rule of law, and that there was already a high level of investment flows between these jurisdictions? What could be the great danger to investors justifying such a privatization of law that operates in favour of private corporations?

As Niels Gheyle emphasizes, organizations such as S2B (Seattle to Brussels) in Europe had already opposed ISDS mechanisms in EU agreements for years, and a lot of the analysis, discourse, and ways of framing ISDS they used preceded their campaign against TTIP. Thus, civil society had the benefit of employing ISDS expertise quickly and efficiently (Gheyle, 2019, 185). An ISDS mechanism was included not only in TTIP but also in CETA that the EU had started to negotiate already back in 2009. But a lot of things had changed since 2009. For instance, important developments after the Romanian 2013 protests against the Roşia Montană mining project drew additional attention to the dangers of ISDS. The Romanian government ultimately listened to the voice of the people and stopped the mining project led by the Canadian company Gabriel Resources. As a result, Gabriel Resources challenged Romania on the basis of a bilateral trade agreement between Romania and Canada that included an ISDS mechanism. The company demanded US$5.7 billion in compensation, the equivalent of 2.7% of Romania's gross domestic product (GDP) (10ISDS Stories, 2019).

The fear that with agreements such as TTIP and CETA such type of cases would become the new normal made civil society players in the EU extremely wary of ISDS. Due to rising criticism, the European Commission called a public consultation on the topic: 97% of the 150,000 respondents rejected ISDS and more than 3 million people signed an independent European Citizens' Initiative rejecting ISDS and more broadly TTIP (Friends of the Earth, 2016).

In order to replace the unpopular ISDS, the Commission proposed a new type of Investment Court System (ICS). Nevertheless, multiple analyzers pointed out that the changes introduced in the new ICS were insufficient, and both ISDS and ICS could force governments to use billions in taxpayers' funds to compensate corporations for public health, environmental, labour, and other public interest policies, government actions, and even court rulings. Neither mechanism was subject to democratic principles or scrutiny or could ensure that private interests would not undermine public policy objectives. In February 2016 the German Association of Magistrates, a Berlin-based judicial umbrella organization, claimed that there was "neither a legal basis nor a need" for ISC because domestic courts were good enough to settle disputes (Nielsen, 2016). This position was strongly contested, as it could be expected, by the European Commission.

But the disputes around ISDS and ICS, even though highly visible in the media, accounted for only part of the opposition to TTIP and later on CETA. As these were such broad agreements that covered many aspects of transatlantic trade, there were many points for which they were criticized by Europeans. The divergence between labour, environmental, and food safety standards in the EU and the US caused widespread concerns among EU citizens who worried about potential imports of genetically modified food from the US and about imports of the, by now emblematic, US chlorinated chickens, which were often used by campaigners as a shortcut for everything that was wrong with the agreement. There were also strong worries about TTIP driving down high EU labour and environmental standards and infringing on the regulatory sovereignty not only of member states but also of the EU. Crucially, Europeans feared that regulatory cooperation as envisaged in TTIP would oblige EU actors to provide elaborate assessments of planned regulations with regard to their impact on trade, thus leading to "paralysis by analysis" and making it much more difficult for democratically elected bodies to regulate (de Ville and Siles-Brugge, 2017, 7, pointed out in personal communication by N. Gheyle).

Of course, presenting the EU as an innocent sacrificial lamb is as far away from the truth as it could be. While European negotiators did not want to open up their agricultural sector and were adamant on protecting geographical indicators such as Champagne, Parmigiano cheese, and Cognac, they at the same time pushed hard to open the public procurement sector of their negotiation partners. A little known fact is that earlier negotiations between the EU and Canada failed in 2006, when Canadian provinces remained sceptical of EU's ambitions in the field of sub-federal-level procurement (Hübner et al., 2017). The EU was also perceived by US civil society as much less strict when it comes to financial regulations. Nevertheless, most campaigning around TTIP in the EU was framed exclusively in terms of dangers coming from the other side of the ocean. The more general critiques towards the current international trading system and the push towards liberalization could be found in discussions about ISDS and "paralysis by analysis" and the way they threatened sovereignty and democratic decision-making.

"Being Isolated From Your Own Citizens"

After a substantive and sustained civil society campaign and intense parliamentary activism against both TTIP and CETA in the Belgian region of Wallonia (Gheyle, 2019), the region vetoed CETA in October 2016, causing an unprecedented stir. Trade policy has been an exclusive EU competence, yet because of the controversies around the agreement, the European Commission made the political decision to make CETA a mixed agreement, meaning it now required national approval as well. As Belgium, a member state of the EU, has a federal system, all provinces had to agree to CETA in order to give it a green light at the national level, and Wallonia refused to give its approval. The stand-off between Wallonia and the European Commission caused great controversy: journalists often compared the situation to a David and Goliath battle, and proponents of CETA argued that it was ultimately undemocratic for a small region to hold hostage the whole European Union on the issue. Accused that Wallonia was self-isolating and causing a diplomatic scandal, Paul Magnette, the Minister-President of Wallonia, responded:

> To be isolated from our own population, to be isolated from our own citizens, in an era, in the beginning of the 21st century, when democracy is so profoundly in crisis, this would be at least as grave as being diplomatically isolated.
>
> *(Bollen, 2018, 335)*

"Being isolated from our own citizens" is a powerful metaphor that aptly describes not only the secretive negotiations of agreements such as TTIP and CETA but also the notable disregard towards democratic opposition to them. The non-democratic nature of economic decisions that affect generations ahead is the common factor behind both austerity policies and the free trade agreements that the EU pursued in the aftermath of 2008. The position of the European Commission with regard to democratic accountability was revealed succinctly by EU Trade Commissioner Cecilia Malmström who, when asked about the mass opposition to TTIP, answered, "I do not take my mandate from the European people" (Hilary, 2015).

Yet the politicization of TTIP and CETA did lead to at least some democratization of trade negotiations. Thanks to the Lisbon Treaty, the European Parliament had been institutionally empowered to veto trade agreements, which it did in 2012 in the case of ACTA. The European Parliament used the controversies around TTIP and CETA to interpret its institutional capacities further and assert itself in important ways (Meissner and Schoeller, 2019; Roederer-Rynning, 2017). The politicization of trade was also used strategically by national parliaments in order to establish direct liaisons with the EU Commission, the European Parliament, and other national parliaments in their attempt to scrutinize trade policy making and influence its direction (Jancic, 2017, 216).

Indeed, somewhat paradoxically, while being constantly accused of secrecy and non-transparency, the TTIP and CETA negotiations turned out to be the negotiations with the greatest involvement of the European Parliament so far, in line with a general trend towards democratization of trade policy making in the

EU. To a large extent, this paradox can be explained with the highly different understandings of transparency of the European Commission on the one hand and activists on the other, who insisted on a much more comprehensive democratic involvement and participation (Gheyle and de Ville, 2017).

TTIP was ultimately abandoned by Trump. And CETA was agreed with only a few concessions by the European Commission that, considering the failure of TTIP, focused all its attention on getting CETA right. The following agreements that the EU negotiated with Japan, Vietnam, and Singapore, among others, were less politicized (de Bièvre and Poletti, 2020), and most NGOs that were at the centre of the Stop TTIP campaign had moved on to work on other topics (interview with Georgi Hristov). Crucially, after the debacle with Wallonia's veto on CETA, the European Commission referred to the European Court of Justice to establish whether the free trade agreement the Commission had negotiated with Singapore could be concluded by the Commission alone, that is, under exclusive EU competence, or had to be agreed upon also by member states, that is it was of mixed competence. The ECJ ruled that the EU had exclusive competence to enter in most commitments of the agreement with some exceptions, such as the protection of non-direct investments and the inclusion of ISDS mechanisms.

While this might have seemed a blow to the EC, the practical effect of it was that the Commission simply started to split trade agreements, leaving the investment clauses aside, and in fact fast-tracked them, away from democratic discussion and contestation. Thus, similarly to the case of ACTA that caused a big stir and was rejected but then its provisions were accepted in a piecemeal manner, TTIP and CETA also caused heated public debates and protests, but it remains to be seen to what extent they were actually "game changers" in the field of EU trade policy (de Ville and Siles-Brugge, 2017). While the politicization of both agreements led many researchers to optimistic assessments of the democratization of trade policy, this might be more of a promise than a reality. The possibility to "split" trade agreements has provided EU negotiators once again with the comfort of "being isolated from their own citizens" and their democratic demands. One thing, however, is certain: with the failure of TTIP and all the controversies surrounding CETA, neither of these agreements marked a "symbolic and practical assertion of Western Renewal".

4.2. "Protectionists and Scaremongers Are Winning in Germany": The Spread of Anti-TTIP Protests

In an attempt to explain the prevalence of protest against TTIP in Germany, the major export country of the EU, *The Economist* published an article with the not-so-neutral title, "Protectionists and Scaremongers Are Winning in Germany" (The Economist, 2016). In the next sections, I show that most European players opposing agreements such as TTIP or CETA were far from protectionists in their views and in fact came from the Green left. It was only later that the far right recognized opposition to TTIP and CETA as its issue and tried to appropriate it, which met strong resistance by Green left NGOs, political parties, and trade unions.

The politicization of TTIP and CETA was not only done from very different standpoints by Green left and far right actors but was also far from equal in various EU member states (de Bièvre and Poletti, 2020; Gheyle, 2020). In some countries these agreements caused a storm, in others they were barely noticed. Focusing on protests as one of the key manifestations of politicization, one cannot fail to acknowledge the increasing scale and geographical reach of anti-TTIP protests. Small protests erupted first in Belgium, in April 2014, attracting wide public attention due to the heavy-handed response of the police, which arrested numerous Green activists and even MEPs (Gheyle, 2019, 314). Activists emphasized the connection between austerity and free trade, claiming that "[t]he continuation of austerity that will come from the proposed EU-US free trade deal is only going to make European citizens and producers poorer, unhealthier, more precarious and lend us further into disaster" (Gheyle, 2019, 314). In late summer 2014, the UK also witnessed protests against TTIP that bridged critique of austerity with critique of liberalization (Milevska, 2014). These early actions were followed by the European Day of Action against TTIP in October 2014 that received little coverage but spurred further cooperation between organizations. In April 2015, a Global Day of Action against TTIP followed: 2,000 people protested in Brussels and 1,000 in Madrid and Helsinki (Euractiv, 2015). One of the most successful Days of Action followed in October 2015 when 15,000 protesters marched through the streets of Vienna and more than 200,000 in Berlin (Reuters, 2015). Finally, in September 2016, 25,000 people protested in Vienna and between 160,000 and 320,000 throughout Germany (Pasquet, 2016), while tens of thousands took to the streets of Brussels (DW, 2016).

The key explanations of the differentiated politicization of TTIP in particular so far have focused on either political opportunity structures (Caiani and Graziano, 2018) or the success of domestic coalition formation, depending on (1) links with transnational advocacy networks; (2) the prior availability of domestic alliances, and (3) inclusive framing in order to establish a diverse coalition (Gheyle, 2020). The explanation in this chapter, based on the players and arenas framework, largely confirms Gheyle's findings. A key addition, however, is that through diffusion processes, a change in the domestic composition of players could occur, leading to new players and coalitions appearing, introducing dynamism in the system. For example, even though mobilization against TTIP and CETA in Bulgaria was small, as in other countries in Eastern Europe, it was made possible by a coalition of traditional Green NGOs but also new left-wing organizations that had appeared in the aftermath of the big anti-austerity protests. In what follows I trace in detail the diffusion of protests against TTIP and CETA and the main players involved.

Proposals for a Transatlantic Free Trade Agreement (TAFTA) between the EU and the US had been made since the 1990s, but they finally materialized when the official negotiations for TTIP started in July 2013. Already in March 2013, a group of civil society actors from both sides of the Atlantic insisted that the negotiation and pre-negotiation texts should be available for public scrutiny and that intellectual property rights such as copyright, trademarks, patents, and geographical indications should be kept out of TTIP (IP Out of TAFTA, 2013). The groups, among which were the European Digital Rights Initiative, the Polish Centrum Cyfrowe, the German Digitale Gesselschaft, the French La Quadrature du Net, and many others which had been active on ACTA, explicitly drew a connection between TTIP and the preceding legal initiatives such as ACTA, SOPA, and PIPA:

> Last year, millions of Americans told their government not to undermine the open internet. We sent the SOPA and PIPA bills down to defeat. Soon after, hundreds of thousands of people took to the streets of Europe to protest against ACTA, a secretive trade agreement that would have violated our rights online and chilled generic drug competition.
>
> *(ibid.)*

Thus, some of the very first opponents of TTIP were the very same organizations that had opposed ACTA in 2012, showing clearly that opposition to these trade agreements should be studied as a continuous phenomenon rather than an episodic one focusing exclusively on individual agreements. At the same time, TTIP was much broader than ACTA, for example, and attracted the attention also of numerous other organizations.

The key organizations that focused on TTIP early on were mostly members of the Seattle to Brussels network, formed "in the aftermath of the World Trade Organisation's (WTO) 1999 Seattle Ministerial to challenge the corporate-driven trade agenda of the European Union and European governments" (S2B, 2020). While the S2B network has members also from the US and Canada, its very creation marked a transition to EU groups taking the lead in resistance to WTO in the early 2000s:

> More importantly, much of the network rested not only on the shoulders of just a few groups, but also of a few specific individuals. For instance, a member of a UK-based development group took the central role through her initial activity in helping both establish S2B and then develop a critique of the GATS. This critique became the master template for groups across Europe, both for those who were directly involved in the network as well as for groups more on the periphery.
>
> *(Strange, 2015, 85)*

Membership in the S2B network is not uniformly distributed across European countries – the best represented and most active countries are Germany, UK, France, the Netherlands, Spain, and also to some extent Belgium (Gheyle, 2019, 183). S2B members had their first coordination meeting on TTIP in December 2013 and quickly realized they could rely on already existing expert analyses to activate the campaign (ibid., 185). A link with S2B through domestic groups was acknowledged as an important factor for early mobilization against TTIP and diffusion of protest in different EU countries: "At least in Belgium, the Netherlands, Germany, France, the UK and Spain, it is extremely clear that it were S2B members that kick-started the process and also built alliances that were bigger" (Gheyle, 2020, 305).

The initial strategy of S2B member organizations seems to have been more lobbying-oriented since in these early days getting favourable news coverage and attracting public attention seemed difficult (Strange, 2015). In March 2014, social movement groups opposing TTIP met in Brussels at what was the biggest transatlantic meeting of TTIP opponents to that date:

> The three day event included a series of presentations on specific topics – environment, health, labour, investment, food and digital rights – as well as strategy discussions, a stakeholder presentation to the European Commission and a small street protest outside the offices of DG Trade. The format reflected the broader strategy where lobbying of negotiators and other social groups was prioritized over any public protest. This reflected the calculation of these groups as to where they were most likely to influence the negotiations, accepting there is too little time to catch public interest.
>
> *(Strange, 2015, 90)*

What happened between March 2014, when NGOs still believed they could not catch public interest, and 2015–2016 when hundreds of thousands people participated in protests against TTIP and CETA? The answer is simple: a massive anti-TTIP and CETA campaign, coordinated at the local, national, and transnational levels that managed to involve thousands of citizens. The March 2014 meeting was followed by several parallel initiatives – the announcement of European Days of Action against TTIP, the establishment of the Stop TTIP network (with key input by the German NGO Mehr Demokratie) that started organizing a European Citizens' Initiative on TTIP, and the establishment of a series of digital platforms and innovative digital instruments that allowed thousands of EU citizens to contact their MEPs and lobby against TTIP. A Bertelsmann Foundation study showed that from 2014 to 2015 there was a 14% increase in public opposition to ACTA in Austria, with as much as 67% of the population opposing the agreement. Of all Germans, 51% opposed TTIP in 2015, 10 percentage points more than in 2014 (Bertelsmann Foundation, 2016, 27). Such dramatic rises in the percentage of population disapproving of the agreement is a testimony to the success of the anti-TTIP campaign in both countries.

Exploring the coordination of the different Days of Action against TTIP allows us to gain important insights into the diffusion of protest against TTIP and CETA. The October 2014 Day of Action, for example, was being organized in a decentralized way across Europe with strong participation of organizations from the S2B network. The hashtag of the October 2014 days of action, #O11DoA (https://twitter.com/search?q=%23O11DoA&src=typed_query), was incorporated in tweets by altogether 20 actors, including NGOs such as Corporate Europe Observatory, Friends of the Earth, the Transnational Institute, Global Trade Watch, Finance Watch, bottom-up activists such as Occupy London, Occupy Manchester, the Indignados media – Take the Square and 15MBcn-int, and also UK's largest trade union Unite the Union, the UK alternative left-wing media *Red Pepper*, the Belgian Pirate Party, Podem Valencia (the Valencia Branch of Podemos), the Spanish Party Partido X that sprung out of the 2011 protests, the Confederal Group of the European United Left/Nordic Green Left in the EP, and finally the website The TTIP of the Iceberg, created by The Greens/European Free Alliance in the European Parliament. Clearly the types of actors spreading information on the protests went well beyond bottom-up activists as the usual suspects and included a wide variety of additional players, including NGOs, media, political parties, and trade unions, among others.

What is particularly interesting about these early days of action was the high involvement of volunteers from grassroots movements such as Occupy and Indignados (Glattauer, 2014) that had been active in resisting austerity and had the necessary expertise in organizing Days of Action. Such bottom-up groups drew on the practice of using collaborative maps in order to visualize the transnational dimension of protest, familiar from the Occupy and Indignados protests. These movements were also very active in popularizing the protest online and tweeted intensely. Displaying high levels of self-awareness, a number of activists promoting the Day of Action also produced analyses of tweets on the event. Tweets came only from a handful of European countries, including France, Germany, the UK, Spain, and the Netherlands, with the UK clearly in the centre of the conversation (Vila, 2014). Another analysis, focusing more on the players themselves, showed several key clusters of tweets with Occupy London, clearly in the centre, accompanied by smaller clusters around the Spanish campaign No al TTIP and the Spanish X-Net collective (Ben, 2014). This type of analysis and visualization produced by the participants of the event is interesting not only because of its content, but also because it shows clearly the blurring of the lines between research and activism, with data visualization as a form of activism in itself. Both analyses showed a clear correlation between a country having active S2B members and the diffusion of protest against TTIP. What is more, these activist-produced visualizations testified to the important role of British NGOs such as War on Want and Global Justice Now that had been among the first to mobilize on TTIP and spread expertise across the EU. John Hilary, executive director of War on Want, UK, for example, wrote the brochure on TTIP of the German Rosa Luxembourg Foundation (Rosa Luxembourg, 2015). In February 2015, UK activists travelled all the way to Brussels to meet allies and lobby MEPs. They also presented the new Trade Commissioner Cecilia Malmström with giant ears "to remind her to listen to the people of Europe" (War on Want, 2015).

By the Global Day of Action on April 18, 2015, the number of players tweeting on the event with the hashtag #April18DoA (https://twitter.com/search?q=%23April18DoA&src=typed_query) had expanded from 20 to 83, with a considerable increase of NGOs among the profiles tweeting. At the same time, the geographical spread of the tweeting profiles hadn't expanded equally considerably. Most tweets came from organizations based in the UK, Spain, Netherlands, and Brussels NGOs. During this Day of Action, the EU's TTIP Team tried to also actively tweet with the same hashtag providing an alternative narrative. The 99 anti-TTIP tweets with this hashtag were countered by only nine pro-TTIP tweets produced by four profiles altogether. In general, the Twitter dissemination of information about the Days of Action gained traction but failed to reach a substantial audience.

Overall, bottom-up activists from the British Occupy and the Spanish Indignados networks together with British NGOs such as War on Want and Global Justice Now and Spanish political parties such as Partido X and Podemos were crucial in the initial dissemination of information on TTIP. Yet, they were soon replaced in terms of importance by transnational networks dominated by German organizations that had more resources to reach out both domestically and transnationally (Bauer, 2016).

German NGOs were instrumental in diffusing protest against TTIP and in setting up the common European platform Stop TTIP (stop-ttip.org) and the European Citizens' Initiative petition, which attracted civil society organizations from different countries. The campaign against TTIP (and subsequently against CETA) used many of the forms of contentious action tried out in the campaign against ACTA but centralized, standardized, and streamlined them. Counting on a high degree of centralization of platforms and strategies allowed the campaign to diffuse a coherent message across the EU. During the mobilization against ACTA, the campaigning community Avaaz had launched a highly successful petition with more than 2.3 million signatures. The mobilization against TTIP and CETA followed this precedent but decided to use the instrument provided by the EU itself. The Stop TTIP initiative coordinated with Avaaz and offered a platform of its own to collect signatures for a European Citizens' Initiative (ECI) – a European Union mechanism introduced with the Lisbon Treaty and aimed at increasing direct democracy (ECI Basic Facts, 2016). An ECI is an invitation to the European Commission to propose legislation on matters in which the EU has competence to legislate (Weisskircher, 2020). As such, in order to be discussed, an initiative has to be backed by at least one million EU citizens, coming from at least seven out of the 28 member states (ibid.). The Stop TTIP ECI was registered in July 2014 by a citizens' committee consisting of seven members from different EU countries: Romania, Germany, the Netherlands, the UK, Finland, Portugal, and Luxembourg (Stop TTIP, 2014). The ECI not only over-fulfilled the requirements for numbers of signatures but also turned into a crucial instrument of diffusing information about TTIP, with activists collecting signatures not only online but also in market squares, at town events, and at mass demonstrations, going beyond digital media in their efforts to disseminate knowledge of the agreement.

Yet, the Stop TTIP ECI was rejected by the European Commission on the grounds that it fell "manifestly outside the framework of the Commission's powers to submit a proposal for a legal act of the Union for the purpose of implementing the Treaties" (ECI, 2014). The Commission claimed that the negotiating mandates on TTIP and CETA were not legal acts but internal preparatory acts between EU institutions and therefore not contestable via an ECI. The organizations responded by claiming that the arguments given by the Commission did not hold legal scrutiny and were politically motivated. A 2017 decision of the European Court of Justice (May 10, 2017) pointed out that the Commission was wrong to refuse registration, as the principle of democracy, which is "one of the fundamental values of the EU" and the objective behind the European citizens' initiatives, required a broader interpretation (Longo, 2019, 195).

When the registration of the ECI was refused, the Stop TTIP initiative had no other option but to continue collecting signatures as a self-organized European Citizens' Initiative, using the same platform. In the period from October 7, 2014, to October 6, 2015, the self-organized European Citizens' Initiative Stop TTIP collected 3,284,289 signatures against TTIP and CETA and reached the country quorum in 23 member states (About Stop TTIP, 2016). The Stop TTIP initiative combined seamlessly opposition to TTIP with opposition to CETA, the Comprehensive Economic Trade Agreement with Canada. While CETA's negotiations had started much earlier, already in 2009, and were concluded in August 2014, activists realized that they had less chance of gaining public attention and successfully defeating the agreement with Canada that was already so advanced and decided to launch a campaign against TTIP first in order to draw public attention and only then to focus full scale on the campaign against CETA as its smaller "sister agreement". Thus, the fact that the campaign initially focused on TTIP and only later shifted all efforts to combating CETA was not a coincidence but a pre-mediated strategic choice (interview with Borislav Sandov).

The very fact that there was one platform against TTIP and CETA that could be consulted by different national organizations proved to be highly important. While the mobilizations against austerity and later against ACTA were largely non-coordinated in advance and consisted of diverse initiatives launched by different players, the mobilization against TTIP was much more coordinated and professionally managed. Securing the transnational dimension of TTIP was to a large extent centralized in the hands of the NGOs participating in the S2B network, and later in the hands of NGOs managing the Stop TTIP initiative. Membership in different national and international NGO networks often over-lapped, thus allowing the networks to expand and make more coalitions both domestically and transnationally. Meso-mobilization players with transnational connections were in fact crucial, even if not sufficient, for the politicization of the agreement in the domestic context (Gheyle, 2020).

The transnational campaign against TTIP (and later against CETA) borrowed from the anti-ACTA campaign not only the petition tactic but also the massive involvement of citizens in lobbying MEPs through sending emails and making phone calls. What the Stop TTIP network did was to streamline these practices through its own platform and with scripts prepared by its experts. To begin with, similar to the practice in the anti-ACTA mobilization, European citizens oppos-ing CETA were encouraged to call their MEPs using a detailed phone script and instructions, after being recommended to go through recommended posts with reasons to oppose CETA. The Stop TTIP initiative also launched a "Fax Friday" campaign inviting people to its office in order to meet, chat, and send faxes to MEPs. Of course, the reference to faxes was highly playful, underlining the dif-ference between the deputies in the EP who were still from the fax generation and the young generation that uses computers. But the Stop TTIP initiative did not ignore its strength in the digital sphere either and urged citizens to use the hashtags #CETAthursday and #CETAtuesday to tweet to MEPs urging them to oppose CETA or thanking them that they've already pledged to oppose it. The campaign again provided template tweets and pictures that could be tweeted, thus making it even easier to take part in the initiative. What is more, citizens could go beyond simply calling their MEPs, writing emails, or tweeting. They could use the "CETA check" tool that completely automated the process of connect-ing to elected representatives and asking questions. One of the most fascinating aspects of the form is a small arrow followed by the text: "Click here to see the text of your email to [name of MEP]". Users did not even have to bother reading the text of their own emails anymore as the professionalized campaign had taken care of it.

NGOs also encouraged the creation of several campaign videos such as the animation created by the Stop TTIP campaign, "TTIP and CETA – A One Way Street of Liberalization", the animation "Freihandelsabkommen TTIP stoppen!", created by Jonas Krammer for Attac Deutschland and later uploaded and popu-larized by the UK NGO 38 Degrees, called "What Is the Transatlantic Trade and Investment Partnership", or *The Guardian* newspaper video, "What Is TTIP? Everything You Need to Know About the 'Super Sexy' Trade Acronym". These videos had a pattern of views that shows a slow but steady increase through the years. In a sense, this pattern testifies to the sustained efforts of NGOs to raise awareness of TTIP and CETA. This pattern of views also points to the benefits of the strategic decision to focus on both agreements, shifting the focus on CETA later. In late summer 2016, it was almost certain that the TTIP negotiations had failed: the German Vice Chancellor and Economy Minister Sigmar Gabriel famously said that the TTIP negotiations were "dead in the water" (Gotev, 2016). At this moment activists focused exclusively on CETA, thus performing a smooth transferral of opposition from TTIP to CETA.

To be sure, it would be foolish to believe that the campaign against TTIP and CETA counted only on digital media practices. While MEP Anne-Marie Mineur, for example, had been actively publishing on TTIP and CETA, the dangers of the agreement gained salience in the Dutch public debate only after they were features in the mainstream TV show with a large viewership "Zondag met Lubach" (interview with Anne-Marie Mineur). In addition, all NGO representatives I interviewed in Austria emphasized the role of the tabloid newspaper *Die Kronen Zeitung* for the mass opposition to TTIP and CETA. The most widely read Austrian tabloid had decided to oppose the agreements and thus caused a dramatic shift in public opinion, making the NGOs campaigning and lobbying work against the agreements substantially easier from a political point of view. In Germany, a documentary by Stephan Stuchlik and Kim Otto, working for West-Deutsche Rundfunk, was aired on the mainstream broadcaster ARD in August 2014 and was subsequently shared and translated multiple times, contributing to increasing media and public attention on the lack of transparency and the potential effects of TTIP negotiations (Gheyle, 2019, 238). Overall, while it is difficult to establish the role of mainstream media for the transnational diffusion of protest, they did prove to be crucial players in raising the domestic salience of the issue.

A key and unexpected type of player that contributed to the diffusion of protest against TTIP and CETA turned out to be cities and regions that started declaring themselves as "TTIP-free zones" and later also as "CETA-free zones". This practice had its origins in earlier campaigns against the General Agreement on Trade and Tariffs (GATS) (Siles-Brugge and Strange, 2020; Gheyle, 2019), yet it received a further push from the rise of the municipalist movement in the aftermath of the 2011 anti-austerity protests, as seen especially in initiatives such as Barcelona en Comú or Catalunya en Comú. The giant inflatable Stop TTIP pencil (Stop TTIP Pencil, 2015; Ryø, 2015; Voss, 2015) became a symbol of the efforts of campaigners to reach out to local communities and collect signatures in places whose inhabitants wouldn't have had the chance to discuss TTIP/CETA otherwise. Moving resistance to cities and regions was particularly important as it also marked another stage of campaigning and an attempt to shift scales from the transnational to the local level.

In April 2016, representatives of 60 European cities met in Barcelona and signed a declaration claiming it was their duty to defend local communities and democratic institutions as spaces for debate and decision-making (Barcelona Declaration, 2016). The mayors pointed out that the provision of services and the administration of public funds to aid people with housing, health, education, food safety, etc. have traditionally been duties of local authorities. Yet, they had no say in the negotiations of TTIP and CETA – both agreements with the potential to affect all of the areas mentioned. In a sense, the Barcelona Declaration attempted to bring back into play the local actors, paying attention to sovereignty as an act of self-governance, direct participation, and governance of the people for the people.

Cities had also declared themselves TTIP-free before the Barcelona Declaration, but the declaration emphasized the truly transnational dimension of these local efforts and gave a name and a map to the campaign. The municipalist impulse coincided with an active period of NGO mobilization, giving rise to important cooperation and synergies between players. NGOs such as Attac had long pursued a bottom-up type of globalization (Pasqualoni and Treichl, 2012, 184) and in fact, shortly before the Barcelona meeting, Attac France created a website for the campaign to provide a centralized map on which each European city that had adopted a resolution could mark itself as TTIP-free. Again, the website provided standardized materials that could be used by activists lobbying city councils and local governments. Among the pieces of advice given to activists was the suggestion to lobby mayors who were already sympathetic to their cause.

Declaring a zone to be TTIP-free has no legal effect and could hardly challenge the provisions of a transnational agreement if it comes into force. At the same time, the motions of local mayors to declare their cities TTIP-free had a strong symbolic dimension and helped spread resistance to TTIP as an exemplary case of governmental activism (Verhoeven and Duyvendak, 2017). Beyond individual citizen action, organized street protests, lobbying by NGOs, and political parties voting in the national parliaments and the EP, cities and regions engaging in the TTIP-free zones initiative aimed to show that territorially organized communities also opposed TTIP and their voice mattered.

It is not by chance that the meeting of local mayors took place in Barcelona, a city whose mayor is the activist Ada Colau, supported by Podemos in the last elections. Barcelona has a flourishing network of collectives experimenting with new democratic forms and variations of the "solidarity economy". The Barcelona city council declared itself a TTIP-free zone in October 2015, several months before the signing of the Barcelona Declaration. By 2016, more than 2,000 cities in Austria, Belgium, Bulgaria, France, Germany, the Netherlands, Spain, and the UK have joined the initiative. As a clear testimony for the collaboration of very different type of players, in the UK, Global Justice Now worked with Unison, the public sector union, to produce a campaign pack, "consisting of briefings, posters, leaflets, badges, stickers and a sample motion for you to use in getting your local council to come on board with the TTIP Free Zone campaign" (Smith, 2015). In September 2016, protesters against TTIP in Germany marched with signs of cities that had declared themselves TTIP-free. In this way, a symbolic connection between various Green left players opposing TTIP at different levels of resistance was established.

This example shows also that trade unions played a key role in the mobilization and diffusion of protest against TTIP and CETA (Gortanuti, 2016). German trade unions, particularly the confederate body DGB and more sector-specific ones such as IG Metal, focused predominantly on workers-rights-related issues in TTIP and the threats it posed to working conditions by encouraging a race to the bottom (Gortanuti, 2016). The European Trade Union Confederation (ETUC) criticized strongly the threats to labour standards posed by these new comprehensive trade agreements, as well as the inclusion of ISDS mechanisms but did not reject the agreements as a whole (interview with Daniele Basso, ETUC). Yet, it was precisely the inclusion within the anti-TTIP coalition of such reformist actors that allowed it to reach out to more workers both domestically and transnationally. Unions brought hundreds of thousands of people to the streets, a mobilization that civil society campaign groups, regardless of their impact, could not have achieved alone. Trade unions were key not only for mobilizing people to the streets but also for diffusing information and protest: Spanish institutionalized actors, for instance, pointed out the important role of the German Trade Union Confederation (DGB) in convincing them to participate in the campaign (Bouza and Oleart, 2018, 96).

Unions were an important ally and source of information also for other actors such as members of the European Parliament. Anne-Marie Mineur, Dutch MEP from the United Left–Nordic Green Left in the European Parliament (GUE/NGL), noted how one of her first sources of information on CETA was in fact Corrie van Brenk, at that time the president of the Dutch officials' trade union ABVAKABO (now merged into the largest Dutch trade union FNV). Van Brenk and Mineur were both members of the city council of De Bilt, and when Mineur was elected as an MEP, van Brenk urged her to get into action on the topic of free trade agreements, which she did, expanding dramatically her contacts and expertise over the following years (interview with Anne-Marie Mineur). This type of national trade union–MEP interaction might often fall under the radar of research but was vital in the mobilization against free trade agreements such as TTIP.

Indeed, not only trade union but also MEP activism has been overlooked by social movement research that presupposes that MEPs are there to be "lobbied" but are not actively seeking information, campaigning, and engaging in activist actions themselves. Contrary to such predictions, as a member of the European Parliament Committee on International Trade, MEP Mineur actively spread information on the dangers of CETA and TTIP, in interaction not only with fellow MEPs (MEPs Say No to TTIP, 2015) and national and European trade unions, but also crucially with a variety of Brussels-based NGOs and national Dutch players. The diffusion of protests was thus not an exclusively bottom-up activists' task, but could be driven also by politicians with expertise and connections such as Mineur and a number of other GUE/NGL MEPs, who managed to serve as a bridge between different types of players.

FIGURE 4.1   250,000 people protest against TTIP/CETA in Berlin, October 10, 2015

Once CETA was ratified at the EU level, campaigning moved to the national level, where Mineur followed up on her work in multiple ways, including drafting a brief for the Dutch Senate, which in turn took up a number of the questions posed in the brief and put them to the government (interview with Anne-Marie Mineur). This level of commitment in fact differed from the pattern of NGO engagement that was extremely active before the ratification but generally tended to move on to other issues once CETA was ratified at the EU level (interview with Georgi Hristov).

Overall, the TTIP protests were influenced by the mobilizations both against austerity and against ACTA in the shadow of the Great Recession. There were key continuities between these mobilizations but also important differences. To begin with, bottom-up activists had been much more active diffusers of anti-austerity protests, while in the case of mobilizations against TTIP and CETA, after an initial phase in which Occupy and Indignados activists drove diffusion together with S2B actors, NGOs took the leading role. Furthermore, while in the case of the anti-ACTA protests, Brussels-based and German NGOs were to a large extent surprised by the protests, in the case of TTIP they were more involved in the organization from the very beginning and consequently much more involved in crafting protest messages, posters, and slogans. Finally, while the campaign against ACTA was marked above all by the productive tensions and conflicts between hacktivists, NGOs, and street protesters (NGOs were surprised by the protests and opposed the actions of Anonymous), the campaign against TTIP and CETA was more controlled and streamlined by NGOs.

The biggest tension in the anti-TTIP and CETA campaign lay, in fact, between radical left and Green left NGOs and radical right parties. Despite the existence of a variety of strategic responses, NGOs in most cases opposed attempts of the radical right to join protests and street marches. Opposition to TTIP and CETA was perceived by the organizers of the campaign as a Green left issue, and they refused to be associated with the far right. I explore in more detail far right attempts to appropriate resistance to TTIP in the next section.

4.3. The Diffusion of Opposition to TTIP and CETA From the Green Left to the Far Right

Green and radical left parties, NGOs, and bottom-up activists were the first political actors to raise awareness about the risks of the TTIP and CETA. These groups conducted research, developed expertise, and ensured that opposition to these agreements would mount. In fact, a type of "new, new sovereigntism" (structurally similar to the "new sovereigntism" in the US) arose among pro-European movements and parties, mostly centre-left and left, seeking to defend EU laws, values, and legal autonomy against a body of international law which was considered procedurally flawed, substantively objectionable, and intruding on the EU's legal order (Pollack, 2017).

However, what is less frequently commented upon is that the radical right also came to contest TTIP and CETA, and often reframed and appropriated leftist critique of the agreements. In cases where authors do acknowledge mobilization on the radical right, they tend to conflate left-wing and right-wing opposition under the common label of "populism" such as in the already mentioned *Economist* article "Protectionists and Scaremongers Are Winning in Germany". Nevertheless, understanding the differences between radical right and Green and radical left critiques is crucial, as they also lead to important differences in the proposed alternatives to existing neoliberal dimensions of international trade law. Amalgamating all opposition to free trade agreements as "anti-trade" or "populist" in fact obscures important ideological tensions and particular agendas which existed within the anti-TTIP and anti-CETA camp.

As already discussed, German civil society groups, which were at the forefront of the opposition to TTIP in the EU, repeatedly expressed concerns over the lowering of food, auto, and environmental safety standards. This was followed by worries about unfair advantage for foreign companies and threats to jobs and wages. Green left NGOs and political parties in Germany provided in-depth expertise in the field of trade policy, explaining not only the threats of lowered standards, job losses, and advantage to foreign corporations, but also the dangers of ISDS, the regulatory chill that "regulatory cooperation" might entail, the secretive nature of the negotiations, and the ways TTIP and CETA might increase inequalities. What is more, they created platforms and video materials that allowed them to actively spread these analyses across Europe.

The left's virtual omnipresence and the strong resonance of its messages put the radical right German party AfD in a difficult situation. AfD was founded in 2013 by a group of Eurosceptics who opposed German-backed bailouts for poorer Southern European countries and wanted Germany to leave the Eurozone (Arzheimer, 2015). Derisively called "the professors' party" due to the high number of economics professors amongst those who had endorsed its manifesto (Hill, 2015), AfD found it difficult to adopt a clear position on TTIP. In March 2014, at the party conference in Erfurt, the chair, economics professor Bernd Lucke, presented TTIP as a positive, constructive agreement in the interests of Germany, including for the car industry. However, another party member, Berlin lawyer Beatrix von Storch, argued that TTIP could threaten consumer and environmental protection, as well as labour standards. Her position won a party vote on the issue (Jahn, 2014) and, two months later, Lucke made a passionate speech against TTIP in Dresden as part of the European elections campaign. He then presented ISDS as a big problem, claiming it would be neither correct nor appropriate for American companies in Germany to avoid being subjected to German jurisdiction in legal disputes (Lachmann, 2014). Nevertheless, contrary to the sentiments of the supporter base and the official party line, economists such as Joachim Starbatty declared themselves fully in support of the agreement (ibid.).

In July 2015, AfD elected Frauke Petry as its new chair. Her election marked the victory of the radical right faction of the party that was more vocal on issues such as migration. Lucke resigned and formed a new party which most of the economic professors joined. In a sense, the inner tension in the AfD between neoliberal support for free trade and national-conservative protectionist positions was resolved by the split in the party. Having lost its economics specialists, AfD had to formulate an economic policy quickly. Regarding TTIP, it drew on the anxiety prevalent in the German public around TTIP and strongly opposed the agreement. To do so, it took up many of the arguments against TTIP that had been formulated by Die Linke. This created a remarkable overlap in their arguments, making it difficult for Die Linke to retain ownership of the issue.

Die Linke responded with an article entitled "Die LINKE and the AfD – No Common Denominator" (fds Hamburg, 2016). Die Linke acknowledged that some of its criticism of TTIP had been appropriated by the radical right, but also observed:

> [AfD's] criticism is directed either against the Americans or the global financial elites, who want to exploit the German people. It thus serves anti-Americanism and anti-Semitism. . . . Die Linke's criticism of CETA, TTIP and similar agreements is directed against their anti-democracy. These agreements are neo-liberal and anti-social. Left answers must describe a design for a better future, the development of our society towards lived solidarity, more democracy, and a peaceful world.
>
> *(ibid.)*

The prevailing position in the Stop TTIP initiative was that TTIP should be stopped specifically to protect higher European standards of work, food, and environmental protection. Opposing TTIP in Germany did not mean opposing the EU. Far from it: both the radical left and the radical right welcomed EU standards. They also wanted to protect small and medium-sized enterprises against big business. Notably, the Green left and radical left activists in Germany categorically refused any support from the AfD in their campaign against TTIP. In August 2016, AfD sent a letter to the coordinator of the alliance against TTIP and CETA, asking how to join the march and make the AfD's rejection of CETA and TTIP clear. Such offers had been made earlier in Hannover. In both instances, the AfD was refused permission to join (Leber, 2016). The coordinator of the Stop TTIP initiative in Germany, Christian Weßling, said their rejection of right-wing populism and free trade criticism was meant to demonstrate that there was no space for anti-Americanism and racism in their initiative. Yet despite the categorical actions of Green left actors, the far right did continue in its attempts to appropriate resistance to TTIP and later on CETA. This example shows that diffusion of protest as well as of specific protest frames can be driven by active adopters (the far right) who appropriate and reinterpret the cause even against the wishes of the original diffusers (the Green left).

The case against TTIP evolved very differently in the UK, and some distinguishing features are worth noting from the outset. First and foremost is the fact that the British population, including the radical left, was extremely divided about the merits or otherwise of the EU. This became clear for all to see in the unexpected result of the Brexit referendum on UK membership announced in June 2016. Remarkably, two years before this, UKIP, the UK party of the populist radical right, had managed to attract no less than 26.6% of the UK vote for the European Parliament, more than any other party in the UK. It is also worth noting how the protection of the National Health Service was widely discussed in relation to TTIP in the UK. This is the only country where this happened so prominently, showing how an international issue can come to be connected to various pre-existing salient national debates.

As in Germany, radical left organizations in the UK such as War on Want had been developing and providing expertise on TTIP as early as 2013 (War on Want, 2013). They opposed the agreement as a neoliberal project that bypassed democracy and entailed deregulation and the lowering of working, environmental, and food safety standards. The main political parties did not accept this criticism. The 2014 manifestos of the Conservative, Liberal Democratic, and Labour parties specifically supported TTIP, although they also all promised to monitor TTIP's impact on the NHS. Only the Green Party opposed TTIP (Green Party, 2014). As for UKIP, its manifesto was silent on it. Moreover, again as in Germany, the British radical right was struggling to form its position on TTIP.

UKIP had often espoused economically liberal positions in the past. The big question for the party was how to reconcile its usual support for free trade with the demands by its supporters that it oppose TTIP. A few months after the European elections of 2014, UKIP was forced to clarify its position after a series of eventful misunderstandings. On the morning of October 20, 2014, the *International Business Times* (IBT) published an article stating that William Dartmouth, UKIP MEP and the party's spokesperson for trade, had confirmed in an email exchange that should a transparent agreement come to pass, the party "wishes to see public services such as the NHS and education included in TTIP" (Bermingham, 2014a). By the afternoon, UKIP had backtracked on this position, explaining that an error had occurred and a member of staff not permitted to speak on UKIP policy had received the answers by Dartmouth on the phone hurriedly and had subsequently confused the words "include" and "exclude" while drafting the email response (Bermingham, 2014b). UKIP's then leader, Nigel Farage, later sent a confusing letter to the IBT, which immediately necessitated further clarification. The clarification took the form of the following statement from Farage's office:

> The trade agreement is being negotiated by the unelected EU Trade Commissioner behind closed doors – all our MEPs can do at the moment is sit and wait until the final agreement is forwarded to the EU "parliament" and then say yes or no to it. Astonishingly, MEPs have no power to make amendments to any agreement the EU makes on international trade, nor does our elected UK government.
>
> Ukip is in favour of free trade but we are opposed to the undemocratic Commission negotiating on our behalf. Of course we look at each trade deal on [a] case by case basis, so if this one is not in the UK's interest, we will have no reservation in voting against. However we have yet to receive even the draft agreement (let alone the final agreement). In the meantime, we share your concerns.
>
> *(ibid.)*

UKIP was seeking to reconcile its stance in favour of free trade with an anti-TTIP position by claiming that TTIP was not free enough since it was negotiated by the EU. Over time, the party's position developed further and introduced subtle distinctions, such as the claim that TTIP was not really about free trade. On June 10, 2015, in a session of the European Parliament, UKIP protested against a decision to cancel the vote on a TTIP resolution, holding up posters with the words: "Free Trade – yes. TTIP – no!". In a June 2016 piece on TTIP for Breitbart, Farage claimed that TTIP, as negotiated by the European Commission, was in fact "corporatist": "[w]hilst TTIP may masquerade as being about free trade, actually it's not. It's about harmonisation, standardisation and a market place in which the giant corporations can dominate" (Farage, 2015). One reason which prompted UKIP to declare itself against TTIP was the barrage of popular protest the prospective agreement attracted. On his own admission, in his 16 years as an

MEP, Farage had "never seen such a vast amount of emails, correspondence, even members of the public phoning my office in Strasbourg as I have recently over the issue of the Transatlantic Trade and Investment Partnership (TTIP)" (ibid.). The source of this pressure was the information campaign waged by Green left and radical left parties and NGOs.

The Breitbart piece by Farage offered a similar analysis to those by War on Want and Global Justice Now. What is more, it specifically acknowledged the expertise of the NGO 38 Degrees and expressed gratitude for receiving "a nice letter from Francis [sic] O'Grady, the TUC's General Secretary, regarding TTIP's dispute mechanism" (ibid.). In 2014, 38 Degrees had approached UKIP at its party conference in Doncaster to provide it with information on TTIP. Consequently, UKIP supporters joined 38 Degrees members and handed out leaflets explaining the dangers of TTIP in August 2015 (UKIP with 38 Degrees, 2015). 38 Degrees, a progressive not-for-profit activist organization, offered the following rationale for approaching UKIP: "No matter what you think of UKIP, they have 24 members of the European Parliament (MEPs) – and they'll all get to vote on TTIP" (Blair, 2014).

That said, the readiness of 38 Degrees to collaborate with UKIP in grassroots campaigning was exceptional. Other left-wing and/or Green NGOs were highly hostile to the way UKIP appropriated the issue. For example, Ruby Stockham from the political blog Left Foot Forward claimed that while UKIP focused on where the deal was negotiated, most parties had problems with the actual content of the deal. What is more, "UKIP would welcome the relaxation of environmental restrictions" and they are "in favour of reduced rights for workers – they want to scrap race discrimination laws, think paid maternity leave is 'lunacy' and want to scrap holiday and sick pay". In a sense, "UKIP are actually in favour of many of the things TTIP stands for; they just they just don't like it being negotiated by the EU" (Stockham, 2015). Morten Thaysen from Global Justice Now passionately argued that the left could not let the fight against TTIP become a platform for UKIP:

> Yes, we need every vote we can get against TTIP in the European Parliament, including UKIP's. But celebrating a party associated with racism and homophobia as a champion of the campaign against TTIP is a mistake. In the fight for social and economic justice we must ally ourselves with the people who are going to be hit the hardest by deals like TTIP, not their oppressors.
>
> *(Thaysen, 2015)*

Sam Lowe from the environmental NGO Friends of the Earth insisted that opposition to TTIP was not a reason to leave the EU (Lowe, 2015). Lowe underlined the benefits of EU membership and claimed that, ultimately, "if we want to stop TTIP, we can only do it as part of the EU, as part of a Europe-wide movement" (ibid.). In contrast, for the director of War on Want, John Hilary, the EU was such a problematic institution that his organization decided not to join the Remain campaign in the Brexit referendum and entertained instead the idea of left exit ("Lexit") (though this did not mean an alliance with UKIP) (Hilary, 2016).

To sum up, the fact that UKIP appropriated resistance to TTIP and framed it as opposition to the EU was far from welcome to, and provoked a series of reactions from, Green and left NGOs that tried to distance themselves from UKIP and underline where the real problems with the agreement lay. But once the genie of Farage was let out of the bottle, it was difficult to put him back. In what was again a clear case of adopter-driven diffusion, UKIP cleverly reframed the issue in ways that obscured the apparent contradiction between their support for free trade and their opposition to TTIP. It was a winning card that could be played, and UKIP did not miss the opportunity.

After Green left players had diffused opposition to TTIP in Europe, they were followed by far right players, above all political parites which emulated each other and exchanged views in an attempt to capitalise on the general public mood against the agreements (Live Le Pen and Salvini, 2016). The appropriation of resistance to TTIP and CETA by the far right was a widespread phenomenon in the EU that went beyond Germany and the UK. In Austria, one of the European countries with the strongest opposition to TTIP, the Freedom Party FPÖ was a prominent opponent of TTIP and CETA, posing important challenges to Green left NGOs such as Attac and Global 2000 that had to devise clever strategies to avoid appropriation of their arguments by the far right (interviews with Reinhard Uhrig and Valentin Schwarz). FPÖ later set a precedent by quickly sacrificing its position on these agreements during the coalition talks with Sebastian Kurz's ÖVP. In May 2018, the Austrian ÖVP-FPÖ government agreed to the ratification of CETA (Szigetvari, 2018). In general, radical right opposition to TTIP and CETA across Europe was more situational and fragile rather than offering an overall challenge to the legitimacy of the current international trade regime. It was also very much adopting and reframing the arguments and expertise of the chronologically earlier Green left mobilization, despite protests by Green left actors.

Thus, labelling all diverse actors opposing TTIP and CETA as "populist" prevents us from distinguishing the distinct reasons why they opposed the agreement (both political and substantial) and the different solutions they offered as an alternative to these agreements. In their opposition to TTIP and CETA, Green left and radical left actors often supported internationalism, and many of them took part in initiating an "Alternative Trade Mandate" (2013) to promote fair trade and use trade agreements to raise regulatory standards instead of lowering them. The "TTIP-Free Zones Initiative" that moved resistance to TTIP and CETA to cities and regions was also a smart way to relocate sovereignty to the local level and counteract radical right narratives. Still, there were some serious challenges for the Green left for resisting discursive appropriation by the far right in the long run.

One of the key challenges was that Green left NGO network that campaigned against TTIP and CETA was largely dismantled. As coordinator of the anti-TTIP and CETA campaign from Solidarna Bulgaria Georgi Hristov noted, once CETA was approved by the European Parliament in February 2017, the majority of NGOs quickly moved to other issues. Due to their professionalization and dependence on project financing, Green left and left NGOs arguably missed a great opportunity to use those already established networks and public support to develop constructive proposals on international trade. Focusing on different new issues, they left the battle primarily to Green left political parties and trade unions. The later especially, however, counted on more traditional media strategies and could not match the NGOs' inventiveness in the digital sphere. Once CETA was ratified by the European Parliament, active coalition and diffusion work diminished, protest activity ceased, and the battle moved to the national legislative sphere. Nevertheless, there were some contexts where protests had failed to diffuse at the start. Why was this the case? I explore this question in the following section.

4.4. The Failed Diffusion of Protests Against TTIP and CETA in Eastern Europe

Bertelsmann Foundation data (2016) on support for TTIP, comparing answers from 2014 and 2015, shows clearly the high public support for the agreement in the countries of Eastern Europe, among which the most supportive is Lithuania with 79% of the population in favour of TTIP, followed by Romania (78%), Poland (71%), Bulgaria (67%), and Czech Republic (62%). What is more, while the general trend has been decreasing support for TTIP (support fell 5% on average and opposition increased 7% on average [Rehn, 2016]), countries like Romania and Bulgaria even increased their support. One of the explanations given for the relative passivity of countries from the former Eastern Bloc when it comes to TTIP is the strong geopolitical dimension of the agreement:

> V4 countries, especially Poland, tend to be sensitive to the signs of a reborn Russian imperialism and, together with other Central and Eastern European countries, have traditionally been Atlantic-oriented. That is, the geopolitical significance of TTIP is perhaps more appreciated here than in Western Europe where alliance with America is just business as usual.
>
> *(Boda, 2015)*

Following the transition period in the 1990s that came with the rise of pro-free market, pro-transatlantic NGOs and disciplines in universities, few organizations in Eastern Europe were ready to declare opposition to a transatlantic trade agreement. When supporters of the Stop TTIP initiative went to the Baltics with a giant inflatable "Stop TTIP" pencil, very few people there even knew what TTIP was. In July 2015, the Stop TTIP supporters organized in Vilnius the first public event on TTIP to take place there, with around 40 participants from trade unions, NGOs, political parties, students, etc. It is indicative that the event was called "Will a Transatlantic Treaty Save Us From Russia?" and during the event German activists such as Jürgen Maier from Germany's "Forum for Environment" and Lora Verheecke from "Corporate Europe Observatory" tried to explain why being against TTIP is not being pro-Russia and how the agreement threatened workers' protection and the environment (Gintalaite, 2015).

Due to the prevalence of pro-Atlantic pro-free trade actors in their civil society, countries such as Bulgaria, Latvia, and Lithuania had fewer players that could mobilize against TTIP and CETA. Considering the few traditions and small experience of Bulgarian activists and NGOs in alter-globalization mobilizations from the late 1990s and early 2000s, the main players to mobilize on the issue in Bulgaria were the traditionally strong Green NGOs. And they did mobilize. The Bulgarian Greens and Za Zemyata, the Bulgarian representative of Friends of the Earth, both well connected to Green actors across Europe, launched a national anti-TTIP campaign. While they pointed to the undemocratic way in which the agreement was negotiated and the dangers of ISDS, they focused especially on the potentially dangerous ecological consequences from TTIP: the way it could open the door to fracking, GMO imports, and imports of toxic pesticides and medicines and the threats it posed to food safety. Connecting opposition to TTIP to opposition to GMO foods and to fracking was a clever strategic move, considering that some of the biggest protests in Bulgaria in the last 10 years had been precisely in opposition to GMO foods and fracking and led to a government moratorium on both. The Green Party and Za Zemyata hoped to make the agreement more relevant to the local context by focusing on issues that were already salient and highly politicized. But the Bulgarian protests against TTIP attracted only between 50 and 300 people in Sofia and a few other big cities and could not be compared to previous mass ecological mobilizations in Bulgaria with thousands of participants.

One reason for this might be the complete absence of the topic in mainstream media as a key player, which only started actively reporting on TTIP in 2017 when the oppositional centre-left Bulgarian Socialist Party (BSP) eventually took a clear position and decided to oppose the agreement. BSP was strongly influenced in this decision by the expertise of the association Solidarna Bulgaria, founded in 2012 to act as a corrective to the increasingly neoliberal BSP. While Solidarna Bulgaria is not a radical left organization, it is one of the few Bulgarian organizations to the left of the social democrats. It focuses on issues such as antiracism, ecology, healthcare, local politics, education, workers' rights and conflicts, welfare provision, and social assistance. With regard to TTIP, the group focused on the potential dangers of TTIP on work regulations, trade union association, and labour rights, leaving the ecological issues to the expertise of Green actors.

Interestingly, Solidarna Bulgaria as a newly emerging organization at the beginning of the campaign against TTIP was not well embedded in transnational activist networks. They first learned about TTIP when Dimitar Sabev, a leading journalist member of the group, was invited to a Brussels event on TTIP by the European Commission in late 2013 and subsequently wrote a critical article on the agreement. Solidarna Bulgaria understood that the agreement was important and started work on the topic, reaching out to other Bulgarian and foreign organizations, including the Stop TTIP network (personal communication with Vanya Grigorova). What this episode shows is that diffusion in Bulgaria did indeed happen based on common membership in larger networks but in the case of Solidarna Bulgaria, at least, it was adopter-driven. Even though they were a latecomer, Solidarna Bulgaria not only played a crucial role in collecting signatures against the agreement and organizing key anti-TTIP protest events, but they also pushed the BSP to mobilize its structures in order to collect signatures for the Stop TTIP Citizens' Initiative. What is more, the organization also pushed the topic as part of the electoral campaign of the independent presidential candidate Rumen Radev (currently the president of Bulgaria) who publicly denounced CETA. It was only after Radev opposed CETA that mainstream media started to pay attention to the issue and dedicated some reporting to it, increasing its public salience. This was not enough, however, to attract mass participation in the Bulgarian street protests against the agreement.

Overall, the campaign against TTIP in Bulgaria remained low key and the issue remained at best a marginal topic in public debate. Green actors, even when supported by left-wing organizations such as Solidarna Bulgaria, could not mobilize their constituency. Furthermore, while at the international level there had been considerable continuity between the campaigns against ACTA and against TTIP and CETA, in Bulgaria there was little such continuity. Internet freedom as a cause was embraced in Bulgaria mostly by right-wing liberal (and, thus, pro-Atlantic) bloggers and media activists, very different from Green left actors opposing further liberalization of trade.

Two cases that seem to differ from the general Eastern European pattern have been Romania and Hungary. Both countries were well represented with a number of organizations in the common European Stop TTIP initiative. NGOs in Romania had indeed been more active against TTIP in comparison to those in Bulgaria, due to the fact that the early phases of the negotiations of TTIP coincided with the mass Romanian environmental protests against the Roşia Montană mining project (Margarit, 2016). Faced with unprecedented and sustained protests, the government stopped the Roşia Montană project, and in July 2015 Gabriel Resources filed a complaint against Romania at the ICSID (the World Bank's International Centre for Settlement of Investment Disputes), thus giving a clear example of the dangers of ISDS clauses in trade agreements (10ISDS

Stories, 2019). With this clear example in mind and thanks also to their strong transnational connections, Romanian NGOs mobilized actively. Yet, Romanian citizens did not come out to the streets to protest against TTIP, due mainly to lack of general media interest and the lack of involvement of players other than environmental NGOs.

Finally, Hungarian civil society organizations, which were strongly represented in the Stop TTIP initiative, found an unexpected ally in the face of the government of Orban, known for his illiberal and often highly protectionist rhetoric (Cooper and Davis, 2016). It was the official position of Hungary that ISDS should not form part of the agreement. What is more, Hungary wrote a GMO ban into their constitution and declared they would veto TTIP if that principle were threatened (Boda, 2015). But again, Hungarian citizens did not mobilize massively against TTIP. Neither did Latvians, Estonians, Lithuanians, Poles, Slovenians, Slovakians, or Czech citizens. In short, Eastern Europe remained unengaged in opposition to the agreement.

The failed diffusion of protests against TTIP and CETA in Eastern Europe confirms that the presence of strong anti-ACTA protests in 2012 does not predict the presence of strong anti-TTIP protests in the period 2014–2016. The best predictor for diffusion of anti-TTIP protests turned out to be the presence of a strong scene of Green left NGOs, political parties, and trade unions opposing liberalization and neoliberalism. The protests against TTIP were organized by Green left and radical left parties and NGOs (and increasingly trade unions) in Germany and Austria, but also in the UK, Spain, Italy, Belgium, and France, among others. Thus, while the legacy of anti-ACTA mobilization mattered in terms of strategy and the use of digital platforms to oppose TTIP and CETA, whether there would be any protest, to begin with, depended on the presence or absence of a legacy from the earlier alter-globalization movement. The strong presence of NGOs defined also the type of protest diffusion observed in the campaigns against TTIP and CETA – while protests against austerity and against ACTA were driven more by bottom-up activists, the mobilization against TTIP and CETA was coordinated by decentralized transnational networks on centralized platforms, allowing both established and newer organizations to share the same expertise. The fact that most national protests happened on common Days of Action shows that while diffusion cannot overcome the lack of strong local players, it can at least allow for the establishment of transnational solidarity and increase media coverage for protests across several countries.

4.5. Conclusions: Avoid Appropriation by the Far Right!

The campaign against TTIP and CETA at the European level demonstrated a remarkable level of coordination and cooperation between a variety of players in different countries and contexts. There was an active involvement by the usual suspects: NGOs, trade unions, and radical left and Green parties, but also by non-traditional actors such as cities and regions. In addition, mainstream media were also instrumental in popularizing opposition to TTIP. The presence of strong organizations taking part in alter-globalization networks was the best predictor of the successful diffusion of protest against TTIP. Nevertheless, the mobilization against TTIP and CETA was marked also by the appearance of a type of player that was much less prominent in previous alter-globalization type of protests in the West: the far right.

As established in this chapter, the far right increasingly adopted the arguments, analyses, and expertise of left-wing players in order to oppose free trade agreements from a strongly nationalist perspective. There were indeed some far right players who tried to appropriate resistance to ACTA in the past, especially in Eastern Europe. Yet, such a large-scale discursive appropriation by the far right of a traditionally "left-wing topic" as seen with TTIP posed serious new challenges. Green and left-wing actors felt uncomfortable hearing their own arguments and analyses from the likes of Frauke Petri or Marine Le Pen, but there was little to be done. Ultimately, the more noise was made around the agreement, the better. Still, this situation allowed proponents of TTIP and CETA to conflate radical left and radical right opposition to the agreement as "populist" or "protectionist", completely ignoring the crucial differences between these positions.

Thus, the crucial takeaway for activists from this chapter has to do with preventing discursive appropriation. At the heart of the conflation between far left and far right players by the mainstream was the fact that they both defended sovereignty. Nevertheless, what liberal pro-trade media missed was that for Green left actors, sovereignty was above all the expression of the democratic will of the people, regardless of whether this will was expressed at the state, EU, or even local level. On the contrary, for far right actors, sovereignty was the ultimate right of the state to decide on its own policy – it was national sovereignty first, and only later democratic sovereignty. Calling both far right and far left and Green actors nationalist and protectionist could not be further from the truth. In fact, the conflicts around TTIP and CETA laid bare the need to reconfigure sovereignty in the EU (Crespy, 2016) and showed that rather than a simple conflict between national and supranational sovereignty, the conflict around these trade agreements was also very much a conflict between popular and parliamentary sovereignty on the one hand and the supranational sovereignty of the EU on the other (Brack et al., 2019).

How can Green left activists emphasize their differences with the far right when opposing transnational agreements? One of the positive steps taken in this direction comes from the way NGOs and city councils moved the whole debate to the local level with the TTIP-free zones initiative to emphasize even more clearly that what is at stake is ultimately democratic decision-making. This argument for democracy, however, can be made also at the state level, and Green left activists can only gain from not shying away from the topic of sovereignty. Instead of completely ignoring the argument for national sovereignty as nationalist, Green left activists have the chance to reconceptualize national sovereignty as primarily a question of democratic participation and to promote popular and parliamentary sovereignty.

Second, a more aggressive media campaign is needed, both on digital and mainstream media against interpretations that conflate all opposition to free trade as protectionist or populist. Opposing agreements such as TTIP and CETA is not enough – what needs to be opposed as well is the false dichotomy between free trade and protectionism as a binary choice. The best way to avoid both appropriation by the far right and mainstream misrepresentation is to develop a much more elaborate vision of what free and fair trade should look like. At the time of writing this book, the website of the broad alliance for Alternative Trade Mandate cannot even be reached online, and the Alternative Trade Mandate page on Facebook has only 600 likes. If anti-free trade activists would simply follow up on this already existing project or start a new project with a similarly democratically informed vision of trade, they could present themselves less as grumpy naysayers and more as visionaries who can fix a broken system. The use of collaborative platforms in order to formulate alternative trade policies can increase citizen participation and popularize the project across national borders.

Following up on issues and thinking of alternatives is something that can be done in person but also online – with the help of mailing lists, online working groups, and tools for collaborative writing. What is more, as the March to Brussels of the Spanish Indignados has shown, sometimes the best way to diffuse ideas and get new ideas is to go directly to people and talk to them in their town squares and homes. A well-coordinated conversation (in the form of inclusive assemblies and/or of deliberation by mini-publics) on free trade and what Europeans expect from it, and what they are ready to sacrifice for it, is more than due.

While different players might overlap in their diagnosis of the present, it is in the prognosis for the future where one can see clearly who is who. Ultimately, Green left activists need to focus more on the elaboration of alternatives in order to situate themselves with respect both to the non-democratic attempt to curb sovereignty and the far right critique of the liberal order that is based on nationalist standpoints. While this is a difficult task, it is not impossible, and the success or failure of Green left players in this respect will define struggles in the years to come.

Note

1 Part of this chapter was published earlier in Rone, Julia (2018): Contested International Agreements, Contested National Politics: How the Radical Left and the Radical Right Opposed TTIP in Four European Countries. *London Review of International Law*, 6:2, 233–253.

References

10ISDS Stories (2019): Suing to Force Through a Toxic Goldmine, Gabriel Resources vs Romania. *10ISDS Stories*. Retrieved from https://corporateeurope.org/sites/default/files/2019-06/Gabriel%20Resources%20vs%20Romania.pdf.

Alternative Trade Mandate (2013): Trade: Time for a New Vision. *Seattle to Brussels Network*, 30 November. Retrieved from www.s2bnetwork.org/trade-time-new-vision.

Arzheimer, Kai (2015): The AfD: Finally a Successful Right-Wing Populist Eurosceptic Party for Germany? *West European Politics*, 38:3, 535–556.

Barcelona Declaration (2016): *Barcelona Declaration*. Retrieved from www.ttip-free-zones.eu/node/70.

Bauer, Matthias (2016): *Manufacturing Discontent: The Rise to Power of Anti-TTIP Groups*. Retrieved from http://ecipe.org/app/uploads/2016/11/Manufacturing-Discontent.pdf.

BDI (2016): *BDI: Europe Needs TTIP*. Retrieved from http://english.bdi.eu/article/news/europe-needs-ttip/.

Ben (2014): *#TTIP Resistance Across Europe #o11DoA UK, Spain, Germany, Brussels, Italy Most Present Networks Nodes #goodjob*. Retrieved from https://twitter.com/cyberbenb/status/520994466501779456.

Bermingham, Finbarr (2014a): TTIP Exclusive: Ukip Wants to Privatise the NHS in Controversial EU – US Trade Deal. *International Business Times*, 20 October. Retrieved from www.ibtimes.co.uk/ttipexclusive-ukip-wants-include-nhs-controversial-eu-us-trade-deal-1470790.

Bermingham, Finbarr (2014b): TTIP: Ukip Backtracks on NHS Privatisation Amid Communication Shambles. *International Business Times*, 20 October. Retrieved from www.ibtimes.co.uk/ttip-ukipbacktracks-nhs-privatisation-amid-communication-shambles-1470926.

Bertelsmann Foundation (2016): *Attitudes to Global Trade and TTIP in Germany and the United States*. Retrieved from www.bertelsmann-stiftung.de/en/publications/publication/did/attitudes-to-globaltrade- and-ttip-in-germany-and-the-united-states.

Blair, James (2014): TTIP at UKIP Conference – This Saturday. *38 Degrees*. Retrieved from https://home.38degrees.org.uk/2014/09/24/ttip-ukip-conference.

Boda, Zsolt (2015): *Attitudes to TTIP in Eastern Europe*. Retrieved from https://stop-ttip.org/blog/attitudestowards-ttip-in-eastern-europe/.

Bollen, Yelter (2018): *The Domestic Politics of EU Trade Policy: The Political Economy of CETA and Anti-Dumping in Belgium and the Netherlands*. PhD Dissertation, Centre for European Studies, Ghent University, Ghent.

Bouza, Louis and Alvaro Oleart (2018): From the 2005 Constitution's 'Permissive Consensus' to TTIP's 'Empowering Dissensus': The EU as a Playing Field for Spanish Civil Society. *Journal of Contemporary European Research*, 14:2.

Brack, Nathalie, Ramona Coman and Amandine Crespy (2019): Unpacking Old and New Conflicts of Sovereignty in the European Polity. *Journal of European Integration*, 41:7, 817–832.

Caiani, Manuela and Paolo Graziano (2018): Europeanisation and Social Movements: The Case of the Stop TTIP Campaign. *European Journal of Political Research*, 1–25.

Cooper, Alexis and Gabriel Davis (2016): *'Trumpian' Attitudes in Central Europe: Causes for Hungary's, Germany's and Poland's Attitudes Toward Transatlantic Trade*. Claremont-UC Undergraduate Research Conference on the European Union, Vol. 2. Retrieved from https://core.ac.uk/reader/70985978.

Crespy, A. (2016): CETA Has Laid Bare the Need to Reconfigure Sovereignty in the EU. *LSE Europe*. Retrieved from https://blogs.lse.ac.uk/europpblog/2016/10/26/ceta-sovereignty-democracy-wallonia-europe.

de Bièvre, Dirk and Arlo Poletti (2020): Towards Explaining Varying Degrees of Politicization of EU Trade Agreement Negotiations. *Politics and Governance*, 8:1.

de Ville, Ferdi and Jan Orbie (2014): The European Commission's Neoliberal Trade Discourse Since the Crisis: Legitimizing Continuity Through Subtle Discursive Change. *The British Journal of Politics and International Relations*, 16, 149–167.

de Ville, Ferdi and Gabriel Siles-Brügge (2015): The Transatlantic Trade and Investment Partnership and the Role of Computable General Equilibrium Modelling: An Exercise in 'Managing Fictional Expectations'. *New Political Economy*, 20:5, 653–678.

de Ville, Ferdi and Gabriel Siles-Brugge (2016): *TTIP: The Truth About the Transatlantic Trade and Investment Partnership*. London: Polity Press.

de Ville, Ferdi and Gabriel Siles-Brugge (2017): Why TTIP Is a Game-Changer and Its Critics Have a Point. *Journal of European Public Policy*, 24:10, 1491–1505.

DW (2016): Thousands Protest Against CETA in TTIP in Brussels. *DW*. Retrieved from www.dw.com/en/thousands-protest-against-ceta-and-ttip-in-brussels/a-19564581.

ECI (2014): *The European Citizens Initiative Official Register: Refused Request for Registration*. Retrieved from http://ec.europa.eu/citizens-initiative/public/initiatives/non-registered/details/2041.

ECI Basic Facts (2016): *Basic Facts: What Is a European Citizen Initiative?* Retrieved from http://ec.europa.eu/citizens-initiative/public/basic-facts.

The Economist (2016): Germans Against Trade: Fortress Mentality. *Protectionists and Scaremongers Are Winning in Germany*. Retrieved from www.economist.com/news/europe/21707241-protectionists-andscaremongers-are-winning-germany-fortress-mentality.

Egan, Michel and Neill Nugent (2015): The Changing Context and Nature of the Transatlantic Relationship. In: Laurie Buonanno et al. (eds.), *The New and Changing Trasnatlanticism*. London: Routledge.

Euractiv (2015): Thousands Across Europe Protest Against TTIP. *Euractiv*. Retrieved from www.euractiv.com/section/trade-society/news/thousands-across-europe-protest-against-ttip/.

Farage, Nigel (2015): Farage for Breitbart: TTIP Is About Giant Corporations Dominating Our Economies. *Breitbart*, 11 June. Retrieved from www.breitbart.com/london/2015/06/11/farage-for-breitbart-ttip-is-about-giant-corporates-dominating-our-economies.

fds Hamburg (2016): *Die Linke und die AfD – kein gemeinsamer Nenner*. Retrieved from www.fdshamburg.org/die-linke-und-die-afd-kein-gemeinsamer-nenner.

Felbermayr, G. (2016): The EU and the U.S.: TTIP. In: Harald Badinger and Volker Nitsch (eds.), *Routledge Handbook of the Economics of European Integration*. London: Routledge.

Friends of the Earth (2016): *Investment Court System: ISDS in Disguise*. Retrieved from http://ttip2016.eu/files/content/docs/Full%20documents/investment_court_system_isds_in_disguise_10_reasons_why_the_eus_proposal_doesnt_fixed_a_flawed_system_english_version_0.pdf.

Gambini, Gilberto, Radoslav Istatkov and Riina Kerner (2015): *USA – EU: International Trade and Investment Statistics*. Retrieved from http://ec.europa.eu/eurostat/statistics-explained/index.php/USA-EU_-_international_trade_and_investment_statistics.

Gheyle, Niels (2019): *Trade Policy with the Lights on*. Brussels: ASP.

Gheyle, Niels (2020): Huddle Up! Exploring Domestic Coalition Formation Dynamics in the Differentiated Politicization of TTIP. *Politics and Governance*, 8:1.

Gheyle, Niels and Ferdi de Ville (2017): How Much Is Enough? Explaining the Continuous Transparency Conflict in TTIP. *Politics and Governance*, 5:3, 16–28.

Gintalaite, Laura (2015): *The Seeds of 'Stop TTIP' Awareness Spread in the Baltics*. Retrieved from https://stopttip.org/blog/seeds-spread-in-the-baltics.

Glattauer, Barbara (2014): European Day of Action: Together, Let's Roll Back Corporate Power! *Open Democracy*. Retrieved from www.opendemocracy.net/en/can-europe-make-it/european-day-of-action-together-lets-roll-back-corporate-power/.

Gortanuti, Giulia (2016): *The Influence of Trade Unions and Social Movements on EU Trade Policy*. Retrieved from goo.gl/qufCxK.

Gotev, Georgi (2016): Germany Says TTIP Dead in the Water. *Euractiv*. Retrieved from www.euractiv.com/section/trade-society/news/germany-says-ttip-dead-in-the-water/.

Green Party (2014): *Green Party, Real Change: Manifesto for the European Parliament Elections 2014*. Retrieved 22 June, from www.greenparty.org.uk/assets/files/European%20Manifesto%202014.pdf.

Hamilton, Daniel and Jacques Pelkmans (2015): Rule-Makers or Rule-Takers? An Introduction to TTIP. In: Daniel Hamilton and Jacques Pelkmans (eds.), *Rule-Makers or Rule-Takers: Exploring the Transatlantic Trade and Investment Partnership*. Lanham: Rowman & Littlefield.

Hill, Jenny (2015): What Next for Germany's Eurosceptic AfD Party? *BBC*, 21 July. Retrieved from www.bbc.com/news/world-europe-33593500.

Hilary, John (2015): I Didn't Think TTIP Could Get Any Scarier, but Then I Spoke to the EU Official in Charge of It. *The Independent*. Retrieved from https://www.independent.co.uk/voices/i-didn-t-think-ttip-could-get-any-scarier-but-then-i-spoke-to-the-eu-official-in-charge-of-it-a6690591.html.

Hilary, John (2016): EU Referendum: How Should the Left Vote? *War on Want*. Retrieved from www.waronwant.org/media/eu-referendum-how-should-left-vote.

Hübner, Kurt, Anne-Sophie Deman and Tugce Balik (2017): EU and Trade Policy-Making: The Contentious Case of CETA. *Journal of European Integration*, 39:7, 843–857.

IP Out of TAFTA (2013): *IP Out of TAFTA*. Retrieved from https://web.archive.org/web/20130418045616/www.citizen.org/documents/IP%20out%20of%20TAFTA%20without%20logos.pdf.

ISDS Fact Sheet (2013): *Investor Protection and Investor-to-State Dispute Settlement in EU Agreements*. Retrieved from http://trade.ec.europa.eu/doclib/docs/2013/november/tradoc_151916.pdf.

Jahn, Joachim (2014): AfD gegen mehr Freihandel mit Amerika. *Faz*. Retrieved from www.faz.net/aktuell/wirtschaft/parteitag-afd-gegen-mehr-freihandel-mit-amerika-12860008.html.

Jančić, Davor (2017): TTIP and Legislative-Executive Relations in EU Trade Policy. *West European Politics*, 40:1, 202–221.

Lachmann, Günther (2014): Freihandel reißt tiefe Gräben in der AfD auf. *Welt*. Retrieved from www.welt.de/politik/deutschland/article133530458/Freihandel-reisst-tiefe-Graeben-in-der-AfD-auf.html.

Leber, Fabian (2016): Anti-TTIP-Bündnis Will AfD-Teilnahme verhindern. *Tagesspiegel*. Retrieved from http://www.tagesspiegel.de/politik/demo-gegen-freihandelsabkommen-anti-ttip-buendnis-will-afd-teilnahme-verhindern/14013694.html.

Leblond, Patrick and Crina Viju-Miljusevic (2019): EU Trade Policy in the Twenty-First Century: Change, Continuity and Challenges. *Journal of European Public Policy*, 26:12, 1836–1846.

Live Le Pen and M. Salvini (2016): *Live: Le Pen and Salvini Gives Press Conference on TTIP and CETA at European Parliament [English]*. Retrieved from www.youtube.com/watch?v¼VjqtyXlN0RA.

Longo, Erik (2019): The European Citizens' Initiative: Too Much Democracy for EU Polity? *German Law Journal*, 20:2, 181–200.

Lowe, Sam (2015): Is the EU's Pursuit of TTIP Reason Enough to Leave? *Friends of the Earth*. Retrieved from www.foe.co.uk/blog/eu-s-pursuit-ttip-reason-enough-leave.

Manrique Gil, Manuel et al. (2015): *The TTIP's Potential Impact on Developing Countries: A Review of Existing Literature and Selected Issues*. Brussels: European Parliament.

Margarit, Diana (2016): Civic Disenchantment and Political Distress: The Case of the Romanian Autumn. *East European Politics*, 32:1, 46–63.

Meissner, Katharina L. and Magnus G. Schoeller (2019): Rising Despite the Polycrisis? The European Parliament's Strategies of Self-Empowerment After Lisbon. *Journal of European Public Policy*, 26:7, 1075–1093.

MEPs Say No to TTIP (2015): *MEPs Say No to TTIP and Support the Global Action Day*, 18 April. Retrieved from www.youtube.com/watch?v=sdzvXqlBUNY&feature=youtu.be.

Milevska, Tanja (2014): UK Anti-TTIP Protests to Focus on NHS Privatisation. *Euractiv*. Retrieved from www.euractiv.com/section/social-europe-jobs/news/uk-anti-ttip-protests-to-focus-on-nhs-privatisation/.

Nielsen, Nikolaj (2016): EU Defends TTIP Investor Court After German Backlash. *EUObserver*. Retrieved from https://euobserver.com/economic/132295.

Pasqualoni, Pier Paolo and Helga Treichl (2012): Post-Democracy and Engaged Citizenship – the Case of Attack. In: Wolfgang Weber, Annette Ostendorf and Lynne Chisholm (eds.), *Democratic Competences and social Practices in Organizations*. Springer Research. Retrieved from https://link.springer.com/content/pdf/bfm%3A978-3-531-19631-2%2F1.pdf.

Pasquet, Yannick (2016): *Protesters Rally Across Germany Against TTIP Trade Deal*. Retrieved from www.yahoo.com/news/protesters-rally-across-germany-against-mega-trade-deal-004030468.html.

Pollack, Mark (2017): The New, New Sovereigntism (or, How the Europe Union Became Disenchanted with International Law and Defiantly Protective of Its Domestic Legal Order). In: Chiara Giorgetti and Guglielmo Verdirame (eds.), *Concepts on International Law in Europe and the United States*. Cambridge: Cambridge University Press.

Rehn, Friederike (2016): *It's EU Official: Opposition to TTIP Keeps Increasing*. Retrieved from https://stopttip.org/blog/its-eu-official-opposition-to-ttip-keeps-increasing/.

Reuters (2015): Hundreds of Thousands Protest in Berlin Against EU-U.S. Trade Deal. *Reuters*. Retrieved from www.reuters.com/article/us-trade-germany-ttip-protests-idUSKCN0S40L720151010.

Roederer-Rynning, Christilla (2017): Parliamentary Assertion and Deep Integration: The European Parliament in the CETA and TTIP Negotiations. *Cambridge Review of International Affairs*, 30:5–6, 507–526.

Rosa Luxembourg (2015): *TTIP Protests Are Going Global*. Retrieved from www.rosalux.eu/en/article/242.ttip-protests-are-going-global.html.

Ryø, Charlotte (2015): *Together We Are Stronger!* Retrieved from https://stop-ttip.org/blog/together-we-arestronger.

S2B (2020): Seattle to Brussels Network. *About Us*. Retrieved from http://s2bnetwork.org/about-us/.

Siles-Brugge, Gabriel (2013): The Power of Economic Ideas: A Constructivist Political Economy of EU Trade Policy. *Journal of Contemporary European Research*, 9:4, 597–617.

Siles-Brugge, Gabriel and Michael Strange (2020): National Autonomy or Transnational Solidarity? Using Multiple Geographic Frames to Politicize EU Trade Policy. *Politics and Governance*, 8:1, 277–289.

Smith, Kevin (2015): *Local Councils Are Starting to Tear Strips off TTIP*. Global Justice Now. Retrieved from https://www.globaljustice.org.uk/blog/2015/aug/28/local-coun cils-are-starting-tear-strips-ttip.

Stockham, Ruby (2015): Don't Buy UKIP's Hypocrisy on TTIP. *Left Foot Forward*. Retrieved from https://leftfootforward.org/2015/04/dont-buy-ukips-hypocrisy-on-ttip.

Stop TTIP (2014): *European Citizens' Initiative Against TTIP and CETA*. Retrieved from https://web.archive.org/web/20140719035403, http://stop-ttip.org/members/.

Stop TTIP Pencil (2015): *The Giant Stop TTIP Pencil Is Coming to Your Town!* Retrieved from https://stopttip. org/blog/giant-stop-ttip-pencil-is-coming-to-your-town/.

Strange, Michael (2015): Implications of TTIP for Transnational Social Movements and International NGOs. In: Jean-Frederic Morin et al. (eds.), *The Politics of Transatlantic Trade Negotiations*. Surrey: Ashgate.

Szigetvari, András (2018): Umfallen vie die FPO. *Der Standard*. Retrieved from www. derstandard.de/story/2000079865324/zustimmung-zu-ceta-umfallen-wie-die-fpoe.

Thaysen, Morten (2015): Why We Shouldn't Let the Fight Against TTIP Become a Platform for UKIP. *Global Justice Now*. Retrieved from www.globaljustice.org.uk/ blog/2015/jul/9/why-weshouldn%E2%80%99t-let-fight-against-ttip-become-plat form-ukip.

UKIP with 38 Degrees (2015). *Braintree UKIP Protests with 38 Degrees Against TTIP in Sudbury*, 25 August. Retrieved from www.ukipessex.org/?p¼3337.

Verhoeven, Imrat and Jan Willem Duyvendak (2017): Understanding Governmental Activism. *Social Movement Studies*, 16:5, 564–577.

Vila, Sol (2014): *Beautiful Visual Display of Anti #TTIP #TAFTA Tweets #O11DoA @ bernardosampa @X_net_@toret*. Retrieved from https://twitter.com/Soltrumbo/ status/521660960441139200/photo/1.

Voss, Anna-Mareike (2015): *The 'Stop TTIP' Giant Pen Visits the City of Wismar*. Retrieved from https://stopttip.org/blog/the-stop-ttip-giant-pen-visits-the-city-of-wismar/.

War on Want (2013): *War on Want, TTIP and Third Countries: A Compendium of Research Studies and Articles Relating to the Impact of EU – US Trade Negotiations on Third Countries, with Special Reference to the African, Caribbean and Pacific Group of States (ACP) (Ram-phal Institute, 2013)*. Retrieved from http://media.waronwant.org/sites/default/files/ TTIP%20and%20Third%20Countries%2C%202016.pdf.

War on Want (2015): *TTIP in 2015: Building the Fightback*. Retrieved from https://waron want.org/media/ttip-2015-building-fightback.

Weisskircher, Manès (2020): The European Citizens' Initiative: Mobilization Strategies and Consequences. *Political Studies*, 68:3, 797–815.

CONCLUSIONS

This book has been the result of a process of writing stretching to almost a decade. I started the book project in 2013, in the aftermath of the 2008 economic crisis, and finished the last chapter during the spring 2020 quarantine caused by the global COVID-19 pandemic. The pandemic has so far led to a crash in the service economy, mass unemployment, and an even further increase in wealth concentration and inequality, but also to a radical rethinking of economic policy and the role of the state. In many respects this is a pre-pandemic book, whose focus on austerity and free trade reflects the political hopes, anxieties, and battles of the decade between the two crises – the 2008 economic one and the 2020 pandemic.

My main aim with this book has been to synthesize first, research on protests against austerity and research on protests against free trade; second, research on protests in Southern Europe with research on protests in Eastern Europe; and third, research on media practices with research on the strategic actions of a number of political players beyond bottom-up activists that have been the focus of most social movement studies so far. I have connected these largely disconnected strands of literature by exploring the diffusion of protests against austerity and free trade within the EU in the aftermath of the Great Recession. Focusing on diffusion allowed me to trace inductively the many players involved in spreading protest, including intellectuals, political parties, trade unions, NGOs, and mainstream media that used a wide variety of media practices to spread protest frames and repertoires. The focus on protest diffusion also allowed me to explore key aspects of the differentiated politicization of austerity and free trade policies in Western and Eastern Europe. Studying how protests in these parts of Europe are connected has been long overdue, since most authoritative research on the cycle of protest after the Great Recession has either focused exclusively on Western

European cases or has *compared* protests in Eastern and Western Europe without paying attention to the ways they have influenced each other, being part of the same complex system.

There have been several reasons to explore austerity and free trade in the framework of a single project. To begin with, as this book shows, imposing competitive austerity in Southern Europe had been conceived as necessary for achieving structural convergence in the Eurozone that was expected to make the more domestic consumption-oriented Southern European economies more export-oriented. Austerity was recommended not only to secure that governments could repay their debt and the economy would grow thanks to supply-side reforms (expansionary austerity) but also as a strategy to increase export competitiveness (competitive austerity): in both respects, austerity had only a moderate success in most countries, while leading to outright failure in others, most notably in the case of Greece. The focus on increasing competitiveness to improve exports made sense mainly in a worldview in which trade was a key source of growth. While the bulk of EU's trade happened internally, between countries of the bloc, in the 2010s the European Commission negotiated several key agreements that would also stimulate trade with third countries. The goal of these free trade agreements was to open foreign markets for EU trade by overcoming important regulatory barriers. In a certain sense, improving export competitiveness through competitive austerity was meant to help the EU overcome not only its internal structural imbalances but also its standing in the world of globalized trade.

Second, not only were austerity policies perceived as an important step for some countries to make full use of trade agreements but there was also a similar anti-democratic logic underlying both types of economic endeavour. This logic can be summed up as disregard for democracy in how these policies were negotiated and imposed (procedural threats to democracy) and as disregard for future democratic decision-making by insulating, through legal means, markets from contestation (substantive threats to democracy). It was this explicitly anti-democratic logic of both austerity and free trade agreements that provoked the indignation of protesters.

Third, austerity policies and the active negotiation of free trade agreements by the EU largely overlapped in time, which means that the protests against them were also close in time and strongly influenced each other. Two of the biggest trade agreements negotiated by the EU – TTIP and CETA (with the US and Canada respectively) gained unexpected salience in the public debate and were highly politicized in the aftermath of the 2011 anti-austerity protests and the 2012 rejection by the European Parliament of the Anti-Counterfeiting Trade Agreement. The campaign against TTIP and CETA emphasized the undemocratic and secretive way of conducting the negotiations and the threats investor-state dispute settlement mechanisms posed to democratic sovereignty. These arguments of the campaign fit perfectly with the rhetoric of earlier Indignados-styles protests that opposed the non-democratic way in which the informal body of the Troika (the

European Commission, the European Central Bank, and the IMF) in cooperation with national governments imposed austerity measures.

Both protests against austerity and free trade opposed the anti-democratic logic of such policies and defended democracy and sovereignty, understood not so much as national sovereignty but rather as popular and parliamentary sovereignty. What is more, actors that emerged from the 2011 anti-austerity protests, such as the municipalist movement, were to play an important role in the subsequent anti-TTIP and -CETA mobilizations. There was a clear continuity between both types of protests not only in terms of rhetoric but also in terms of some of the players involved. Anti-austerity protests and anti-free trade protests have been the two sides of the same coin, closely intertwined in multiple ways in the same protest cycle. At the same time, there has not been a complete overlap between anti-austerity and anti-free trade protests. Far from it.

Both EU's Southern and Eastern peripheries were affected by austerity, but mass Indignados-style protests took place only in the South (in Portugal, Spain, Greece, and Italy), while protests in countries such as Bulgaria and Romania were more often framed in right-wing liberal or nationalist terms. What is more, while free trade agreements such as CETA and TTIP were strongly politicized by players with traditions in the alter-globalization movement in Germany, Austria, or Spain, they passed almost unnoticed in Eastern Europe. Eastern European countries did protest against one trade agreement, though – the Anti-Counterfeiting Trade Agreement that threatened Internet freedom and the right to privacy. One common thread that united all these different types of protests, beyond left–right distinctions, was the demand for more democracy and democratic decision-making. This demand in the South came from a left-wing anti-austerity perspective and in the East mainly from right-wing liberal ecological or anti-corruption perspectives. Of course, corruption had been present as a topic in the South as well, but it was not as dominant an issue as in the East and was articulated with broader left-wing anti-austerity ideas as well.

What does this all tell us? Certainly, that it makes sense to speak of protest cycles, since there was a heightened protest activity all across the EU with protests following each other closely in space and time. Certain key aspects of the protest narrative such as demands for more democracy, critique of corruption, and faith in digital technology diffused successfully and marked protests both in the West and in the East. Yet, there were also crucial differences in the ways protests were conceived: left-wing frames and ideas diffused only to a small extent from the West to the East, emphasizing that while these protests did form part of the same cycle, they had very different profiles depending on the local players that drove them. In general, protests against austerity and free trade were framed in Western Europe in mostly left-wing terms, while in Eastern Europe, as seen in the 2012 mobilization against ACTA or the 2013 protests in Bulgaria and Romania, the opposition came mainly from the liberal or conservative right. Still, protests do have an eventful character, and some, albeit marginal, left-wing players emerged from the 2012–2013 protests in the East as well. This is important since it shows that diffusion *is* possible, and this is precisely what drives the appearance of *new* types of political players.

The classic explanation why protests succeed in some countries but fail in others has to do with the political opportunity structure, understood in broad terms as the levels of repression, political enfranchisement, divisions in elites, and levels of political pluralism, among others. Yet, such an approach presupposes that political opportunities are present or absent for players to seize. It does not explain *how* these players appear or why would they want to seize the opportunities to mobilize. In countries such as Bulgaria and Romania in 2013, there were both political opportunities present and large protests, but these protests were not against austerity since the players who organized them were not left-wing players. The successful diffusion of particular types of protest can thus be explained only by the presence or absence of constellations of players that want to "adopt" these particular protests and the protest frames and repertoires associated with them. In the absence of such players, there is either no diffusion whatsoever, as in the cases of the remarkable lack of anti-austerity protests in Latvia and Lithuania, or partial diffusion of some frames only (pro-democracy, anti-corruption, and pro-digital tech use) as in the case of the 2013 protests in Bulgaria and Romania.

If there were no diffusion whatsoever, one would expect countries to always experience the same kinds of protests that they had before because they have the same kinds of players with their established protest traditions. Yet, as the analysis of the spread of protest from Western to Eastern Europe has shown, new left-wing organizations did appear in the East after 2013. Most of these organizations were founded by intellectuals who had studied in the West or by local activists engaged with the trade union movement and labour rights. These organizations started developing a new language of protest on a variety of independent websites and media. It was these organizations that later on teamed up with local environmental NGOs in organizing protests against TTIP and CETA and adopting the frames diffused by transnational NGOs. Even though protests against these free trade agreements did not diffuse successfully in the East, the very fact that they were attempted shows that diffusion is possible, even if takes time. New players can appear and change is possible.

These examples of West–East diffusion point to the third important message of the book: protests are diffused not only by bottom-up activists but also by a variety of other players such as intellectuals, trade unions, political parties, NGOs, and mainstream media. Each of these players has very different media practices, and who takes the lead in diffusing protest impacts strongly the way protest is diffused. Anti-austerity protests were actively diffused by Southern European, especially Spanish, activists who made an enthusiastic and innovative use of digital media, reaching out to activists across the world in organizing global events. Spanish activists engaged heavily in using online platforms, often free and open source ones, in order to mobilize, organize, and disseminate protest. They also engaged in innovative practices such as data theatre but also in analogue non-digital actions such as marches throughout Europe during which they set local meetings and discussions in every new city they reached. Yet, with the exception of the US, their message was mainly adopted in other Southern European countries such as Portugal, Greece, and Italy, with which they had already existing strong connections. The cultural proximity between Southern European countries meant also that mainstream media often reported on protests in neighbouring countries, thus further increasing their prominence. This shows that diffusion is a difficult process in which digital media connections often follow the pre-established paths of offline and mass media communication. When such paths were absent – as in the case of Eastern Europe, the enthusiasm of diffusers fell on deaf ears: in order to "adopt" protest, protest frames and repertoires local adopters first had to establish their own platforms and alternative media, allowing them to popularize their causes at home, while at the same time reaching out to transnational allies. Intellectuals were crucial early adopters that diffused anti-austerity messages to the East.

Contrary to the experience of predominantly bottom-up-driven diffusion of anti-austerity protests, the diffusion of protest against TTIP and CETA was driven mainly by NGO networks such as Seattle to Brussels and the Stop TTIP initiative, which established a common European digital platform for collecting signatures in multiple EU member states. Anti-austerity activists were instrumental for organizing the first Days of Action against TTIP, but their role was gradually taken over by the Stop TTIP initiative that disseminated standardized frames and made use of ready-made templates for citizen participation. Again, the campaign was the most successful where NGOs with alter-globalization traditions were most established. Yet, support by mainstream media players was also crucial: in countries such as Germany, Austria, or the Netherlands, mainstream media played an important role in popularizing the cause and attracting people to the streets. On the contrary, mainstream media in Eastern Europe showed much less interest in the agreements leading to their low salience.

Why does any of this matter? It matters because if we understand under what condition diffusion succeeds or fails, we can diffuse protests better. What is more, understanding better the way various types of players diffuse protest allows us to predict whether we could expect more bottom-up-driven diffusion, as with protests against austerity that remained very much enclosed within different nation states, or a more centralized one, as in protests against free trade that ended up being more transnational in terms of frames and repertoires. Each type of diffusion comes with its own trade-offs: bottom-up-driven diffusion often risks not being able to reach beyond transnational activist circles, while NGO-driven diffusion comes with the risk of depoliticizing protest in order to achieve efficiency at the institutional level.

The book has offered several practical takeaways for bottom-up activists in particular. First, Southern European players should make more efforts to reach out to the East and diffuse ideas and protest in former socialist countries. This is as valid for bottom-up activists as for trade unions and radical left and Green parties. An important way to make the diffusion of progressive left-wing protests in the East work is to engage in direct contact with the few local left-wing activists there and help them develop their capacities. This would include not only online and live seminars but also common activities, lecture series, discussions, and debates in which transmitters and adopters can negotiate what is being transmitted. Such types of exchanges clearly have to predate the diffusion of protest itself in order to guarantee that there will be players interested in adopting protest. In the absence of proactive effort to make such exchanges of ideas possible, it might be safe to assume that left-wing protests will rarely diffuse to the East. Yet, EU's South and East are locked in the same union, and many of the problems they face are the result of being part of this union with its free movement of people, goods, and services. Issues such as labour exploitation or social dumping are hard to solve or even to address unilaterally. What is more, in the long term, even when social movements from the South manage to change the discourse or reach positions of power, as is the case of Podemos in Spain that grew out of the Indignados movement, they still need to negotiate with Eastern European politicians. Having strong left-wing social movements in the East pressuring these politicians can make a difference. What is more, rather than one-sided diffusion from the West to the East, a proper left-wing dialogue might encourage left-wing actors in the East to rediscover their own protest traditions and left-wing legacy, bringing important insights both in theory and in practice. More connections and diffusion of ideas and practices between different Eastern European countries is also key for formulating common struggles and devising more efficient strategies to mobilize against policies that assault not only citizens' economic wellbeing but also the very principle of democratic sovereignty of the people.

Furthermore, bottom-up activists should avoid the depoliticization of their causes by NGOs by uncritically borrowing NGO expertise but rather engage in a dialogue and produce expertise *together* with NGOs and trade unions. Crucially, all left-wing players should follow up on their issues and engage with topics in a sustained way over time. The analysis of protests against both ACTA and TTIP and CETA showed that once the agreements were rejected (or in the case of CETA ratified by the European Parliament), NGOs counting on project funding moved to new issues. Yet, many of ACTA's components were still adopted in a secret handshake way. Similarly, a group of organizations campaigning against TTIP and CETA developed an "Alternative Trade Mandate" for a fairer free trade, yet the project was somewhat abandoned after CETA was ratified. This has been highly problematic, because the diffusion of protest against trade agreements is not enough. What needs to diffuse across the EU are also positive visions of how things can be done in a better way. Intellectuals and activists alike have a key role in developing ideas to reform existing institutions and inform future protests.

Developing positive proposals and programmes on how things *should* be done is also crucial for clarifying the important differences between left and Green players on the one hand and far right players on the other. While all these actors have opposed free trade agreements such as TTIP and CETA because they saw them as threatening sovereignty, they had very different visions of what the alternative to these agreements was. While the far right was primarily concerned about national sovereignty understood in a nativist sense and put forward protectionist arguments, Green left players were concerned about threats to parliamentary and popular sovereignty, be they at the national, transnational EU, or local level. Thus, one of the key steps in avoiding discursive appropriation by the far right passes through the well-thought-out and explicit articulation of alternatives, based on democratic sovereignty.

Indeed, the far right has appeared only episodically in this book. Yet, far right movements, subcultures, and political parties have risen dramatically in the decade after 2008 across both the East and the West. In fact, far right actors have been extremely efficient in diffusing their ideas and forging transnational alliances. In most of what I wrote, I focused primarily on the interactions *among* various players diffusing protest against austerity and free trade. What I did not focus on were the interactions between these players and the institutions of the EU and its member states or the interactions between these players and the far right. These are fascinating topics that deserve further exploration and will add even more complexity to the already complex topic of resistance to free trade and austerity.

Meanwhile, however, a new exogenous shock has taken place that has reshuffled the cards and thrown away many of the economic and political postulates that seemed unshakeable. The COVID-19 pandemic that started in 2020 was met with swift actions by states that not only incurred increasing debts but also engaged in dramatic fiscal stimulus in order to support demand and protect citizens in times of deep recession and rising unemployment. What is more, the COVID-19 crisis pushed French and German leaders to think of a proposal for a common European debt that would allow countries such as Spain or Italy, hit especially hard by the pandemic, to borrow at favourable rates. Clearly all this is unprecedented.

What is more, global trade, including cross-border service provision, took a strong blow. The outburst of the pandemic exposed the vulnerabilities of global production chains. As Western countries struggled to produce COVID-19 tests and protective equipment, the consequences of outsourcing pharmaceutical production or crucial parts of it to China became clear, and calls for funding "national" firms resonated strongly. Yet, when it comes to trade, COVID-19 only intensified trends that had already started long ago. Already back in 2016, when Donald Trump was elected as president of the United States, he stopped the negotiations for both TTIP and TPP. Since then, the US has escalated a trade war rhetoric, attacking mostly China but also when needed the EU. While China has remained a strong and staunch supporter of free trade (as the international actor who gains the most from it), it has also made substantial efforts at developing its domestic market to decrease dependence on trade. In this precarious international situation, EU's bet on export competitiveness and trade at the expense of domestic consumption might have been premature. Counting on exports in time of trade war comes with its own risks. Thus, it might be reasonable to expect in the coming future the EU and its member states to invest more in stimulating domestic markets. Meanwhile, the exit of the UK from the EU in the beginning of 2020 combined with the rise of the nationalist far right across the EU continue to pose challenges to integration and leave the future of the union uncertain.

Because of all these developments, the fight against austerity and free trade in the EU might seem outdated, an inter-crises development with no lasting legacy. Yet, this cannot be further from the truth. First, free trade agreements continue to be negotiated as I write these sentences. Second, protests against austerity and free trade were both motivated by strong demands for more "real democracy now". And the threats that austerity and free trade negotiations posed to democracy are here to stay. During the pandemic, states assumed emergency powers in order to fulfil their mission understood purely in technocratic "expert" terms and not in political ones. This concentration of power beyond parliamentary and popular control has posed serious threats to democracy, and only time will tell what the consequences of this period will be. A strong state is returning, but is it a fairer and more social state? Calls for more citizen participation in decision-making are more relevant than ever. Many of the players that mobilized against austerity and free trade in the EU left long-lasting legacies in terms of discourse change, innovative media use, new political parties, and new players appearing across the EU. Considering the rise of the far right throughout the EU, it is up to these players to guarantee that citizens will be able to continue controlling their representatives, as symbolized beautifully by the dome of the German Reichstag building that allows visitors to literally walk "above" the parliamentarians.

In 2011, outraged citizens from all across Spain started protest marches towards Madrid that ended up going all the way to Brussels and beyond. These citizens walked together for weeks on end, sharing food, ideas, and hopes as their shoes wore out. Marching throughout the continent, they stopped in small villages and big cities and engaged people in conversations and discussions. Sometimes, they blogged about it or posted on Facebook about their upcoming meetings. Sometimes they didn't. They diffused their ideas by their very way of living and by getting to know other people and other ideas. When they arrived in Brussels in October 2011, they must have looked slightly shabby after the long travel, not too many, generally unimpressive. And they certainly did not change much in the day-to-day political process in the capital of the EU. Yet, almost a decade later Podemos, a party born out of these same marches and protests, is in a ruling coalition in Spain and participated in the introduction of basic income in the country. And it was after a massive offensive by Spanish, Portuguese, and Italian politicians, supported by intellectuals from all across Europe, that French and

German leaders saw themselves forced to at least negotiate the possibility for a common European debt. Almost a decade after the 2011 anti-austerity protests, some, albeit small, left-wing actors are fighting for workers' rights and more progressive taxation in the East. Similarly to people, ideas march slowly. But each mobilization leaves a trace. And at some point of the long march, through countries and institutions alike, change might come.

INDEX

Printed in the United States
By Bookmasters